T0340038

Power and Money

Power and Money

A Marxist Theory of Bureaucracy

ERNEST MANDEL

VERSO
London · New York

First published by Verso 1992
© Ernest Mandel 1992
All rights reserved

Verso
UK: 6 Meard Street, London W1V 3HR
USA: 29 West 35th Street, New York, NY 10001–2291

Verso is the imprint of New Left Books

ISBN 978-0-86091-548-5

British Library Cataloguing in Publication Data
A catalogue record for this book is available from the British Library

Library of Congress Cataloging–in–Publication Data
A catalogue record for this book is available from the Library of Congress

Typeset in Times by York House Typographic Ltd, London
Printed in Finland by Werner Söderström Oy

To my dearest Anne,
Whose inspiration, love and care
Make it all so much sunnier.

Contents

Contents

Introduction

I

The death agony of the bureaucratic regimes in Eastern Europe, together with the break-up of the Soviet Union, have posed in the sharpest possible way the problem of their social nature and place in history – a problem largely identical with that of the specific nature of the bureaucracy in these societies.

Events have been rather cruel to most of the theories offered in answer to this question. For example, right-wing ideologues – and pseudo-left ones like Cornelius Castoriadis – consistently maintained that the Stalinist and post-Stalinist regimes were 'totalitarian', in the sense that they could not be shaken internally and would reproduce themselves for an indefinite length of time. The events of 1989 to 1991 have refuted that thesis. For their part, a number of Marxists like Paul Sweezy argued that it was impossible to call a regime 'transitional' when it had lasted for seventy years. But what about a regime which is shaken to its foundations after seventy-two years? Could that not be transitional after all?

The question of the restoration of capitalism is now posed in Eastern Europe and the former Soviet lands – and that is exactly how the matter is understood by all social and political forces, both nationally and internationally. Those who identified the USSR with state capitalism are thus left in a quandary: how can capitalism be restored if the state is already under capitalism? It is of no avail to argue that state capitalism is different from private capitalism. For if the difference is qualitative, what is the point of calling them both capitalism? And if the difference is only quantitative, it becomes impossible to explain how such minor changes

1

could have produced a profound, systemic upheaval in several East European countries. It would hardly seem a minor difference whether or not an economy is ruled by the law of value, but in the cases of the former GDR, Poland or Hungary that is now precisely what is at issue in the transition from one system to another.

All those who characterized the bureaucracy as a new ruling class look even more misguided in the light of events in Eastern Europe. What kind of new ruling class is it which goes so far towards liquidating itself, which abdicates a large part of its power with lightning speed, in Poland and Hungary not even under the pressure of a revolutionary mass movement? A new ruling class which proves incapable of reproducing its rule after being in existence for three-quarters of a century? A new ruling class which rules through no distinctive form of appropriation of the social surplus product?

One cannot make head or tail of the history of the USSR after 1923 without understanding it as a *three-cornered* fight between the bureaucracy, the working class and petty-bourgeois and pro-bourgeois forces. Neither in the crisis of 1928–33 nor in that of 1941–42 did Stalin restore capitalism; and he did not maintain it in Eastern Europe in 1947–48.

Paraphrasing Trotsky, we might say that the bureaucracy, in its own way and with barbaric means, tried neither to build a socialist classless society nor to restore capitalism, but to defend and extend its own power and privileges. Although it had not the social or historical roots or the economic function of a ruling class, it did have a *relative* autonomy which enabled it to defend itself, provided that it was not directly challenged by a revolutionary mass upsurge. The real historical basis of its power was first the decline and then the disappearance of independent mass activity. As long as that condition prevailed, the relative autonomy could persist.

From the point of view of long-term historical development, the Soviet bureaucracy may indeed be seen as a transmission-belt for capitalist pressure on the Soviet Union. But this does not imply that during a transitional period it acted in each grave crisis in the immediate interests of the international bourgeoisie. There is nothing apologetic in this Marxist interpretation. On the contrary: the blows that the bureaucracy delivered at various points in history against bourgeois or pro-bourgeois forces came after periods in which it had itself weakened the USSR and the Soviet proletariat, and were accompanied by further heavy blows against the workers and peasants. Terrible, unnecessary losses and sacrifices weakened the masses and the country in the long run, making impossible any fresh advances in the direction of a classless society. From that overall point of view, the globally counter-revolutionary nature of that bureaucracy appears undeniable.

Only the revolutionary Marxist interpretation of the USSR and the

Soviet bureaucracy emerges unscathed from the momentous upheavals of the last few years. The Soviet Union was a post-capitalist society, frozen in a transition stage between capitalism and socialism as a result of, on the one hand, its international isolation from the most advanced industrial countries and, on the other, the negative effects of bureaucratic dictatorship in all fields of social life. It could regress towards capitalism. It could, if the bureaucracy's power was overthrown by a political revolution, make significant advances towards socialism. No coherent alternative explanation of that society and dictatorship has been offered.

To the question of how the collapse in the East was possible, we offer a clear answer: power was usurped by a bureaucracy whose political base disintegrated. The point is not that the people in power were bad or inspired by wrong ideas, but that economic, political, cultural, ideological and psychological forces interacted in ways that this book will seek to analyse.

This view of a *socially distinct* bureaucracy justifies our use of the term to characterize the ruling layer in the USSR at a number of successive moments – say, 1930, 1937, 1945, 1956, 1970, 1986 and 1990. Political conditions were, of course, quite different before and after Stalin's bloody purges, before and after victory in the Second World War, before and after Khrushchev's initial de-Stalinization, at the beginning of Gorbachev's rule and in August 1991. But what they expressed were various forms of rule by the same social stratum. In a similar way, the German imperialist bourgeoisie ruled under Bismarck in 1880, the Kaiser in 1900, the Weimar Republic in 1920, the Nazis in 1935 and the Federal Republic since 1948, but through very different political systems.

Furthermore, the internal cohesion of the bureaucracy was much greater in the period 1950–70 than it was in 1930–39 or than it was to be after the late seventies. The degree of cohesion reflected, but also powerfully interacted with, the relative stability or instability of society as such. Thus the growing and conflictual decomposition of the bureaucracy itself increased the speed of disintegration of Soviet society and of the Soviet Union as a state.

II

When we say that the revolutionary Marxist interpretation of the Soviet bureaucracy is the only one to have resisted the acid test of events, we do not mean to imply that it has provided an answer to every question. Far from it. In our approach to the transitional character of Soviet society, and the peculiar nature of the Soviet bureaucracy, our focus has been on the *rise* of that social layer, and the relative stability of its power and privileges. But the problem posed today is the *decline* and now decomposition of that same social layer. The dialectics of decline are not identical with the dialectics of ascent. Two points should be stressed in this regard.

The relative positions of the world bourgeoisie and the Soviet bureaucracy were quite different in the 1930s (world economic crisis!) from what they are today. During the rise of Stalinism, especially after 1928, the bureaucracy behaved as parvenus flushed with success. Even when Khrushchev succeeded Stalin, he still felt able to declare to the US bourgeoisie: 'We shall bury you.' Today, however, the Soviet bureaucracy, like the Chinese, operates in a world context where the economic relationship of forces with the leading imperialist countries is actually worsening. It is profoundly conscious of this deterioration, even exaggerating its depth and duration. It no longer has anything of the parvenu's cheek: it is marked rather by senile despair. Thus, for both objective and subjective reasons, it is much more vulnerable to imperialist pressure, and substantial forces within its own ranks are ready to link up with the international bourgeoisie.

Furthermore, after the Second World War, as a result of the objective strengthening of the USA, the spread of revolutions and the effects of many of the crimes of the Soviet bureaucracy, imperialism succeeded in establishing an international alliance that contrasted with the deep rifts it knew in the 1929–45 period. While inter-imperialist rivalries have continued to operate, they do so within the framework of that alliance. The fragmented world market of the thirties and forties gave breathing-space to the reactionary utopia of 'socialism in one country'. The unified world market of the last few decades has rained hammer blows on that utopia.

On the other hand, the overthrow of the bureaucratic dictatorship by a *victorious* political revolution appears today as a possibility which may be pre-empted by the achievement of capitalist restoration. The objective relations of forces between the proletariat, the bureaucracy and the pro-restorationist forces, to be sure, give great weight to the working class at least in Russia and Czechoslovakia, and even in Romania and Poland. The level of working-class activity and mobilization has been rising in several of these countries. However, a victorious outcome also requires a high level of class consciousness, self-organization and political leadership on the part of the working class, with a clear content and dynamic of class power – conditions which are still lacking in every East European country and, to a lesser extent, in Russia itself.

It is for this reason that we witnessed in East Germany a process which, in some respects, recalls Marx's analysis of France in 1848: namely, the rapid turning of a political revolution into a social counter-revolution. This, too, is why restorationist forces have come to the fore in several

4

other East European countries and are now developing on a larger scale in the USSR. Of course, if we leave aside what is involved in a simple swallowing up of the GDR by the Federal Republic, the restoration of capitalism is nowhere a foregone conclusion. The process follows a classical three-stage pattern. A first phase of general democratic euphoria is followed by one of reactionary counter-offensive, under conditions of profound political confusion and disorientation of the working class. But then, in a third phase, the workers, despite their lack of political clarity or objectives, start to defend their immediate material interests not only against the openly restorationist forces but also against the 'democratic' governments which they themselves helped to elect. This phase has already begun in Poland. It will develop elsewhere.

Restoration of capitalism is possible only if that resistance is defeated, or at least so fragmented as to become practically inoperative. Such an outcome, however, is by no means certain. It is not inevitable in the former USSR, which has the strongest working class in the world, and one of the most skilled and most cultivated. The awakening of that mighty social force, with its first moves of independent intervention, is one of the most positive aspects of world developments in the last five years which could largely neutralize and even reverse the negative trends in Eastern Europe. But all this being said, it remains a fact that the low level of class consciousness of the East European and Soviet working class has created a situation which restorationists can exploit.

We have to admit that revolutionary Marxists seriously underestimated the disastrous long-term effects of Stalinism and bureaucratic dictatorship on the average level of consciousness. The balance-sheet which the great majority of toilers in these countries have drawn from their experience is that bureaucratic dictatorship totally failed to assure the level of consumption and freedom to which they aspire. As decades of Stalinist indoctrination – supported by the bourgeois ideological offensive – told them that these bureaucratic regimes were socialist, the bankruptcy of Stalinism appeared in their eyes as the bankruptcy of communism, Marxism and even socialism *tout court*. This created in their midst a tremendous ideological–moral vacuum. And since society, like nature, abhors a vacuum, ideological currents distinct from and opposed to socialism – from pro-capitalist social democracy and bourgeois liberalism to religious fundamentalism, racist chauvinism and outright fascism – have found it possible to penetrate these societies and make considerable headway.

In order to regain a level of consciousness and leadership adequate for the task of taking and directly exercising state power – that is, of leading a victorious political revolution – the Soviet and East European working classes will have to go through a whole series of practical experiences in mass struggle. No propaganda or education, however necessary, can substitute for this, the only real source of collective mass consciousness. Any attempt to make short-cuts in this long and painful process – for example, through new experiments in substitutionism – will only lead to fresh disasters.

III

Throughout the world, virtually all currents and tendencies of the Left are today posing the same series of questions. How was the disaster possible? What are its deeper historical causes? How can a repetition be averted? Does the socialist project still have any future whatsoever? Will it survive the shipwreck of Stalinism and post-Stalinism? It is impossible to give a convincing answer to these questions without presenting a systematic theory of the labour bureaucracy – of the bureaucracies emerging from working-class organizations and workers' states. This is the purpose of the present book.

The bureaucracy is a many-faced monster and has to be apprehended as such. Its roots are economic and institutional. Its process of development involves political–strategic options. It is reflected through processes of ideological self-justification and degeneration. Its rise to power is mediated by mechanisms of negative cadre selection. All these aspects of bureaucratization are analysed in the first three chapters, where the guiding thread is the definition of the bureaucracy as *a new social layer* appropriating administrative functions previously exercised by the masses themselves. This results from the introduction into the labour movement, including the ruling party in a workers' state, of the social division of labour. Workers are henceforth managed and 'bossed' by people arising out of their own ranks. They become oppressed and exploited by their own functionaries.

The economic causes and consequences of this oppression in Soviet Russia have by and large been understood by Marxists since the 1920s. The institutional causes and consequences were laid bare by Rosa Luxemburg in 1918, by the Left Opposition and Rakovsky's brilliant analysis in the 1920s, and by Trotsky's magisterial synthesis in the 1930s. Many sensational revelations about the Soviet Thermidor have been published in the USSR within the new framework of glasnost, but they add nothing really new to the fundamental analysis.

In the USSR and similar countries, the ambivalent and hybrid character of the workers' bureaucracy was seen most clearly in the relationship between administrative power and money wealth. The non-capitalist nature of that bureaucracy was expressed in the fact that it essentially *ruled* not through money but through a monopoly of political power. Its non-socialist nature, on the other hand, was expressed in its inability to free itself from the *influence* of money and money wealth. The fact that it was not a new ruling class was expressed through its inability to free itself from the whole hybrid combination of power monopoly and money power, and to base itself on fundamentally new mechanisms of rule.

Now, the undeniable growth of state, para-state and private bureaucracies in the capitalist countries, which is dealt with in Chapter 4, has to be put in the real framework of class power. Nowhere has any sector of the bourgeois bureaucracy been able to break the decisive power of money wealth. On the contrary: whereas in post-capitalist societies money wealth is in the final analysis subordinated to political power, in capitalist societies political power is in the final analysis an emanation of money wealth. Whenever it achieves an unusually high degree of autonomy, this becomes either an avenue for primitive accumulation of private money wealth or a means of penetration into the upper layers of the bourgeois class.

Thus, the idea of the 'bureaucratization of the world' is based upon a false perception of capitalist reality. It presupposes the break-up of Big Business's control over the main mechanisms of producing and distributing material wealth, and therefore over society as a whole, when in fact such a process has not even begun in any of the developed capitalist countries.

It is true that there are two common social sources for the parallel – not identical – processes of bureaucratization of working-class mass organizations, workers' states, bourgeois states and private Big Business: namely, the increasing complexity of social and economic life since the decline of 'freely competitive' capitalism; and the growing need of all ruling classes and social layers to keep the workers and all 'bossed over' people under tighter control than before, given the greater objective strength of the world proletariat and its higher potential to destabilize and overturn existing power structures. Bureaucracies of an otherwise different nature correspond to this dual phenomenon.

Paradoxically, it is not so much any basic weakness of the working class as its relative strength and *partial victories* which give rise to bureaucracies, insofar as these victories remain only partial and lead to *partial defeats*. Ultimately, then, the phenomena of bureaucratization express the unstable equilibrium of class forces that has characterized the world situation since 1917. The world proletariat has been unable to extend the October Revolution to the leading industrial nations, and to bring society under the conscious control of the producers and consumers. Imperialism has still been unable to restore its rule over the whole world and decisively to break the labour movement in the capitalist countries. This unstable equilibrium cannot last forever. The fate of the bureaucracies will be decided by the final outcome of the class struggle on a world scale.

IV

Prospects for a new breakthrough towards socialism hinge on a radical marginalization of the weight of bureaucracies within the mass movement in the capitalist countries as well as in the Stalinist, or formerly Stalinist, states. The possibilities for a withering away of the bureaucracy, which are examined in the final chapter, will obviously be assisted by a deeper theoretical understanding of the whole phenomenon. In this sense, the author's aim has been to make a modest contribution to the historical task of preventing any return to or reproduction of the horrors of Stalinism.

In the end, however, Marxists have to share Marx's own belief that the future of socialism is indissolubly bound up with the struggles of the actually existing working class – that is, with its immediate interests as seen by itself. They have also to share Marx's conviction that the possibility of socialism arises out of the contradictions of capitalism, that the constitutive elements of the new society develop in the womb of the most advanced capitalist societies themselves. Socialist revolution essentially means the setting free of these constitutive elements.

In this sense, just as the process of bureaucratization hinged on a decline of the working class's control over its own organizations and the workers' state, so the withering away of the bureaucracy hinges on a radical increase in the self-activity and self-organization of the toilers – blue-collar and white-collar united – and in their capacity to take the reorganization of society into their own hands under relatively favourable conditions of material wealth. This is not a matter of speculation. It is a question which has to be answered on the basis of empirical evidence, in the light of unfolding historical trends. This evidence may be summarized as follows: while it is true that up till now, the toilers have not been able to prevent with lasting effect the bureaucratization of their mass organizations, they have been able at various moments to challenge it quite significantly in a series of countries, as a function of mass mobilizations and qualitatively increased self-activity. An analogous process has begun to unfold in the Soviet Union in the last two years.

Similarly, while it is true that the mass of wage- and salary-earners have nowhere yet been able with lasting effect to become the direct rulers of society, they have periodically taken major steps in that direction in the wake of vigorous explosions of mass struggle. This trend has not stopped. There are many signs that it will rise and not decline in the years to come.

One significant indication is the growth of massive extra-parliamentary mobilizations on a series of important political issues: the struggle against war and militarism; the campaigns against nuclear energy; the defence of the environment; the questions raised by the rise of feminism; the new vistas for direct democracy; the extension of workers' rights; and issues relating to the 'quality of life' in general. All these movements are, at this stage, disconnected from one another, fragmented on a 'single-issue' basis, without an overall political perspective, without a coherent vision of an alternative model of society. For this reason, they can be at least partially recuperated and reintegrated into traditional establishment politics. And yet they do express an instinctive trend of the toilers towards another way of practising politics. More direct democracy versus an *exclusively* indirect, representative democracy that is ever more associated with authoritarian repressive traits, not to say outright dictatorship: this is beginning to emerge as a political alternative for the years to come.

It is also closely linked to a socio-economic orientation: neither state despotism nor market despotism; let the producers decide for themselves what they produce, how they produce it and how they divide the product. This vision will grow in the states still encumbered by a Stalinist system, like China, but also in these states which have rejected Stalinism without discovering a viable alternative. It dovetails with the logic of the third technological revolution, which demands the withering away of work processes hierarchically organized from the top down. The future of socialism and of human freedom, the future – even the physical survival – of humankind itself depend upon the conscious and organized fusion of these trends.

This book was written at a time when many of the Communist governments of Eastern Europe had been overthrown, at a time when the old bureaucratic order was everywhere in some sort of crisis but prior to the abortive coup in Moscow in August 1991 and the subsequent rejection of Communist rule and break-up of the Soviet Union. These latter events constitute a development of the very processes analysed in this book, especially of the three-cornered struggle between pro-capitalist forces, the bureaucracy and the newly independent workers' movement.

The rise of workers' struggles, such as the miners' actions of 1989 and 1990, made a large contribution to challenging the legitimacy of the rule of the CPSU but did not become sufficiently generalized, focused and programmatically informed to present an independent political alternative against the nomenklatura and the pro-capitalist forces, many of them within the old bureaucratic order. So it was these forces which could take the political initiative. The victory achieved by Yeltsin, and his proclamation of the supposed virtues of privatization and the free market confirm in their own way the argument that the bureaucratized economy was a deeply contradictory and unstable social formation, obliged to move either towards socialism or towards capitalism. But the undoubted political fact that, for the time being, the option of the Russian government is to build capitalism does not by itself eliminate the old three-cornered struggle. Significant remnants of the old Stalinist bureaucracy survive. And the workers' organizations continue to develop their own independent dynamic as they confront the policies of new authorities – the deliberate creation of mass unemployment, rampant inflation, the dismantling of social services, privatization and the like.

The class struggle in the former Soviet lands thus enters a new stage. While the government wishes to establish capitalism, we should not take its wishes for reality. The social forces and the political options which are discussed in these pages remain as relevant as ever in the former Soviet republics, just as they do in Eastern Europe and, with appropriate variations, in those states which still call themselves Communist.

1

Bureaucracy and Commodity Production

The main characteristic of the USSR and similar societies was the hypertrophy of the state. In the Soviet Union itself, the economic system came to be almost universally described as a 'command economy', and it is a historical fact that state control over all sectors of social life marked nearly sixty years of bureaucratic dictatorship. Hence the first question which arises is the following: on what material foundations does the state rest? What is its place in human societies?

The general relationship between scarcity, the social division of labour, the attribution of certain social functions to a separate group of people (the bureaucracy) and the origins and continuing existence of the state was established by Marx and Engels:

It is clear that so long as human labour was still so little productive that it provided but a small surplus over and above the necessary means of subsistence, any increase of the productive forces, extension of trade, development of the state and of law, or foundation of art and science, was possible only by means of a greater division of labour. And the necessary basis for this was the great division of labour between the masses discharging simple manual labour and the few privileged persons directing labour, conducting trade and public affairs, and, at a later stage, occupying themselves with art and science.[1]

The second distinguishing feature [of the state] is the establishment of a *public power* which no longer directly coincides with the population organizing itself as an armed force. This special public power is necessary because a self-acting armed organization of the population has become impossible since the split into classes. . . . This public power exists in every state; it consists not merely of armed men but also of material adjuncts, prisons and institutions of coercion of every kind, of which clan society knew nothing.[2]

11

1. The Social Division of Labour, the State and Scarcity

The withering away of the state and of social classes – which Marx and Engels saw as parallel processes – presupposes a level of the forces of production such that scarcity can be overcome and individuals are enabled to achieve their full development. Under such circumstances, it is no longer inevitable that individuals will be subject to the tyranny of the *social* division of labour. Or, to paraphrase Engels, the 'common affairs of society' can henceforth be conducted by *all men and women* and no longer by a *special apparatus*.

> Only the immense increase of the productive forces attained by modern industry has made it possible to distribute labour among all members of society without exception, and thereby to limit the labour-time of each individual member to such an extent that all have enough free time left to take part in the general – both theoretical and practical – affairs of society.[3]

Engels explicitly asserts that these 'common affairs of society' include all those functions which, in a class society, are performed by the state. The withering away of the state is thus a return to the performance of these functions by society itself, without any need for a specialized apparatus, or bureaucracy.

In *The German Ideology* (1845–46) Marx and Engels had already grasped that a prerequisite for communism was 'a great increase' and 'universal development of the productive forces', because 'without it want is merely made general, and with destitution the struggle for necessities and all the old filthy business would necessarily be reproduced . . . '[4] It follows from this fundamental thesis of historical materialism that the absence of socialism (that is, the first, lower stage of communism) in the Soviet Union and other such societies is attributable to three material causes: (1) the inadequate level of development of the productive forces; (2) the isolation of these societies from the hegemonic industrial nations; and (3) the renewed struggle for the satisfaction of material needs, with its inevitable consequence in a return to 'all the old filthy business'.

Trotsky expressed this most clearly in *The Revolution Betrayed*:

> If the state does not die away but grows more and more despotic, if the plenipotentiaries of the working class become bureaucratized and the bureaucracy rises above the new society, this is not for some secondary reasons like the psychological relics of the past, etc., but is the result of the iron necessity to give birth to and support a privileged minority so long as it is impossible to guarantee genuine equality. . . . The basis of the bureaucratic rule is the poverty of society in objects of consumption, with the resulting

struggle of each against all. When there are enough goods in a store, the purchasers can come when they want to. When there are few goods, the purchasers are compelled to stand in line. When the lines are very long, it is necessary to appoint a policeman to keep order. Such is the starting point of the power of the Soviet bureaucracy. It 'knows' who is to get something and who has to wait.[5]

The state, as the organ which oversees and conducts the 'common affairs of society' (that is, accumulation of part of the social surplus product, military affairs, enforcement of the rules governing cohabitation between citizens, creation and maintenance of the infrastructure, etc.), as distinct from the immediate economic activity of production and distribution, is embodied in special apparatuses which, as Engels shows in *Anti-Dühring*, conquer their own autonomy in society, becoming its masters rather than its servants.

In this sense, the state has always performed a dual function: it guarantees the rule of the ruling class over the exploited classes, and it assures the general interests of the ruling class as against the private interests of its members. This is true for all stable class societies, but above all for capitalism where private economic interests are much more compelling. Private capitalists cannot, for example, effectively assume the role of a central bank, because they cannot make abstraction from their private interests. State bureaucracies, unlike those of private slave-owners, feudal lords or capitalist entrepreneurs, act through a rigid system of formal, hierarchically organized rules, regardless of the immediate effect these might have upon the personnel who adhere to them. The rules can be changed only by collective decision of the ruling class. Failure to apply them would not be part of 'the game': it would be due to such factors as the corruption or incompetence of individual functionaries. The army, with its iron 'regulations' and chain of command and its insistence on blind obedience, is an admittedly caricatural model of the state bureaucracy. It is supposed to be completely detached from the quest for private pecuniary advantage, and although plunder and corruption have accompanied the rise to eminence of armies in all class societies, the ruling classes have normally been able to keep these 'excesses' under control.

With an insight astonishingly close to Marxism, Hegel recognized in *fixed income* and *security of tenure* the material basis of the bureaucracy. These he opposed to the fluctuating income and insecurity of 'civil society' (that is, the basic classes of bourgeois society).[6] If one adds, as Hegel did, the *hierarchical* nature of the bureaucracy (that is, the prospect of rising income through promotion), then one has indeed discovered the three distinctive social pillars of the bureaucracy, as distinct from those of the bourgeoisie or the proletariat.[7]

But the social situation of the bureaucracy is not defined only by its difference from the social classes surrounding it. It is also determined by its simultaneous immersion in 'civil society'. When Hegel magnifies and exalts the 'disinterested' character of the state functionary (based upon guaranteed income and security of tenure!), he seems to forget that in a society ruled by wealth the power of attraction of money, and hence of corruption, is quite formidable. Especially in the upper echelons, state functionaries will tend to discover myriad ways of becoming part of the 'egoistic', profit-hungry bourgeois class.[8] We might say that the specificity of the Soviet bureaucracy lies precisely in the fact that it is immersed in a society in which money wealth, and private wealth in general, though not absent, play a qualitatively smaller role than in either bourgeois, feudal or mature slave-owning society, or in the classical societies of the 'Asiatic mode of production'.

Be this as it may, it is obvious that the state did not even begin to wither away in the Soviet Union. On the contrary, it continued to expand as a powerful independent force set up over society as a whole, and the CPSU leadership – as we can see as late as the Party programme of 1986 – quite openly advocated its further strengthening. The Soviet experience of bureaucratization reflected not only historical backwardness but also deep social tensions, far removed from a classless society. The management of these contradictions required the existence and hypertrophy of the organs of the state, that is, the bureaucracy. As Engels put it: 'The state is, therefore, by no means a power forced on society from without. . . . Rather, it is a product of society at a certain stage of development; it is the admission that this society has become entangled in an insoluble contradiction with itself, that it has split into irreconcilable antagonisms which it is powerless to dispel.'[9]

Revolutionary Marxists do not accuse the Stalinist faction and its successors in power of having 'caused' the monstrous growth of the state and the bureaucracy through their 'betrayals' or 'political errors'. In fact, the opposite is the case. Revolutionary Marxists explain the victory, the political line and the ideology of the Stalinist faction and its successors by reference to the material and social conditions outlined above. The reproaches that may be directed against them, insofar as reproaches serve any purpose within the context of scientific socialism, are the following:

1. They conceal social reality and breed 'false consciousness' by offering special ideological justification for the bureaucracy. Through this departure from Marxism and the historical–materialist interpreta-

tion of society, they deceive the working class of their own country and the world at large and give great assistance to the international bourgeoisie and its ideologues.[10]

2. In the name of 'communism' and 'Marxism', they unleashed large-scale processes of exploitation and oppression of workers, young people, peasants, women and national minorities, all of which constituted a crime against socialism and the proletariat.

3. Their policies have in practice led to conditions which, far from limiting shortages and bureaucratic excesses to a minimum, have greatly encouraged their development. They have thus not acted, and are not acting, in the interests of socialism and of the proletariat as a class, but have subordinated these interests to the particular ones of the privileged bureaucracy.

This Marxist analysis of the hypertrophy of state and bureaucracy in the Soviet Union poses a crucial historical question. Were not the Mensheviks right after all when, in opposition to Lenin and Trotsky, they opposed the October Revolution on the grounds that Russia was not ripe for socialism and that any attempt to 'leap over' the development of capitalism was 'voluntarist' and 'Blanquist'? Was the Russian Revolution not a historical mistake if, as the post-1945 development of the productive forces has shown, capitalism had not yet realized all its economic potential on a world scale?[11]

The reply to this question is that the *process of socialist world revolution* must be distinguished from the illusion of completing the construction of a socialist society in one country. Without a doubt, Russia was not 'ripe' for the establishment of such a society, and until 1924 this view was shared by all revolutionary Marxists, not only Lenin, Trotsky, Luxemburg, Bukharin, Zinoviev, Lukács, Gramsci, Thalheimer, Korsch or Radek, but also Stalin himself. And yet *the world* was ripe for socialism. This distinction and this certainty had already been explained by Engels in *Anti-Dühring*, and what was true in 1878 was incomparably truer in 1917.

Now, the appropriation of the means of production by the workers' state is a *political* act linked not only to the already prevailing material conditions but also to the existing political and subjective conditions. Basing himself on the discovery of the law of uneven and combined development, Trotsky was able to predict as early as 1905–6 that, *in the framework of the imperialist world*, the proletariat of a less developed country like Russia could utilize a unique combination of socio-economic backwardness and political maturity to overthrow the state power of capital before anything similar took place in the more developed industrial nations.

At one and the same time, imperialism hampers the full development both of the objective conditions for socialism in the backward countries (that is, the complete development of capitalism) and of the subjective conditions for socialism in the highly industrialized countries (that is, the full development of proletarian class consciousness). It is precisely the combination of these two processes that determines the concrete form of the world socialist revolution. This may *begin* in countries like Russia but will lead to the full development of a socialist society only if it is extended to the industrially most advanced nations. The whole tragedy of the twentieth century is contained in this prognosis.

That the October Revolution was indeed a driving force of the world socialist revolution, and not simply a means towards the 'development of socialism in one country', was from the outset the historical justification assigned to it by Lenin, Trotsky, Luxemburg and their comrades. Let us just listen for a moment to Luxemburg:

> Let the German government socialists cry that the rule of the Bolsheviks in Russia is a distorted expression of the dictatorship of the proletariat. If it was or is such, that is only because it is a product of the behaviour of the German proletariat, in itself a distorted expression of the socialist class struggle. All of us are subject to the laws of history, and it is only internationally that the socialist order of society can be realized. The Bolsheviks have shown that they are capable of everything that a genuine revolutionary party can contribute within the limits of the historical possibilities. They are not supposed to perform miracles. For a model and faultless proletarian revolution in an isolated land, exhausted by world war, strangled by imperialism, betrayed by the international proletariat would be a miracle. What *is* in order is to distinguish the essential from the non-essential, the kernel from the accidental excrescences in the politics of the Bolsheviks. In the present period, when we face decisive final struggles in all the world, the most important problem of socialism was and is the burning question of our time. It is not a question of this or that secondary question of tactics, but of the capacity for action of the proletariat, the strength to act, the will to power of socialism as such. In this Lenin and Trotsky and their friends were the *first*, those who went ahead as an example to the proletariat of the world: they are still the *only ones* up to now who can cry with Hütten: 'I have dared.'[12]

The First World War, which exacerbated the internal contradictions of imperialism and of the capitalist mode of production, issued in a virtually uninterrupted series of revolutions. Although these received considerable impetus from the Russian October and the founding of the Soviet state, they constituted a *real world process* that carried with it a prospect of revolutionary victory in industrially advanced countries like Germany,

Austria, Italy and Finland. During this period the possibility of achieving socialism on a world scale was progressing, in spite of the impossibility of realizing socialism in Russia. The October Revolution is thus, historically speaking, fully justified.

The Russian Revolution was a conflict of massive social forces unleashed in an elemental way which could not be controlled by moderate or 'reasonable' liberal conciliators. In this extreme polarization the real alternative was not liberal democracy or 'Bolshevik dictatorship', but rather dictatorship of the proletariat or a murderous dictatorship of an extreme right-wing, semi-fascist nature.[13] Thus, the Ukrainian counter-revolutionary Petlyura, by no means the most right-wing of the political leaders active in the civil war, killed a hundred thousand Jews during pogroms in 1919 – the greatest number of victims of right-wing terror until Hitler's extermination camps. Even before the October Revolution could occur, there was General Kornilov's attempted *coup d'état*, when the counter-revolutionaries were prepared to bring the German army to occupy Petrograd. This would have led to a massacre of the Petrograd proletariat, some idea of which can be gained from the bloodbath perpetrated by German militarism and the Mannerheim forces in the Finnish civil war.[14]

We do not need to speculate on the price that would have been paid if the October Revolution had not taken place – historians who carefully add up the costs of revolution almost never take such 'counter-factuals' into account. What we can base ourselves on, however, is the tragic example of Germany. When the German revolution broke out in 1918, social democracy tried to crush it with the help of the Reichswehr and the Freikorps – the nuclei of the future SA and SS – thereby unleashing a process of gradual counter-revolution that would eventually culminate in Hitler's taking of power in 1933 and the loss of tens of millions of lives. We can say that the price of a victorious socialist revolution in 1918 would have been incomparably lower, and that the Stalinist degeneration of Russia, with its huge costs, would thereby also have been avoided. The historical balance-sheet thus eloquently confirms the legitimacy of the October Revolution in the light of Germany's alternative path.

As to the adaptability of international capitalism expressed in the new 'long wave' of economic development after the Second World War, it has been paid for at a tremendous price: 20 million deaths as a result of the first war; 80 million as a result of the second war; and an even greater number due to 140 'local wars', Third World misery and various technological disasters since 1945. Does this not prove the correctness of the Marxist thesis that, unlike in the pre-1914 period, the negative results of capitalism now far outstrip its positive effects? Again: is not the price humankind has paid for not realizing world revolution incommensurably higher than the costs of that revolution would have been?

2. Scarcity and Commodity Production

In exploring the economic roots of the bureaucracy in scarcity, we now need to consider the question of commodity production. The contradiction between commodity production and a society of freely associated producers (that is, a socialist society as the lower phase of communism) is one of the basic tenets of historical materialism.

It is true that for Marx and Engels the scope of commodity production was by no means restricted to the capitalist mode: 'Political economy begins with *commodities*, with the moment when products are exchanged, either by individuals or by primitive communities.'[15] But in Chapter One of the first volume of *Capital*, Marx states that products become commodities only when they are the result of different *private labours conducted independently of each other*. From the moment when labour loses its private character, becoming immediately and directly social, its distribution among the various sectors of activity is determined not by spontaneous decisions of individuals, production units or firms but by the a priori decisions of society as a whole. Commodity production then disappears:

> Within the cooperative society based on common ownership of the means of production the producers do not exchange their products; similarly, the labour spent on the products no longer appears as the *value* of these products . . . for now, in contrast to capitalist society, individual pieces of labour are no longer merely indirectly, but directly, a component part of the total labour. . . . We are dealing here with a communist society, not as it has *developed* on its own foundations, but on the contrary, just as it *emerges* from capitalist society. In every respect, economically, morally, intellectually, it is thus still stamped with the birthmarks of the old society from whose womb it has emerged. Accordingly, the individual producer gets back from society – after the deductions – exactly what he has given it.[16]

Thus, from a Marxist standpoint, the partial existence of commodity production in the Soviet Union and similar social formations, together with the hypertrophy of the bureaucratic state apparatus, is conclusive proof that there does not yet exist a *socialist* economy or society, a complete socialization of the means of production, the processes of production or the processes of labour. Marx and Engels did, of course, consider the distribution of social labour 'in definite proportions' to be a

18

rule valid for all societies, with the force indeed of 'a natural law'. But when Marx dealt with this question, he immediately added:

> What can change in historically different circumstances is only the *form* in which these laws assert themselves. And the form in which this proportional distribution of labour asserts itself, in a social system where the interconnection of social labour manifests itself through the *private exchange* of individual products of labour, is precisely the *exchange value* of these products. . . .
> The essence of bourgeois society consists precisely in this, that a priori there is no conscious social regulation of production. The rational and naturally necessary asserts itself only as a blindly working average.[17]

And even more clearly in the *Grundrisse*: 'Thus, economy of time, along with the planned distribution of labour time among the various branches of production, remains the first economic law on the basis of communal production. It becomes law, there, to an even higher degree. *However, this is essentially different from a measurement of exchange values (labour or products) by labour time.*'[18]

Thus, the statement that under socialism *conscious* proportional allocation of quantities of labour will by and large determine planning in no way implies – quite the opposite – that commodity production and value still prevail. For the commodity and value are *specific* forms in which the allocation of labour quantities occurs in a blind, anarchic manner, 'behind the backs of the producers'. By definition, this prevents the producers from determining their own preferences, from controlling their own conditions of work and life.

The Soviet bureaucracy's attempts to revise these fundamental aspects of Marxist theory started with a famous article which appeared in 1943 in the magazine *Pod Znamenem Marxizma* (Under the Banner of Marxism), signed by the editors but probably written by the academician Leontiev: 'In socialist society,' it argued, 'the product of labour is a commodity; it has use value and value. . . . The value of a commodity in socialist society is determined not by the units of labour actually expended on its production, but by the quantity of labour socially necessary for its production and reproduction.'[19] If that were true, there would be no fundamental difference between socialism and capitalism. For the essential rationality of commodity production, let us repeat, is the private character of labour.

Stalin himself codified this revision of Marxism in 1952, in his article 'Economic Problems of Socialism in the USSR'. There he stated categorically that 'the law of value does exist and does operate' in the Soviet Union.[20] One of the more sophisticated neo-Stalinist theoreticians, the East German economist Fritz Behrens, subsequently since tried to develop a subtler justification of 'socialist commodity production', which he saw as linked to the insufficient absolute level of development of the productive forces, the private ownership of labour power, and the growing complexity of relations among productive units. If we leave aside the pragmatic and unscientific character of some of the formulations ('commodity/value relations persist because they should and must be used for more efficient planning'), Behrens's thesis boils down to an admission that labour is not yet immediately social labour. So it is still partially private labour.[21] But does not that simple fact confirm that we are not yet dealing with a socialist society?

Some might consider this whole debate essentially dogmatic, if not downright scholastic. Why pay so much attention to what Marx and Engels wrote or to an interpretation of their writings? Would it not be preferable to focus on what actually occurred in the USSR and is occurring in China? Such an objection, however, misses what is key to the debate. It is not a question simply of portraying economic phenomena and developments in the Soviet Union and similar societies, essential as this may be. The point is to understand and explain them. This is impossible without analytical–theoretical tools. And that is where Marx and Marxism come in.[22]

Apologists for the Stalinist bureaucracy, supported by the benevolent smiles of bourgeois and petty-bourgeois ideologists in the West, seek to refute this line of argument in two ways. On the one hand, they claim that Marx and Engels were mistaken regarding the 'real movement' of socialism, which has been shown in practice to be not incompatible either with a 'strong state' or with commodity production. Moreover, it is argued, the two masters never tired of repeating that communism is not a goal to be achieved but a real movement which abolishes the 'existing state of things', namely private property. This reductive stance is based upon a blatantly false intepretation of a passage from *The German Ideology*:

> With the abolition of the basis of private property, with the communistic regulation of production (and, implicit in this, the destruction of the alien relation between men and what they themselves produce), the power of the relation of supply and demand is dissolved into nothing, and men get exchange, production, the mode of their mutual relation under their own control again. Communism is for us not a *state of affairs* which is to be established, an *ideal* to which reality [will] have to adjust itself. We call communism the *real* movement which abolishes the present state of things. The conditions of this movement result from the premises now in existence.[23]

Marx and Engels, then, clearly state that the abolition of 'the present state of things' must not be limited exclusively to private ownership of the means of production. It must also include at least the following: (1)

abolition of commodity production and the gradual disappearance of money ('the power of the relation of supply and demand dissolved into nothing'); (2) abolition of trade in consumer goods, at least within the commune; (3) control by the freely associated producers over the product of their labour and over their working conditions, including access to consumer goods; (4) control by the people over 'the mode of their mutual relation', which rules out a repressive apparatus separate from society. It follows, from the experience of the Soviet Union and elsewhere, that *there has not yet been a real movement which has abolished the 'present state of things'*. There is no socialist society in existence anywhere.

Another accusation levelled by apologists for the bureaucracy against revolutionary Marxists and other 'left critics' is that they deliberately jacked up the demands of socialism in such a way as to show that reality in the Soviet Union and elsewhere failed to live up to the ideal.[24] This, so the argument goes, is a symptom of the substitution of 'historical idealism', 'normative utopia' or 'moralism' for the categories of historical materialism.

Our reply to this is that it is precisely one of the central tenets of historical materialism that scientific categories (as well as 'ideals') are the products of *real social relations* and not of 'false reasoning' or some demonic 'anti-communism'. The survival of such 'categories' as the commodity, value and money in the Soviet Union and similar societies has a *material base* in the insufficient socialization of production. Labour is not yet completely and immediately social in character. The producers, who do not yet constitute a free association, do not have direct access to the means of production and to consumer goods. Accordingly, private labour and private property have not yet been completely abolished.

In other words, it was not because social conditions in the USSR failed to comply with Marxist 'ideals' that they were 'bad' and non-socialist. Such reasoning would indeed be idealist and 'normative'. No, these conditions were non-socialist because they were still exploitative, extremely oppressive and alienating, because they did not correspond to the real criteria for socialism. These criteria, as defined by Marx and others, are neither idealist projections nor utopian concepts but *objective conditions* necessary for the advent of a non-exploitative and non-oppressive classless society. 'Actually existing socialism' turns out not actually to have existed in the Soviet Union or anywhere else.

The bureaucracy and its ideologues asserted the opposite because it was in their own interests to do so, to conceal or condone the inequality, material privileges and power monopoly in the USSR. For its part, the international bourgeoisie was happy to play along in presenting the

Soviet Union as socialist, in order to prove in the eyes of workers in the West and elsewhere that 'socialism' is a very bad form of society indeed.

A further argument that is sometimes heard in less instructed circles is that the 'left-opportunist' critics of Soviet society were confusing socialism with communism, and that what is demanded of a socialist society is possible only in a higher, communist one. However, these apologists forget Lenin's unequivocal description of what is commonly called socialism:

> It is this communist society – a society which has just emerged into the light of day out of the womb of capitalism and which, in every respect, bears the birthmarks of the old society – that Marx terms the 'first', or lower phase of communist society. The means of production are no longer the private property of individuals. The means of production belong to the whole of society. Every member of society, performing a certain part of the socially necessary work, receives a certificate from society to the effect that he has done such and such an amount of work.[25]

The apologists also forget that this definition of socialism is to be found in the passages we have already quoted from Marx and Engels, and that the whole Marxist tradition from 1875 to 1928, starting with Bebel, was based upon it. Up until June 1928 it was even repeated by Stalin himself.[26]

But is it simply a matter of definitions? Certainly not. It is possible to maintain that commodity production and the law of value continue to rule in a socialist society only if one rejects the whole of Volume One of Marx's *Capital*, his analysis of commodities, value, exchange-value (form of value) and the law of value. This would be to discard not only Marx's definition of socialism but also his analysis of capitalism and the origins of classes and the state. It would be to leave altogether the ground of Marxism and historical materialism.

Marx's argument in the *Critique of the Gotha Programme* that 'bourgeois right' continues to prevail under socialism (the first, lower phase of communism) can under no circumstances be taken to imply the survival of commodity production and the law of value. Our earlier quotes from that Critique explicitly state the opposite. *In spite of the disappearance of commodity production and value under socialism*, 'bourgeois right' continues to predominate because there is still *only formal equality*. Identical quantities of individual labour, immediately recognized as social labour, give rise to identical shares in the consumption fund. But since different individuals have differing needs and differing capacities to produce quantities of labour, some are able to satisfy their needs and others not.[27]

What existed in the Soviet Union was precisely not that *formal equality* in the distribution of consumer goods to which Marx referred in his use of the term 'bourgeois right', but rather a tremendous, and ever growing, *formal inequality*. In exchange for eight hours of labour an unskilled manual worker received x amount of consumer goods, while for the same eight hours a high-ranking bureaucrat, enjoying not only his salary but also special access to luxury goods and services in kind, received $10x$ or $20x$ consumer goods. *This* bourgeois right extends far beyond Marx's account of the first, socialist phase of communism. In Stalinist apologetics, it appears as the 'distribution norm' of 'to each according to the quantity and *quality* of labour', which is supposed to distinguish socialism from the communist norm of 'to each according to their needs'. But once again this is in flagrant contradiction to Marx's own formulas in the *Critique of the Gotha Programme*, where there is no reference to the 'quality of labour' or any such notion, and with Engels's polemical treatment of the same question in *Anti-Dühring*.[28] As for the Stalinist political onslaught on 'egalitarianism', qualified as a form of 'petty-bourgeois asceticism', this broke with the whole socialist tradition and with explicit positions taken by Lenin.[29]

It followed from this regime of distribution in the USSR, as it did from the persistence of commodity production and value, that the 'struggle for existence', the general fight for personal enrichment, the cold calculation of 'personal advantage', selfishness, careerism and corruption, continued to dominate Soviet society, even if to a lesser extent than they do capitalist society. This social dynamic did not derive primarily from 'vestiges of capitalist ideology' or 'the influence of the West' but was principally the result of *the prevailing socio-economic structure of the USSR*.

Here we encounter once more the phenomenon of scarcity, the same inadequacy in the development of the productive forces which has already served to explain the survival and hypertrophy of the state and the bureaucracy. There is no way in which distribution, law, legal or power relations can operate at a level qualitatively superior to that made possible by the development of the productive forces. The organization of distribution, the manner and agency of its regulation, ultimately depend on the quantity available – that is, on how much has been produced.[30] No amount of good intentions, voluntarist endeavour or idealist yearning can alter this constraint in the long run. As long as the society of the Soviet Union was unable to unite with the potential of the most advanced industrial sectors in Western Europe, North America and Japan, there could be no socialism. The fate of socialism has always depended on the fate of international capitalism, on the victory or defeat of the world proletariat – in other words, on the future of the world revolution.

This enables us to dispel another misunderstanding. When revolutionary Marxists argued that the survival of market relations in the Soviet Union and elsewhere proved that a socialist society did not yet exist, they were not thereby 'demanding' that 'the party' or the working class should immediately do away with commodity production and money or some such 'leftist' absurdity. Commodity production and value, like the state, cannot be arbitrarily 'abolished'; they can only *gradually wither away*. The fact that they continue to flourish and expand in China, instead of withering away, is essential to a scientific, Marxist, objective analysis of Chinese and similar societies. But it is not a ground for irresponsible and irrational proposals. Under the given internal and external conditions, the overnight 'abolition' of commodity production and the circulation of money would actually ensure an even swifter disintegration of the existing relations of production, not in favour of socialism but ultimately in favour of the restoration of capitalism.

Neither in the Opposition's proposals for a reform of the Soviet economy and society between 1922 and 1933, nor in the programme for a political revolution later drawn up by revolutionary Marxists in the USSR, was there ever any talk of an immediate end to commodity production. They called rather for its inclusion, and even expansion, within a system of socialized production and planning, aimed simultaneously at the optimum *long-term* development both of the productive forces and of *genuinely socialist relations of production*. The one cannot be arbitrarily separated from the other.[31]

Without expansion of the productive forces based upon another technology, respecting humankind and nature, there can be no socialism. But it is equally impossible to build socialism in the absence of truly socialist relations of production. The aim cannot be to produce 'in the first instance' such and such a quantity of steel and cement or cars and houses, leaving until the future day when the producers suddenly (by what miracle?) become masters and mistresses of their working and living conditions. Simultaneous progress has to be made, by a process of constant interaction, both on the front of production and labour productivity and in the growth of social equality, workers' self-management and socialist democracy in the economy and state administration. Otherwise, the sources of further development of the productive forces will gradually, one after the other, dry up.

By the same token, it is quite inappropriate to suggest, as did Lukács, that for revolutionary Marxists the only choice is between 'socialism through revolutionary warfare or a return to the circumstances that prevailed before the 7th of November, in other words, the dilemma of having to choose between adventurism and capitalism'. 'With regard to this dilemma,' Lukács concluded, 'a rehabilitation of Trotsky is not historically justified. With regard to the strategic issues of the time Stalin was completely right.'[32]

This distortion of history takes at face value legends of the bureaucracy that are directly refuted by all the documents relating to debates within the CPSU and the Comintern between 1923 and 1933. Far from having been prisoners of the dilemma described by Lukács, Trotsky and the Left Opposition maintained – first against Stalin and Zinoviev, then against Stalin and Bukharin, and finally, once the CPSU had become totally monolithic, against the Stalin faction alone – that communists had two key tasks, and that these had to be accomplished together. On the one hand, they had to speed up the gradual industrialization of the Soviet Union, introducing economic planning, raising the technical conditions of agriculture and reorganizing it – *though only with the peasantry's freely given consent* – upon a cooperative basis. But at the same time, they had also to extend the revolution on the international front *in accordance with the internal laws and requirements of the class struggle in each country* (and not in accordance with what happened to be the economic or diplomatic needs of the Soviet Union at a particular time). This line constituted a rejection of both surrender and adventurism, as is indicated by Trotsky himself in his 'Critique of the Draft Programme of the Communist International':

> During the Third Congress [of the Comintern], we declared tens of times to the impatient Leftists: 'Don't be in too great a hurry to save us. In that way you will only destroy yourselves and, therefore, also bring about our own destruction. Follow systematically the path of the struggle for the masses in order thus to reach the struggle for power. We need your victory but not your readiness to fight under unfavourable conditions. We will manage to maintain ourselves in the Soviet republic with the help of the NEP and we will go forward. You will still have time to come to our aid at the right moment if you will have gathered your forces and will have utilized the favourable situation.[33]

Finally, within the framework of the theories of permanent revolution and uneven and combined development, it is obviously not the case that the peoples of the less industrialized countries can take no steps towards their own liberation, while awaiting the victory of the proletariat in the industrially advanced nations to create the foundations for the successful building of socialism. On the contrary, Trotsky reached the conclusion that a socialist revolution in the backward countries was the only means of freeing them from the barbarous heritage of the past that weighed upon them so heavily.

In the age of imperialism, the bourgeoisie is incapable of cleaning out the Augean stables as, for the most part, it did in the West. This alone is full and sufficient justification for socialist revolutions in the Third World, for only they can resolve the unaccomplished tasks of the national-democratic revolution and *begin* socialist development. Nevertheless, this process cannot be *completed* on the exiguous economic and social foundations of these countries; it must be extended to the leading industrialized countries whenever the current state of the class struggle allows it.

3. The Hybrid Combination of Market Economy and Bureaucratic Despotism

It may be asked whether it follows from our analysis in the previous sections that the bureaucracy had become either a 'state capitalist class' or 'a new ruling class'. The answer to this question is: not in the least. But in order to refute such mechanistic notions, we need to examine more closely the contradictory combination of, on the one hand, commodity production and the operation of the law of value and, on the other, the despotic power of the bureaucracy. This has, in turn, to be incorporated into the more general problematic of societies in transition between 'progressive' historical modes of production, to use the famous expression coined by Marx.

As we have already argued, to restrict the functioning of commodity production to the age of capitalism would be to contradict one of the basic theses of historical materialism. Exchange, exchange-value and commodity production, and hence also the play of the law of value, were in existence centuries before the emergence of the capitalist mode of production. What distinguishes capitalism from various forms of petty commodity production is that the production of commodities and of value becomes *generalized*; only within this mode do the means of production and labour power become, in a general way, commodities. Although capital, capitalism and their contradictions are already present embryonically in petty commodity production, they are there precisely as no more than embryos. For them to develop to the full, a whole series of *further* economic and social conditions have to be created. In the West, and in the great civilizations of the East, this process took thousands of years. In the less developed countries, it is not yet completed today.

The obstacles on this path are truly formidable. We shall mention but one, namely, the need to separate peasant producers from all direct access to the land, their elementary means of production and subsistence, and to transform them into wage-earners. Clearly this requires a huge transformation of property relations in the countryside – the elimination of the slave plantation and land owned by the state, as well as

26

of the original village communities where peasants have de facto use of the land (whether in the framework of the 'Asiatic mode of production' or under 'pure feudalism').[34]

Additional economic, social and political changes in production and trade, in both town and countryside, are also necessary. The slow pace of this development entailed, even in the advanced regions of Western Europe, long periods of coexistence of petty commodity production, preponderantly non-capitalist production relations, and gradually emerging capitalist relations.[35] This phase of transition from feudalism to capitalism produced a hybrid combination of commodity production and simple use-value production. The law of value did operate in the commodity sphere, in a form peculiar to this transitional society. But at village level, for a long period, it operated scarcely or not at all.

A European peasant during the early Middle Ages, an Indian or Chinese peasant in the eighteenth century, a Mexican or African peasant in the middle of the nineteenth century, did not alter the volume or nature of his production in accordance with fluctuations in market prices, so long as output was intended first and foremost for his own subsistence. Land rent, taxes, wars or famine may have diminished, in some cases quite drastically, the proportion of total use-values remaining for his own consumption. But this fact did not transform him into a producer of commodities dependent on the market, that is, on the law of value. For that to happen, a change in *property relations* in the village was necessary – property relations being understood not in an essentially legal but in an economic sense. A de facto separation of the peasant from free access to the land was required.

The logic of a hybrid society of this kind may be expressed by saying that the law of value *operates* but does not predominate. Distribution of the socially available productive resources among the different sectors is determined above all by custom and tradition, by peasants' needs and habits, their production techniques, the organization of their communities, the despotic encroachments of the state, and so on. Marx's analysis of this state of affairs is well known.

Such hybrid relations of production do not necessarily lead to stagnation of the productive forces and of society. The contradiction between the transitional economy and commodity production unfolds gradually, one element being the expansion of usury and of commercial (later manufacturing) capital. It may in the long term produce an economic and social dynamic that eventually leads to the predominance of the law of value and the capitalist mode of production. Nonetheless, we are dealing with a *gradual historical process*, which has to be studied concretely and whose reality has to be empirically demonstrated. It cannot be deduced by means of abstract reasoning of the type: emergence of commodity production = automatic predominance of the law of value = capitalism = domination of a capitalist class, of the bourgeoisie.

The analogy with the economic and social structure of the Soviet Union and other societies organized along the same lines is striking. As in the pre-capitalist societies, commodity production persists in the transition between capitalism and socialism. But in both cases, one is faced with a non-generalized, only partial form of commodity production. Consumer goods and the means of production exchanged between agricultural cooperatives and state enterprises are commodities, as are the products channelled into foreign trade. But the bulk of the large-scale means of production are not commodities, nor is the greater part of labour power: there is no market for them in the proper sense of the word.[36] For this reason these economies cannot be meaningfully called 'capitalist', since the basic laws of motion of the capitalist mode of production do not apply.

Machinery and the labour force do not shift from sectors with a lower to sectors with a higher 'rate of profit'. Prices and 'profits' (which, in any case, serve mainly for accounting purposes insofar as prices are fixed administratively) are not signals that shape or redirect investment. It is not the law of value but the state (that is, the bureaucracy) which ultimately determines what proportion of the social product will be invested and what will be consumed, as well as deciding on the dynamic to be followed by the economy as a whole. The Soviet-type economy is thus not a generalized market economy. *It is an economy of centralized allocation of resources*, a centrally planned economy.

Yet it is not a 'pure' centrally allocative economy but a *hybrid combination* of an allocative and a commodity-producing economy, in which the law of value operates but does not hold sway. And this influence of the law of value *ultimately sets immovable limits to bureaucratic despotism*. This is what the theorists of 'bureaucratic collectivism', from Burnham and Shachtman to Castoriadis, fail to see.

First of all, the bureaucracy's scope for arbitrary action is restricted by objective internal constraints, by the limited material resources that the economy is in a position to allocate. It is true that the bureaucracy may command that certain sectors of industry will have a special claim on scarce resources in the field of, say, high technology. It may thus successively give priority to heavy industry, armaments, aerospace, gas pipelines to Europe, and so on. But what it cannot do is free itself from the laws of expanded reproduction.[37] Each disproportionate allocation of resources in favour of one sector leads to greater disproportions in the economy as a whole, ultimately undermining labour productivity in the priority sector itself. This means, for example, that a portion of Soviet economic resources then had to be diverted to the import of foodstuffs, rather than of machinery or modern technology.[38] What is more, the non-market sectors were in countless ways enmeshed in commodity–money relations – all the terror, pressure and despotism of the bureaucracy notwithstanding. Second, the arbitrariness of bureaucratic behaviour is restricted by pressure from the world capitalist market, where there is ultimately only one price structure and the law of value does hold final sway. All the Soviet bloc's foreign trade (even within Comecon) was in the final analysis conducted on the basis of world-market prices.

The hybrid nature of the Soviet-type society in transition is clearly reflected in the *dualistic structure of internal prices*, one set being determined by the law of value, another being arbitrarily fixed by the planning authorities. It is still this second group of 'prices' that predominated – which is why it was an economy of centralized allocation, protected by the state monopoly of foreign trade. Yet the greater the proportion of gross national product that is connected with foreign trade, the greater is the influence of the law of value on the 'planned' prices and on the distribution of resources within the state sector. The room for manoeuvre of the planned economy – that is, the centralized allocation of the decisive material resources – is thus clearly circumscribed. And conflicts between the 'political' and the 'technocratic' wing of the bureaucracy, between the central planning authorities and the business managers, is in the end a reflection of these objective contradictions.

For the same reason, each 'national' ruling bureaucracy, while sharing most of the characteristics of its Soviet prototype, combines them with a number of national specificities. These reflect the moment and the way in which it came to power, the history of its country and labour movement, the pre-existing socio-economic and political structure, the political traditions of the ruling and the middle classes, and – most important of all – the country's specific insertion in the world market. Events in 1989–90 confirmed these points in a spectacular way.

Although the persistence of commodity production and the despotic domination of the bureaucracy are both attributable to the isolation of the socialist revolution in a part of the world that is relatively backward in industrial terms, this despotism remains tied to the collective ownership of the means of production, to the planned economy and to the state monopoly of foreign trade. Commodity production and the operation of the law of value cannot in the long run become generalized without breaking the despotism of the bureaucracy.

Here we see the decisive reason why the bureaucracy did not become a ruling class. It could not do so by evolving in the direction of a new ruling class, but only by turning into a classical capitalist class. *For a 'new', 'bureaucratic' non-capitalist mode of production to emerge, the Soviet bureaucracy would have to have liberated itself once and for all from the influence of the law of value.* However, this would have required not only the disappearance of relations of distribution based on exchange within the Soviet Union itself, but also the total emancipation of the USSR from the world market, that is, the elimination of capitalism on a world scale, or at least in the most important industrialized nations.[39] This, in turn, depends on the final outcome of the struggle between capital and labour on a world scale, and a victory for the world socialist revolution would be unpropitious in the extreme for a conversion of Stalinist bureaucracy into a ruling class.

A new ruling class presupposes a new mode of production, with its own internal logic, its own laws of motion. Until now, no one has been able to do so much as outline the laws of motion of a 'new bureaucratic mode of production' – for the simple reason that no such mode exists. On the other hand, it has been possible to identify the laws of motion specific to the Stalinist economies. The empirical data of the last thirty years abundantly confirm their operation.[40]

As far as revolutionary Marxists are concerned, the partially positive aspects of the Soviet state derived precisely from the fact that it was still a workers' state, albeit an extremely bureaucratized one. As for its non-proletarian aspects, everything which related to the particular interests and the specific nature of the bureaucracy as a social stratum – its hostility to the working class, its appropriation of part of the surplus product, its conservative role in the international arena – all were profoundly and utterly reactionary.[41]

Historically, ruling classes have been able to maintain their dominance in the long term only on the basis of property. The fate of state officials under the Asiatic mode of production is highly illustrative in this respect.

In China during the early phases of each dynasty, the objective function of the bureaucracy was to protect the state and the peasantry from the claims of the landed nobility in order to enable expanded reproduction (irrigation work, centralization of the surplus product, guarantees of adequate labour productivity in the villages, and so on). This in turn permitted the – often extremely generous – remuneration of the bureaucracy by the state out of the centralized surplus product. The bureaucrat, however, remained dependent on *the whim of the state*, in the shape of the court and the emperor. His position was never secure.[42] He could have no assurance that his son would obtain the same good position in the bureaucracy that he himself occupied.

This is why, during the second half of each dynastic cycle, there was a general tendency for the landed nobility (or gentry) to merge with the bureaucracy. Bureaucrats would gradually become owners, first of money and movable property, and then of land – this being an 'illegal' process, comparable to the appropriation of stocks of raw materials and finished products by bureaucrats in the Soviet Union.

To the extent that state bureaucrats fused with the gentry, the centralization of the surplus product was undermined, the state power grew weaker, the pressure on the peasantry intensified and its income was reduced. The productivity of agricultural labour declined. Rural exodus, peasant revolts, banditry and insurrection became general phenomena. The dynasty lost 'the mandate of Heaven' – that is, its legitimacy – and eventually collapsed. A new dynasty, often springing from peasant origins, then restored the relative independence of the state and its bureaucracy vis-à-vis the landed nobility.

One of the best works on traditional Chinese society is Etienne Balazs's *La bureaucratie céleste*. It is true that Balazs sometimes calls the mandarins a class, but this general definition does not stand up to the concrete characteristics that he successively identifies, nor to his remarkable concrete analysis of its social behaviour and fundamental lack of stability.

> A long and painful process [took place under the Zhou dynasty], the most notable result of which was the birth of a new intermediate social layer between the nobility and the common people. . . .
>
> This new, highly educated, fearful and ambitious layer, barely conscious of its own role and its future autonomy, wished to save the whole of society, and in the first place itself, from the prevailing general insecurity. . . .
>
> The highly educated officials responsible for the administration of the unified Empire, founded by the 'First Emperor' Qin Shihuangdi (221–210 BC) and continued by the Han dynasty, were, generally speaking, also property owners. But – and this is very important for an understanding of imperial China – the source of their power was not their property but their position, active fulfilment of which determined their privileges. This fact explains the permanent character of two contradictory aspects of agrarian history in China. On the one hand, the privileged class of educated officials/property owners, which adopted as its faithful expression the paternalist Confucian doctrine, vigorously opposed the formation of latifundia and the power of the big landowners because the excesses of the nobles, the behaviour of the feudal barons, jeopardized the unity and even the existence of the Empire. At the same time, these very officials were naturally inclined to invest their fortune in land, commerce and industry, though these occupations were theoretically incompatible with the honour of a gentleman. Hence the continuous vacillations in agrarian policy.[43]

We can see here a three-cornered fight among big landowners, mandarins and peasants – four-cornered if the incipient urban bourgeoisie is included. There is again a striking analogy with the USSR, where the three corners were represented by workers, bureaucrats and an incipient bourgeoisie in town and country – and a fourth by the labouring peasantry. An analogy is, of course, not an identity. Private property and personal enrichment played a much greater role among the mandarins of ancient China than within the Stalinist and post-Stalinist nomenklatura. But in both cases we are dealing with a hybrid social layer, combining monetary and non-monetary access to the social surplus product. The hybrid – and therefore fundamentally unstable – nature of that social layer reflects the hybrid character of the social relations of production themselves – that is, of the social structure in its totality.

As long as the absolute shortage of consumer goods persisted in the Soviet Union – broadly speaking, from 1928 to the early 1950s – the necessity of satisfying their own immediate needs impelled the bureaucrats to force the workers to work twice or three times harder. But once these immediate needs were assuaged, Soviet society was faced with the problem that has been a feature of all pre-capitalist societies. *Where the privileges of dominant classes or strata (castes, etc.) are mainly confined to the realm of private consumption, they have no objective long-term interest in a sustained increase in productivity*. This is why the growth in production and in the consumption of luxury goods goes hand in hand with waste, senseless extravagance and personal decadence (alcoholism, orgies, drug-taking). In this respect, the behaviour of the nobility in the Roman Empire, the eighteenth-century French court nobility, the nineteenth-century Ottoman Empire and the Tsarist Empire on the eve of the Revolution is to all intents and purposes identical.

The parallel with sections of the upper strata of the Soviet bureaucracy, and with parasitical propertied strata under monopoly capitalism, is obvious. Only the class of capitalist entrepreneurs is *compelled by the pressure of competition* (that is, by the generalization of private property and commodity production) to behave in an essentially different manner. If competition wanes, Marx pointed out, capitalism shows a tendency to stagnate. But competition is a corollary of private property (in the economic sense of the term) and loses all meaning in its absence.

In the fifties, critics of our thesis – according to which the USSR was still a society in transition – vociferously argued that 'production for production's sake' held sway there and would lead to permanent levels of relatively high growth. Our own analysis enabled us to predict that the opposite would come to pass. Now history has decided the issue. The more Soviet economic growth slowed down, the more a sector of the bureaucracy pushed for decentralization of control over the means of production and the social surplus product, on the grounds that what is 'objectively' required is greater rights for managers and a legal appropriation of resources for *private* consumption and *private* profit. This 'liberalization' gradually erodes central planning. It leads to a more powerful role for the law of value and finally to a tendency to restore capitalism.

In a parallel process, the bureaucracy is subject to internal divisions and, above all, to growing opposition on the part of the working class. For the workers observe in practice that private property can gain decisive ground *only at the expense of full employment and even greater inequality*, and the massive strikes of 1988–90 confirm that they are prepared to fight for these with determination. Some call this 'conservatism'. One might just as well describe as 'conservative' the mentality of workers in capitalist countries who resist wage-cuts and redundancies![44]

For these reasons, workers' self-management of the Yugoslav type, where it is combined with a so-called 'socialist market economy', merely masks rather than resolves the contradiction. There is no genuine *power of decision-making* by the workers' collectives (and hence no genuine self-management) if the closure of a factory can be imposed upon them by the law of value. There is no genuine 'market economy' if worker collectives can effectively *prevent* fluctuations in employment.

Now, in the Soviet Union and other such societies, it is possible to observe an embryonic transformation of parts of the bureaucracy into a capitalist class. Such a process requires a generalization of commodity production – that is, the transformation of the means of production *and of labour power* into commodities. To reach completion, it would have to destroy collective ownership of the means of production, the institutional guarantees of full employment, the dominance of central planning, and the state monopoly on foreign trade. It would also have to involve a further historical defeat of the Soviet working class at the social and economic levels. Such a defeat has not yet taken place.[45]

The October Revolution and the bureaucratic domination that resulted from its isolation can be explained only by *a combination* of, on the one hand, the limits of Russian 'internal development' (a 'barbarous' capitalism in a semi-feudal state subject to strong imperialist influence from outside, with a relatively stronger, more concentrated and more conscious working class) and, on the other, the prodigious development of world capitalism and the world proletariat in the imperialist epoch. For this same reason, the Russian bureaucracy cannot turn into a 'new ruling class' as long as the fate of capitalism has not been decided internationally one way or another. That 'dirty old business' which re-emerged in the USSR after the victory of the Revolution could not take the form of a new class society but became enshrined in a bureaucratization of the society in transition between capitalism and socialism.

33

4. The Impact of Bureaucratic Policy on Social Reality

The revolutionary Marxist analysis of the Soviet Union was not based on an 'objectivist', still less on an 'economistic' view of history. Nowhere do we assert that the subjective factor – the class consciousness of the workers and the political line taken by the state and party leadership – has been or is purely marginal in its impact. Objective circumstances – above all, the degree of development of the productive forces – clearly do set strict limits on the policy variants that are open to the state and the party. Even the most highly accomplished revolutionaries in the Soviet Union in 1990 (not to speak of 1920, 1927, 1933 or 1953) could not completely abolish commodity production, the role of money, the state and the bureaucracy. Nevertheless, within these objective constraints, the range of possible policies was and remains broader than is generally believed. Twenty-eight years ago, in Chapter 16 of *Marxist Economic Theory*, we tried to elucidate the consequences of these options. To date, no one has offered a refutation of our argument.

In every society where there is more or less continuous expanded reproduction, the social product subdivides into three, and not two, basic sectors: the productive consumption fund (A), which enables the labour power and means of production depleted in the course of production to be reconstituted; the accumulation fund (B), comprising the sum of means of production and means of consumption for *additional producers*, which is made available by the expanded reproduction *expressed in use-value*;[46] and the non-productive consumption fund (C) – including arms production – which makes no contribution to future expanded reproduction in terms, once again, of use-value.

The bureaucracy's economic ideology, supported by countless Western ideologues and various pseudo- or semi-Marxists, insists that the productive consumption fund had to be kept depressed in order to assure a high level of accumulation for economic growth, and *in the long term* for 'optimum growth' of consumption. This is supposed to explain the high rate of accumulation in the Soviet economy – on average, 25 per cent of annual national income. In both theory and practice, however, this thesis is mistaken for the following two reasons.

First, it fails to take into account that the consumption fund for direct producers is a fund of *indirect means of production*. Every shortfall with regard to the basic consumption expectations of the direct producers results in a relative or even absolute decline in labour productivity. Additional investment made possible by the relative or absolute fall in producers' consumption therefore leads to *diminishing rates of increase in final output*. The 25 per cent rate of accumulation translates initially into 7 per cent annual growth, then into 5 per cent, 4 per cent, and

Table 1 Distribution of social product in the Soviet Union (%)

	A	B	C
Initial situation	55	15	30
Beginning of bureaucratic industrialization	35	30	35
Long-term result	35	20	45

eventually just 3 per cent. Western economists speak in this respect of a 'rising coefficient of capital' in the USSR. Official Soviet economists refer to the same phenomenon by the term 'deceleration of the rotation of fixed funds'.[47]

Second, this ideology disregards the fact that the producers who consume fewer or shoddier goods than they expected, and who are dissatisfied with their working and living conditions (including the absence of civil and political rights), are also indifferent to their work and may indeed deliberately slow its pace. Disclaiming all responsibility for production, they have to be *forced to work*.

Now, in a capitalist economy this compulsion operates essentially through the labour market, by means of wage fluctuations, job insecurity, periodic bouts of mass unemployment, and so on. In the Soviet Union, however, these constraints functioned marginally or not at all: *it is for this reason that it was not a capitalist society*. Instead of the laws of the market, the coercive factors are administrative control, pressure and repression – in other words, the despotism of the bureaucracy. *These are precisely the circumstances which explain the hypertrophy of officialdom and the repressive apparatuses, and of the non-productive consumption fund (category C) that we identified above. Thus, B declines by more than would be the case if A were to rise at a reasonable rate. The expansion of non-productive expenditure reduces or cancels those extra advantages that it was thought possible to achieve by holding down the consumption of the producers.* Table 1 sets out the approximate evolution of national income, as distributed among the three categories.[48]

This, then, is the secret essence of the bureaucracy's political and economic history, of its initial successes and its ever more blatant failures. Instead of 'production for production's sake' and a 'systematic drive to expand capital accumulation', we find a huge growth of category C and a growing indifference to the expansion, not to mention optimization, of category B. On account of the internal contradictions of its

35

management and planning, the bureaucracy increasingly becomes a fetter on the expansion of the productive forces – a fetter that must be removed if progress is to be resumed. After the revelations of glasnost, it is hard to deny this overall judgement.

In the Soviet Union the size and reach of the bureaucracy, as well as the dynamics of commodity production, were much greater than is objectively inevitable. In fact, *the interaction between objective inevitability and actual bureaucratic policy* (that is, the product of specific bureaucratic interests) *determined the dynamic of Soviet reality.* The consequences of this interaction may be summed up in a single formula: colossal waste. A former head of the bureaucracy, Yuri Andropov, estimated that *one third of annual working hours* were wasted. Gorbachev has since confirmed that assessment. There could hardly be a more damning indictment of the bureaucracy's management of the Soviet economy.

To see the source of the bureaucracy's power in 'central planning as such' is a typical case of reified, fetishistic thinking which does not ask the question: which social forces plan and in whose favour?[49] Moreover, it leaves aside the main aspect of the Soviet economy, which is precisely the hybrid *combination* of central allocation and the partial survival of commodity production. Ever since the first five-year plan, we have seen only partial, and therefore largely distorted planning, a concentration of resources on 'crash' projects side by side with huge inbuilt disproportions.

The most striking of these disproportions can be seen in the tremendous underdevelopment of the service sector in the broadest sense of the term (trade, transport, storage, banking, etc.), which accounts for only 15–20 per cent of national expenditure, compared with 40–50 per cent in industrialized and even semi-industrialized capitalist countries. (This latter percentage, however, would have to be substantially lowered if one were to take into account the *faux frais* of capitalist production, capitalist distribution and capitalist accumulation in finance and trade, which are also highly wasteful.) The notorious queues in Soviet cities, which eat up so much time for women and men – primarily women – are due at least as much to this long-term underinvestment in the service sector as to insufficiencies in output. For example, although the USSR is by far the largest producer of potatoes in the world, 75 per cent of its output does not manage to be 'serviced' to reach the final consumer.

Such disproportions weigh heavily on living conditions and labour productivity in the Soviet Union, but they can in no way be described as inherent in, or inevitable consequences of, central planning. On the contrary: the huge dysfunctions and waste that they imply run counter to the elementary logic of planning, which is after all an attempt at proportional development of the economy. They only reflect preferences of the bureaucracy, despotically imposed on the mass of producers/consumers.

As to the thesis that central planning 'in and of itself' breeds bureaucracy, and that 'Marxian socialism' therefore equals general and despotic power of the bureaucracy – a thesis first formulated by Max Weber and picked up by von Mises – no logical proof has ever been proposed in its support. It is in fact basically a tautology, *provided* one assumes that the only possible form of planning is planning from above, through a hugely expanded state. But this embodies a strong measure of elitist prejudice, in supposing that the mass of producers/citizens are unable consciously to coordinate (that is, plan) their preferences from below.

If one looks at the historical evidence, the causal chain actually has to be reversed. It is not the intrinsic nature of planning which has produced the hypertrophy of the Soviet bureaucracy, but rather the power of the bureaucracy which has produced the specific forms of planning in the USSR and similar societies.

Another conception now widely circulating in the USSR alleges that bureaucratic despotism is a result of the 'barracks communism' already initiated in the period of War Communism. This is said to have receded somewhat under The New Economic Policy (NEP) but then to have been generalized after 1928 through Stalin's 'leftist–voluntarist' drive to modernize Russia at all costs and by means of ruthless pressure. The fact is, however, that there was hardly any bureaucracy under War Communism. The bureaucracy only rose to power under NEP, as the figures for full-time functionaries in the Russian Communist Party after 1922 clearly demonstrate. If the generalization of planning after 1928 took a monstrously bureaucratic form, this was precisely because it was imposed by the bureaucracy, in order to extend its power and privileges.[50]

In spite of its partial character, Soviet planning contained a hard core of real planning. To portray the Soviet economy *merely* as an 'economy of waste' – as some authors have done – does not explain how an essentially agrarian country could, within less than two generations, become the second industrial power in the world. A good number of American and Japanese factories are currently applying Soviet patents. Is that all a result of 'waste'?[51]

In a system of free and democratic decision-making by the masses, of democratically centralized self-management, the scope for bureaucratic distortion of planning would be sharply reduced. But a number of authors, from different standpoints, suggest that self-management is impossible without the predominance of the market, that the only possible 'real' socialism is market socialism. The historical experience of Yugoslavia has already refuted this assertion, since the radical market reforms of 1971 led not to the strengthening of workers' self-management but to its gradual self-liquidation. If the market imposes massive redundancies or even closures on the workers – in most cases, through no 'fault' or responsibility of their own – how can they be considered free or self-managing in any meaningful sense, except in that of being free to sack themselves?

Marx's analysis of the inevitable consequences of a predominantly market economy have thus been fully confirmed, despite a variety of recent attempts to square the circle. Peter Ruben, for instance, tries to marry a defence of 'market socialism' – including entrepreneurial profits and huge, compulsory fluctuations in employment – with Marx's vision of workers' emancipation through the replacement of class society by an association of free individuals. But this completely misses the point that there are no 'freely associated producers' if they are subordinated and alienated by the law of value, if their economic fate is *imposed* on them behind their backs, independently of their conscious choice.[52]

Mikhail Gorbachev expresses this contradiction even more clearly. On the one hand, he correctly recalls that for Marx socialism meant the free development of all individuals: human beings had to conquer control over their material production; the very essence of socialism lay in freedom. But then comes the *salto mortale*. In Gorbachev's thinking, freedom and control are reduced to the producers' appropriation of the means of production (diversified instead of 'monopolistic' property relations). Social justice is correlated with so-called economic efficiency – that is, with determination of the economy's long-term dynamic by competition and extensive market mechanisms. But how can producers control their material production and labour conditions if these are imposed by the laws of the market and competition, against their own free will?[53]

In this regard, the policy of the CPSU leadership was neither objectively predetermined nor without influence on the evolution of the country and the world: it simultaneously fostered the spread of commodity production and the expansion of the bureaucracy. In the end it has significantly accelerated both processes, thereby rendering the social contradictions more acute. Far from being a weapon of the proletarian masses (of the proletariat as a class) against the bureaucracy, as Lenin hoped and wished, the Party itself became an instrument of bureaucratic dictatorship. Instead of raising the proletariat to the position of directly ruling class during the dictatorship of the proletariat, the Party increasingly turned into a separate bureaucratic apparatus remote from the working class. Bureaucratization of the Party merged with bureaucratization of the state to oppress the proletariat once again.

It is clear that this whole problematic is closely bound up with the question of Thermidor, which was the object of one of Trotsky's most famous analyses. What is much less known is that, as early as 1921, Lenin himself raised the possibility of a Thermidor in his notes for the Tenth Party Conference: 'Thermidor? Reason surely dictates that we admit the possibility. Whether or not it will come to that, only time will tell.'[54]

It should be stressed once more that the outcome was not automatically given by 'objective circumstances' or the 'relationship of forces', but was strongly co-determined by a whole series of decisions taken, first, by the majority of the CPSU leadership, then by Stalin and his faction at the head of the Soviet state, and later, during a third phase, by the summit of the bureaucratic dictatorship after Stalin's death. The following options, in more or less chronological order, were particularly fraught with consequences:

- the refusal to implement the 1923 resolution on inner-party democracy, the stifling of debate and criticism, and the consolidation of a party regime based upon the rule of a non-elected and essentially irremovable apparatus that was monstrously expanded after 1921;

- the destruction of workers' self-expression and of the remnants of Soviet democracy;

- the delay in gradually accelerating industrialization between 1923 and 1927, and especially in creating a tractor industry as the basis for a growth of voluntary producers' cooperatives in agriculture;

- the subordination of the Chinese Communist Party to the bourgeois Kuomintang until after Chiang Kai-Shek's coup – a policy that led to the defeat of the Chinese Revolution in April 1927;

- the forced collectivization of agriculture and mass deportation of so-called kulaks after 1928;

- the precipitate industrialization, with no cost-accounting, after 1928, accompanied by a steep decline in real wages and brutal anti-working-class legislation and repression;

- the theory and practice of 'social fascism', which helped Hitler to take and consolidate power in 1933–34;

- the strangling of the Spanish revolution of 1936–37;

- the massive purge of the CPSU and Red Army between 1934 and 1938, and the institutionalization of terror;

- the Hitler–Stalin Pact of 1939–41, with its disastrous political and military effects;

- the attempts to stifle the mass upsurge for national liberation in India and Indonesia between 1942 and 1946 and the working-class mass upsurge in capitalist Europe in 1943–48;

- the structural assimilation of the East European 'buffer zone' to Stalinist Russia, through methods rejected by the majority of the toiling masses of these countries;

- the break with Tito and Mao at state level;

- the military intervention against the political revolution in Hungary in 1956 and against the Prague Spring in 1968.

All these decisions were avoidable. If others had been taken in their place, they would not have guaranteed a victory of world revolution, but they would certainly have created a world quite different from that which has developed since 1924.

5. The Contradictions of the Bureaucracy's Factory Organization

The Soviet Union's hybrid combination of despotic central planning and partial operation of the law of value has also been clearly expressed at the level of factory organization.

The aftermath of the October Revolution was marked by a great thrust of working-class self-organization in the factories.[55] However, the lack of coordination of the economic system was not spontaneously overcome in this way, and the Bolshevik government tried to combine the workers' initiatives from below with centralization from above.[56] The pressures of civil war and 'war communism' operated in the same direction. With the introduction of NEP in 1921, this new equilibrium was finally stabilized through the 'troika' system of dividing power between the manager, the trade-union secretary and the Party secretary.[57] The trade unions functioned as the main safeguards and transmission-belts of workers' interests, which were by no means systematically sacrificed to those of the management. Indeed, although inequality increased in the NEP period, together with unemployment, the workers' standard of living rose significantly.[58]

The consolidation of Thermidor, of the bureaucratic dictatorship, brutally destroyed this equilibrium. Trade-union rights were reduced to nil. One-man managerial command became an iron rule in the factory. Primitive 'productivism', essentially geared to gross physical output regardless of economic and social cost, became the goal to which both trade-union and Party organizations in the factory had to devote themselves body and soul. Strikes and any other form of working-class resistance were prohibited as 'sabotage'.

The United Opposition strenuously opposed these trends from the beginning. On 21 September 1926 Trotsky pointed out that 'measures of war communism and intensified pressure' could be effective only for a limited period, and that 'in conditions of the long-term building of socialism, workers' discipline must rest more and more on the self-activation of the workers and on their interest in the results of their work.'[59]

The system of bureaucratic management drew massively on a crude Taylorism and deskilling of part of the labour force.[60] Speed-up and piece-work, with a radical, Stakhanov-type fragmentation of the working class according to the technical division of labour, rapidly became the norm. Against the initial resistance of Lunacharsky, People's Commissar of Education, the whole system of vocational training was reorganized to replace general polytechnical and cultural guidelines with an ever greater specialization and narrow occupational horizons.[61]

It would appear at first sight – and this is one of the main points raised by 'state capitalism' (or 'state socialism') theorists – that the new orientation was just a total imitation of capitalist factory organization. One should not think that there is not a kernel of truth here: the symmetry between American and Soviet Taylorism is undeniable. But there is also an asymmetry, which again confirms the specificity of the relations of production in the USSR.

The capitalist entrepreneur is not concerned only with micro-economic maximization of surplus labour. Under the whip of competition, *maximization of realized profit in money form* is an absolute precondition for the accumulation of capital. There is no point in increasing surplus labour if this leads to a reduction of profit. Now, one of the key mechanisms of profit maximization is the substitution of the production of relative surplus-value for the extended production of absolute surplus-value. The tendential rise and periodic revolutions in labour productivity, through improved technology and 'rationalized' work organization, make it possible to produce the equivalent of the workers' wages (including increased real wages) in a shorter and shorter part of the working day. That is one of the main aspects of economic growth under capitalism.

Under the bureaucratic dictatorship, factory managers do not operate under the same constraint. There is no whip of competition; there is no inescapable drive to reduce production costs at the micro-economic level

41

of the factory; there is no obligation to maximize 'profits'. The only basic compulsion is a political one. Under Stalin, the price for poor performance could be loss of freedom or even of life itself.[62] Since Stalin's death, such extra-economic sanctions have steadily declined, and managers in general now enjoy a large degree of security of tenure. If a member of the nomenklatura is dismissed from one job, he will almost automatically be 'reintegrated' elsewhere.

A general lack of responsibility, and indifference to the factory's performance, is therefore a characteristic feature of the system and threatens the USSR with stagnation and decline.[63] In fact, as the only essential criterion of economic rationality is the fulfilment of physical targets, managers tend actually to undermine efficiency by accumulating excessive stocks, cutting the quality of products, wasting energy and raw materials, engaging in 'grey-market' operations, and so on.

It might be objected that the system of bureaucratic planning, though greatly inferior to capitalist competition (capitalist market economy) in micro-economic efficiency, is nevertheless superior from the point of view of macro-economic results. It is certainly undeniable that, for decades, the average rate of growth of the Soviet economy outstripped that of the West. But even if we leave aside the questions 'At what cost?' and 'Why didn't it last?', this line of argument evades the key problem of the *differentia specifica*, in terms of human labour and machinery (technology), of the Soviet factory system.

Precisely because the extraction of surplus labour from the Soviet worker is not geared to micro-economic maximization of profit, it is at once worse and less oppressive than it is under capitalism. Compared with their counterparts in North America or Western Europe, Soviet workers have to spend longer hours in the factory for a much lower wage, but they actually work for considerably less of the time.

The overall waste of economic resources is probably higher under capitalism than in the USSR: in the region of 50 per cent, against 40–45 per cent. It essentially appears as unsold goods, unused means of production and the selling of useless or harmful products. In the Soviet Union, it largely takes the form of hours of labour not actually worked – something that is not often seen under capitalism.

In the sphere of technology, where there is no equivalent to the constant pressure on capitalist entrepreneurs,[64] the great strides in fundamental research and prototypes have not led to their massive introduction in the factory. In fact, this is resisted by the bureaucrats as harmful to the goal of fulfilling a plan that was fixed before the innovations had taken place.[65]

The Soviet manager seeks to combine the behaviour of a typical bureaucrat with that of a would-be entrepreneur.[66] On the one hand, he will strictly follow the rules, whatever the economic results for 'his' factory (precisely because it is not *his* factory) and the economy as a whole. On the other hand, he will try to 'fulfil the plan' at the expense of the workers, with little or no regard for their well-being and by violating many of the rules.

For their part, the workers defend both their rights as consumers (real wages, real consumption, real social services) and their position as producers, whatever the apparent contradictions between the two. Just as the threat of competition is lacking for the bureaucratic manager, so the whip of possible unemployment is lacking for the worker.[67] The result is a factory regime – that is, real relations of production even 'at the point of production', not to say for the economy as a whole – which differs substantially from that of capitalism. Despite all the hierarchies of labour control, the changed relationship of forces at shopfloor level, together with the mentality of 'anything for a quiet life', mean that Soviet managers will for the most part rapidly cave in to workers' demands.[68]

The distinctive feature of the bureaucracy is to work on the basis of formal rules. But 'to work to rule', in the public sector of capitalism, means literally to disorganize the economy, to practise a particular form of strike – quite unlike 'working for profits'. Who does not grasp that does not understand the specificity of capitalism.

Naturally, this analysis should not be construed as an apology either for bureaucratic mismanagement or for capitalist exploitation. Both are oppressive from the point of view of the working class. Both are wasteful in terms of allocating material resources, of protecting the integrity of labour and nature. The point is that they are different.

The most fundamental parallel between capitalist and Soviet-bureaucratic management is that, in their different ways, both tend to combine technological innovation with methods for maintaining or increasing control over labour at the point of production.[69] Walter Süss has shown convincingly how the mechanical and uncritical introduction of Taylorism in the USSR, especially after the launching of the first five-year plan, was precisely designed to achieve the partial deskilling of labour, to enforce greater control over labour-time, and to weaken the resistance to speed-ups.[70] In the ideology of the extreme proponents of 'Soviet Taylorism', like Gastev, this expressed itself in a view of socialism in which the proletariat would not only survive as a class but become (we would rather say, degenerate into) 'social automats'. Trotsky, on the other hand, placing himself in the tradition of Marx and Engels, strongly opposed such conceptions. For him, socialism meant not the perpetuation but the disappearance of the proletariat as a class.[71]

6. State-Commodity Fetishism: The Heart of Bureaucratic Ideology

The evolution of Stalinist and post-Stalinist ideology strikingly reflects the hybrid and contradictory social reality of the USSR. The bureaucracy does not have an ideology of its own. It continues to rely for a substitute on a systematically deformed version of Marxism, whose core has gradually crystallized out of the cynical realpolitik that led the Kremlin to impose numerous changes of direction on its unfortunate ideologues.

The first element is a *fetishization of the state* pushed to its extreme limit. In his *Critique of Hegel's Doctrine of the State*, Marx presented this fetishization as a basic ideological feature of any bureaucracy. His brilliant and penetrating description applies to the letter of the Soviet bureaucracy's ideology:

> The bureaucratic mind is a Jesuitic, theological mind through and through. The bureaucrats are the Jesuits and theologians of the state. The bureaucracy is the religious republic. . . . The bureaucracy appears to itself as the ultimate purpose of the state. As the bureaucracy converts its 'formal' purposes into its content, it comes into conflict with 'real' purposes at every point. It is therefore compelled to pass off form as content and content as form. The purposes of the state are transformed into purposes of offices and vice-versa. The bureaucracy is a magic circle from which no one can escape. Its hierarchy is a hierarchy of knowledge. The apex entrusts insight into particulars to the lower echelons while the lower echelons credit the apex with insight into the universal, and so each deceives the other. . . .
>
> The bureaucracy holds the state, the spiritual essence of society, in thrall, as its *private property*. The universal spirit of bureaucracy is *secrecy*, it is mystery preserved within itself by means of the hierarchical structure and appearing to the outside world as a self-contained corporation. Openly avowed public spirit, even patriotic sentiment, appears to the bureaucracy as a *betrayal* of its mystery. The principle of its knowledge is therefore *authority*, and its *patriotism* is the adulation of authority. Within itself, however, *spiritualism* degenerates into *crass materialism*, the materialism of passive obedience, the worship of authority, the *mechanism* of fixed, formal action, of rigid principles, views and traditions. As for the individual bureaucrat, the purpose of the state becomes his private purpose, *a hunt for promotion, careerism*. . . .
>
> While in one respect the bureaucracy is a crass materialism, in another respect its crass spiritualism is revealed in its wish *to do everything*. That is to say, it makes *will* the prime cause because it is nothing but active existence and receives its content from outside itself, and can therefore only prove its own existence by moulding and limiting that content. For the bureaucrat the world is no more than an object on which he acts.[72]

Let us see how this works itself out in the writings of the ideologues of the Soviet bureaucracy. We find, first of all, a doctrine which denies the parasitical nature and the historically limited, transitional character of the state. L.S. Mamut, for example, writes:

> Taking a retrospective view of the reality of the state, it is to be observed that, on the scale of world history, it develops an ever higher level of political freedom for society and its subjects. . . . According to Marx, freedom can be created only with the help of the [state] institutions; to this end, they undergo fundamental transformation and, much more important, must be placed under the effective control of the workers of the new society . . . . After the victory of the revolutionary proletariat over the bourgeoisie, the freedom of society will include the freedom of *every* worker. A *collective* freedom which has not as a precondition the freedom of *each* of the associated individuals is, according to Marx and Engels, simply absurd. Society cannot become free without freeing every individual.[73]

Except for the last two sentences, which were written by Marx and Engels, this passage is theoretically and empirically preposterous. The 'victory of the revolutionary proletariat over the bourgeoisie' took place in the Soviet Union seventy-three years ago. Did *every* Soviet worker, under Stalin, Khrushchev, Brezhnev and Andropov, have the freedom to found a trade union, a political organization or a monthly publication without prior authorization from a state body? Does he or she enjoy this freedom even today? Does the working class effectively control the KGB? Where? How? When? How can intelligent cynics not be ashamed to put such nonsense on paper? Where is the 'control of Soviet workers' over the central bodies of state, the very ones which are supposed to guarantee 'an ever higher level of political freedom for society and its subjects'?

Even if the workers were in effective control of state institutions, this would not turn the state into a means of assuring 'ever greater freedom'. How remote such conceptions are from the insights of Marx and Engels may be gauged from the following quotation from Engels, which provides a trenchant summary of their theory of the bureaucracy:

> Having public power and the right to levy taxes, the officials now stand, as organs of society, *above* society. The free, voluntary respect that was accorded to the organs of the gentile [clan] constitution does not satisfy them, even if they could gain it; being the vehicles of a power that is becoming alien to society, respect for them must be enforced by means of exceptional laws by virtue of which they enjoy special sanctity and inviolability. The shabbiest police servant in the civilized state has more 'authority' than all the organs of gentile society put together; but the most powerful prince and the greatest statesman, or general, of civilization may well envy the humblest gentile chief for the unstrained and undisputed respect that is paid to him.[74]

Furthermore, Engels actually wrote to Bebel the *exact opposite* of Mamut's ponderings on the state as guarantor of freedom: 'So long as the proletariat still *uses* the state, it does not use it in the interests of freedom but to hold down its adversaries, and as soon as it becomes possible to speak of freedom the state as such ceases to exist.'[75]

As to the Marxist conception of the difference between the bourgeois state (or the state of all earlier ruling classes) and the proletarian state (dictatorship of the proletariat), Lenin was even more radical. Summing up the experience of the Paris Commune, he wrote as follows in *The State and Revolution*:

> It is still necessary to suppress the bourgeoisie and crush its resistance. . . . But the organ of suppression is now the majority of the population, and not a minority, as was always the case under slavery, serfdom and wage slavery. And since the majority of the people *itself* suppresses its oppressors, a 'special force' for suppression is *no longer necessary*! In this sense, the state *begins to wither away*. Instead of the special institutions of a privileged minority (privileged officialdom, the chiefs of the standing army), the majority itself can directly fulfil all these functions, and the more the functions of state power devolve upon the people as a whole the less need is there for the existence of this power. . . . This shows more clearly than anything else the *turn* from bourgeois democracy to proletarian democracy, from the democracy of the oppressors to the democracy of the oppressed classes, from the state as a 'special force' for the suppression of a particular class to the suppression of the oppressors by the *general force* of the majority of the people.[76]

Lenin later characterized the Soviet state in similar terms: 'The Soviet power is a new type of state, without bureaucracy, without a police force, without a standing army.'[77] It is ironic to consider that if, between 1928 and 1986, anyone in the Soviet Union had published and disseminated this quote from Lenin, they would have been sentenced to between five and ten years of forced labour in the gulag for the crime of 'anti-Soviet agitation' or 'slandering the Soviet authorities'. Worse still, they might well have been committed to a psychiatric hospital for years, and subjected to a course of brain-washing treatment. For one would indeed have to be mad – as mad as Lenin – to imagine a Soviet state without bureaucrats, without a police force, and without a standing army!

Stalin did not hesitate to defend quite openly the necessity and functions of the bureaucracy. A forthright statement was contained in his organizational report to the Twelfth Party Congress, in April 1923:

> Once the correct political line is determined, the main task is to select the functionaries in such a way that the posts are filled by people who understand how to carry out the directives, to make sense of the directives, to consider

these directives as their very own and to convert them into reality. . . . That is the reason why huge significance is acquired by the registration and allocation department, the Central Committee organ whose job it is to register and allocate our most important functionaries [that is, the future nomenklatura list!].[78]

The fetishism of the state sometimes borders on the grotesque. Ideologues of the bureaucracy, showing themselves to be, in the final analysis, ideologues of the police, tranquilly envisage that the KGB will continue to exist even in a 'fully developed' communist society without a state. 'The state withers away but the organs remain!' How indeed can one imagine one's own disappearance as a distinct and privileged social group without denying oneself?

This is only part of the story, however. In the ideology of the bureaucracy, fetishization of the state is combined with a *classical fetishization of commodities* – a feature of any society with a significant degree of commodity production, whether partial or general. The law of value was said to prevail in the USSR by virtue of an 'objective necessity'. Sometimes, reference was made in this context to Engels's formula: 'freedom can only be the acknowledgement of necessity'. But what is not mentioned is that Engels was speaking here explicitly of the *laws of nature*. Whereas, for Stalinist and post-Stalinist ideologues, the 'law of value' takes on the force of a 'law of nature', for Marx and Engels it was a law which, precisely, was neither natural nor eternal. It was strictly tied to particular, temporally limited, social conditions, those prevailing in societies where producers work separately from one another on account of private property and enter into mutual relations essentially through exchange of the products of their private labours.

Quite logically, the hybrid combination of state and commodity fetishisms comes to take on the specific form of a justification for the role and function of the bureaucracy itself. The bureaucracy is supposed to make use of (the young Marx said 'petrify') the 'objective laws' in order to direct the economy. The despotic state manipulates 'the law of value', in other words: it violates it at every step. But at the same time, bureaucratic planning has to bow before the 'material acquisitiveness' of the producers (in fact, of the bureaucrats) and *cannot* base itself on the workers' needs democratically defined in terms of 'use-values', because 'the law of value forbids it'. And so this law 'prevails' in spite of state despotism.

Stalin combined these points and expressed these contradictions in his own inimitable style:

Wherever commodities and commodity production exist, there the law of value must also exist. In our country, the sphere of operation of the law of value extends, first of all, to commodity circulation, to the exchange of commodities through purchase and sale, the exchange, chiefly, of articles of personal consumption. Here, in this sphere, the law of value preserves, within certain limits, of course, the function of a regulator.

But the operation of the law of value is not confined to the sphere of commodity circulation. It also extends to production. True, the law of value has no regulating function in our socialist production. But it nevertheless influences production, and this fact cannot be ignored when directing production.[79]

So it is clear, isn't it? The law of value 'influences' production but does not 'regulate' it, under 'socialism'. No, it isn't clear at all. For Stalin also states:

> It is said that some of the economic laws operating in our country under socialism, including the law of value, have been 'transformed', or even 'radically transformed', on the basis of planned economy. That is likewise untrue. Laws cannot be 'transformed', still less 'radically transformed'. If they can be transformed, then they can be abolished and replaced by other laws. The thesis that laws can be 'transformed' is a relic of the incorrect formula that laws can be 'abolished' or 'formed'.[80]

And that is not possible. For the law of value is like a 'natural law', under socialism as well as under capitalism. And 'natural laws' cannot be abolished: they are applied 'independently of the will of man'. Here we have commodity fetishism in its purest form.

The law of value is a 'natural' law which cannot be transformed. So it reigned in the USSR. But at the same time, the law of value did not regulate production in the USSR. So it has after all been 'transformed', as it obviously regulates production under capitalism. Conclusion? Commodity fetishism + state fetishism = complete incoherence at the level of ideas, expressing a massive economic dysfunctioning at the level of practice.

Minor disciples of the great leader, like Professor Malych, were expressing themselves in the same vein fifteen years later, albeit with a little more clarity:

> One should not fall prey to the opposite extreme: if commodity production prevails, then the anarchy of the market, the law of value acting spontaneously, production for an unknown and free market would be inevitable, given the regulatory role of this law, etc. The spontaneity is prevented by the socialist state, since it is in a position to curb the negative aspects [!] of commodity–money relations and to subordinate their instruments . . . to consciously planned goals. Thanks to Marxist–Leninist theory and to the practice of building socialism and communism, the great economic potential

of the socialist state as subject and organizing force of the economic mechanism has been discovered [!] and demonstrated. It would, however, be a mistake to believe that under socialism the determination of the quantity [of the measure?] of work and of consumption depends exclusively [!] on the state. To an important extent, this function is performed by the law of value.[81]

According to Marx, the law of value operates in a market economy in an objective manner, quite independently of the will of human beings. It determines in the medium term – not on a day-to-day basis – the prices of the goods and hence also of the commodity labour-power, to the extent that this is a commodity. But what about a socialist society? Is the producers' consumption fund determined here by conscious decisions to devote, say, 35 per cent rather than 65 per cent of production to consumer goods? No, replies our professor. The socialist state (not, of course, the freely associated producers) is not free to determine on its own the size of this fund: 'to an important extent' this function is performed by the law of value.

This would imply that labour-power is still a commodity! For otherwise, how could it have a price determined by the law of value? But if labour-power is a commodity, like the means of production, how can the 'socialist state' then prevent the law of value – a law which operates independently of human will – from determining the price of *all* the commodities and hence investment and the structures of economic growth? No, says Malych: the socialist state is able to 'curb' this law.

If this whole reasoning has any meaning at all, it is to demonstrate that the disorder in the 'theory' of the bureaucracy is commensurate with the disorder in its actual economic management. The culmination is reached in the concept of the survival of the state not only in socialism but even in full communism – the complete disappearance of class society notwithstanding. What purpose will this strange state serve? 'The withering away of the state will depend first and foremost on the success with which the remnants of capitalism are obliterated from men's minds.'[82] In other words, there is a need for an apparatus of repression, 'armed bodies of men', solely in order to enforce ideological discipline (monolithism). The police confines itself to the policing of minds, because it has nothing else to do. But it still has to survive in order to perform this vital function.

Is it not obvious that we are dealing here with an ideology of self-justification which reflects the material existence of the bureaucracy? What must survive at any cost is an apparatus which arrogates functions previously performed by society without any need for a special apparatus – functions that society could tomorrow exercise in the same way but is not 'authorized' to carry out.

This fetishization of commodity–money relations also breaks through in the analyses of the most intelligent theoreticians of the bureaucracy. Thus Leonid Abalkin, formerly director of the Institute of Sciences Academy of the USSR, then vice prime minister and one of Gorbachev's key advisers, has written: 'Experience shows that the socialist nature of production relations does not as such guarantee society against negative phenomena.'[83] He then went on to quote Gorbachev's words to the 27th CPSU Congress, according to which 'the currently prevailing forms of production relations were constituted in the context of extensive development of the economy and are no longer appropriate to the requirements of intensive development'. Abalkin stresses in this connection that the current system of financial autonomy and economic stimuli, price, finance and credit mechanisms, 'do not, in the light of scientific and technological progress, provide suitable conditions for ensuring a rapid tempo. The enterprises producing routine and often out-of-date goods are in a better situation than those which innovate.'[84]

Nevertheless, if the financial autonomy of enterprises – which the current reforms are intended to strengthen – enables them partially to decide upon the scale and content of production, this shows precisely that they have partial control over the means of production, that these are therefore not fully socialized. The fact that in the enterprises and at the level of society as a whole it is the bureaucracy (the state), and not the freely associated producers, which takes and sanctions decisions, merely serves to confirm that the production relations prevailing in the USSR are not yet socialist in nature.

The historic role of the anti-bureaucratic political revolution, and its objective necessity, can be grasped only if we simultaneously understand the objective role of the bureaucracy and the objective function of socialist democracy in the USSR. It is not a case of applying 'idealist criteria'. What is at issue are *socio-economic necessities*, which derive from the immanent contradictions of Soviet society.

As soon as the state takes control of all the large-scale means of production, appropriates the social surplus product and allocates it from one central point, the question of the management of the various stages of this process becomes decisive for the dynamic of society, including the crucial distribution of resources among the three principal departments. If there is no effective articulation with the clearly recognized and democratically expressed needs and preferences of the great mass of producers and consumers, social despotism (that is, oppression) and economic dysfunctioning are inevitable. *For this reason*, the arbitrary despotic nature of the economy of central allocation in the Soviet Union does not reflect some 'essence' of collective ownership, still less of economic planning. The bureaucracy may implement reforms to correct this arbitrariness. It may resort to additional doses of market economics.

But bureaucratic centralism is condemned to remain despotic and wasteful.

There is only one non-capitalist alternative to bureaucratic arbitrariness: a system of management and planning in which the mass of workers *themselves centrally allocate resources and democratically determine the priorities*. A system of this kind requires that the masses articulate their own needs as producers, consumers and citizens – in other words, that they take control of their living and working conditions, and that they free themselves of the despotism both of the bureaucracy and of the market (the tyranny of the purse).

Such emancipation, however, can only be gradual. During the whole transition period, both conscious, democratic planning and the use of market mechanisms will grow side by side. Trotsky expressed himself quite unmistakably on this question:

> The innumerable living participants in the economy, state and private, collective and individual, must serve notice of their needs and of their relative strength not only through the statistical determinations of the plan commission but by the direct pressure of supply and demand. The plan is checked, and to a considerable degree realized, through the market. . . . The blueprints produced by the departments must demonstrate their economic efficacy through commercial circulation.[85]

Only thus can the irresponsibility and incompetence of the bureaucracy be overcome in practice. A satisfactory solution of the relations between production and needs presupposes *democratic* centralization – that is, the self-centralized administration of the economy, planned and carried out by the workers themselves. This is possible only if commodity production has no regulating role and, in the longer term, is gradually withering away.

NOTES

1. Friedrich Engels, *Anti-Dühring*, Moscow 1954, pp. 251–52. We deal in Chapter 5 below with the general question of the definition of scarcity.

2. Engels, 'The Origin of the Family, Private Property and the State', in Marx and Engels, *Selected Works*, London 1968, p. 577.

3. *Anti-Dühring*, p. 252.

4. Marx and Engels, *The German Ideology*, London 1965, pp. 46–47.

5. Leon Trotsky, *The Revolution Betrayed*, London 1967, pp. 55, 112.

6. See Hegel, *The Philosophy of Right*, London 1967, para. 294, pp. 191–92.

7. The conditions for job security and especially advancement are obedience and the withholding of individual judgement. This is the materialist explanation for the specific ideology of all bureaucracies. Churches, with their ban on the questioning of revealed dogma, are perhaps the best example of this unity between bureaucratic hierarchies and institutionalized obedience. Ideology certainly plays an important role in the internaliza-

tion of obedience, and thus in the objective cohesion of the bureaucracy. See the recent Vatican document which proclaimed that, by definition, a papal (that is, a centrally led and hierarchically structured) organization cannot be democratic. Indeed it can't. Roman Instruction of the Congrégation pour la Doctrine de la Foi, 25 May 1990.

8. Even in a pre-capitalist society such as Manchu China, at the zenith of its power and prosperity, an intelligent French Jesuit immediately recognized this duality of behaviour of the Mandarins. He evidently had the background to understand this basically contradictory nature of bureaucracies. Louis Lecomte, *Un Jésuite à Pékin*, Paris 1990.

9. 'The Origin of the Family, Private Property and the State', p. 576.

10. The greatest ideological assistance was the designation of Soviet and similar societies as 'actually existing socialism'. The result is obvious today: all those who reject Stalinism and its evils now tend to reject socialism as well.

11. For the Menshevik theses see among other sources Julius Martow, *Sein Werk und seine Bedeutung für den Sozialismus*, Berlin 1924; and Karl Kautsky, *The Dictatorship of the Proletariat* (1918), University of Michigan Press 1964, *Terrorism and Communism* (1919), New York 1920, 'Die Lehren des Oktoberexperiments', *Die Gesellschaft* No. 4, 1925, and 'Das Proletariat in Russland', *Der Kampf* No. 10, 1925. See also Massimo Salvadori, *Karl Kautsky and the Socialist Revolution*, London 1979, which contains an extensive discussion of Kautsky's views on this question. In general Martov represented the left-Menshevik and Kautsky the right-Menshevik position.

It is interesting to note that a series of 'liberals' in the USSR today adopt a neo-social-democratic position on the historical and political illegitimacy of the October Revolution. See, among others, Mikhail Lobanov in *Moscow News*, 17 December 1989, A. Tsypko in *Soviet Weekly*, 8 March 1990, and, more surprisingly, Colonel-General Volkogonov in *Nouvelles de Moscou*, 4 March 1990. There are also signs that social democracy is re-emerging as a political force in the Soviet Union. See *Nouvelles de Moscou*, 4 March 1990.

12. Rosa Luxemburg, 'The Russian Revolution', in *Rosa Luxemburg Speaks*, ed. Mary-Alice Waters, New York 1970, p. 395.

13. Typical of a host of their kind are the memoirs of Princess Catherine Sayn-Wittgenstein, who is consumed by an intense class hatred of the peasants and workers of Russia even if this is mitigated by growing feelings of guilt. The memoirs get under way in a fervent spirit of anti-German Russian chauvinism, but end up saluting the German army as liberators from the revolutionary masses. See *Als unsere Welt unterging*, Frankfurt 1988.

14. On the horrors of the Finnish civil war, see Anthony Upton, *The Finnish Revolution, 1917–1918*, University of Minnesota Press, 1980.

15. Engels, 'Karl Marx's "Contribution to the Critique of Political Economy" ', in Marx, *A Contribution to the Critique of Political Economy*, London 1971, p. 226.

16. Marx, 'Critique of the Gotha Programme', in *The First International and After*, Harmondsworth 1974, pp. 345–46.

17. Marx to Kugelmann, 11 July 1868, in *Marx–Engels Selected Correspondence*, Moscow 1975, pp. 196–97.

18. Marx, *Grundrisse*, Harmondsworth 1973, p. 173. Emphasis added.

19. The article was reproduced by the *American Economic Review*, September 1944.

20. J.V. Stalin, *Economic Problems of Socialism in the USSR*, Peking 1972, p. 18.

21. Fritz Behrens, *Ware, Wert, Wertgesetz*, East Berlin 1961.

22. As for the empirical evidence, I have tried to present this in the relevant chapters of *Marxist Economic Theory*, London 1968, and *Beyond Perestroika*, London 1989.

23. *The German Ideology*, pp. 47–48. Cf. Engels: 'This solution can only consist in the practical recognition of the social nature of the modern forces of production, and therefore in the harmonizing of the modes of production, appropriation and exchange with the socialized character of the means of production. And this can only come about by society openly and directly taking possession of the productive forces which have outgrown all control except that of society as a whole. The social character of the means of production and of the products today reacts against the producers, periodically disrupts all production and exchange. . . . But with the taking over by society of the productive forces, the social character of the means of production and of the products will be utilized by the producers with a perfect understanding of its nature. . . . With this recognition, at last, of the real

nature of the productive forces of today, the social anarchy of production gives place to a social regulation of production upon a definite plan, *according to the needs of the community and of each individual.* Then the capitalist mode of appropriation, in which the product enslaves first the producer and then the appropriator, is replaced by the mode of appropriation of the products that is based upon the nature of the modern means of production; on the one hand, direct social appropriation, as means to the maintenance and extension of production – on the other, direct individual appropriation, as means of subsistence and of enjoyment.' *Anti-Dühring*, pp. 386–88.

24. See, for example, P.N. Fedoseyev et al., *The Marxist–Leninist Teaching of Socialism and the World Today*, Moscow 1978, pp. 102–103.

25. V.I. Lenin, *The State and Revolution*, Peking 1965, p. 110.

26. 'We often say that our republic is a socialist one. Does that mean that we have already achieved socialism, done away with classes and abolished the state (for the achievement of socialism implies the withering away of the state)? Or does it mean that classes, the state, and so on, will still exist under socialism? Obviously not.' J.V. Stalin, 'Letter to Kushtysev', 28 December 1928, in *Collected Works*, vol. 11, pp. 325–26.

27. See 'Critique of the Gotha Programme', pp. 346–47.

28. 'And now let the reader fathom Herr Dühring's brazenness in imputing to Marx the assertion that the labour-time of one person is in itself more valuable than that of another. . . . In a socialistically organized society, these costs [of acquiring skills] are borne by society, and to it therefore belong the fruits, the greater values produced by compound labour. *The worker himself has no claim to extra pay.*' *Anti-Dühring*, pp. 277, 279, emphasis added. Compare this with Stalin's opposite formulations in *Economic Problems of Socialism in the USSR*, and with the original statement in the *Under the Banner of Marxism* article quoted earlier: 'The difficulty is that the labour of citizens of a socialist order is not qualitatively uniform. . . . Work of one category requires more training than that of another. . . . In other words, there exist differences between skilled and unskilled work, and between work of various degrees of skill. . . . All this signifies that the hour (or day) of work of one worker is not equal to the hour (or day) of another. As a result of this, the measure of labour and measure of consumption in a socialist society can only be calculated on the basis of the law of value.'

29. Socialism, Lenin argues, and not just the higher phase of communism, involves the achievement of 'equality for all members of society in relation to ownership of the means of production, that is, *equality of labour and equality of wages*' (*The State and Revolution*, p. 118, emphasis added). In a debate with Bukharin in 1918 Lenin stressed: 'And . . . when Bukharin says that [higher retribution for bourgeois specialists] is no violation of principle, I say that here we do have a violation of the principle of the Paris Commune.' (*Collected Works*, vol. 27, p. 311.) Finally, the official Party programme of 1919 set as its eventual goal 'to secure equal remuneration for all labour': 'Programme of the Communist Party of Russia', in Bukharin and Preobrazhensky, *The ABC of Communism*, Harmondsworth 1969, p. 449.

As for Stalin, his ravings against 'petty-bourgeois egalitarianism' would fill a whole pamphlet. They started with an attack on Zinoviev's *Philosophy of the Epoch* (1925), and reached full expression in an interview with the German writer Emil Ludwig in 1931, where he stated that 'equalitarianism has nothing in common with Marxist socialism'. *Collected Works*, vol. 13, p. 121.

30. 'But strangely enough it has not struck anyone that, after all, the method of distribution essentially depends on *how much* there is to distribute, and that this must surely change with the progress of production and social organization, and that therefore the method of distribution will also change.' (Engels, 'Letter to Conrad Schmidt', 5 August 1890, in *Marx–Engels Selected Correspondence*, p. 393.) In *Anti-Dühring* (p. 206) Engels further pointed out that after the downfall of capitalism, the new mode of production 'can secure the distribution which is suitable to it only in the course of a long struggle'. Marcel van der Linden is therefore wrong when he reproaches Trotsky's theory of Soviet society for having rejected Marx's supposed conception of complete coherence between modes of production and modes of distribution. Such coherence only applies to historically stabilized modes of production, not to periods of transition between two modes. Van der Linden's

book (*Het westers marxisme en de Sovjetunie*, Amsterdam 1989) offers one of the most comprehensive accounts of the international Marxist debate on the nature of the Soviet Union; Gerd Mayer's *Sozialistische Systeme* (Opladen 1979) having appeared, at least previously, to be the most complete such review.

31. We have dealt with this problem in greater detail in our essay 'Trotsky's Alternative Economic Platform 1923–1934', a shortened version of which appeared in 'Trotsky Vivant', a special issue of *Rouge*, October 1960. The full text will be published in *Trotski als Alternative*, Dietz-Verlag, Berlin 1991.

32. 'Letter to Alberto Carocci', in *Forum* (Vienna), 1963, here quoted from Lukács, *Schriften zur Ideologie und Politik*, West Berlin 1967, p. 661. Dominique Desanti (pp. 179–80) has shown how Lukács, even in the worst years of Zhdanovism, convinced many progressively inclined intellectuals to become or remain Stalinists.

33. L. Trotsky, *The Third International after Lenin*, New York 1970, p. 89.

34. Cf. Marx, 'Forms Which Precede Capitalist Production', pp. 471–514 of *Grundrisse* on the role of communal property as an impediment to capitalist production relations and even to the production of exchange-value in the village. 'The first presupposition [of large-scale industry] is to draw the land in all its expanse into the production not of use-values but of exchange-values' (p. 511). The most significant passage on this subject, however, is to be found in *Capital* Volume One, London 1976, pp. 477–79.

35. The American Marxist George Novack is the first to have dealt systematically with the problem of periods of transition throughout history. Perry Anderson's classic *Lineages of the Absolutist State* (London 1974) and Miroslav Hroch and Josef Petran's excellent *Das 17. Jahrhundert. Krisen der feudalen Gesellschaft* clearly indicate the transitional character of the social system (or social crisis) of the seventeenth century. This expressed itself most strikingly in the contradictory character of the rise of absolutism as a late-feudal state which could promote either a consolidation of feudal relations of production combined with an extension of capitalist relations, or else a decline of the feudal economic system through a combination of petty commodity production – still prevalent at the time – with growing capitalism.

36. We cannot enter here into a detailed analysis of Soviet 'wage labour'. The concept of 'wages' covers two realities or processes which combine under capitalism but do not do so in pre-capitalist or post-capitalist societies, or at least not according to the same dynamic. On the one hand, it implies indirect access to consumer goods, in exchange for, and limited by, monetary income. In *this* sense the Russian worker is certainly still a wage worker. But on the other hand, wage labour also involves the existence of a labour market, where producers are *compelled* to sell their commodity labour power for a price that is set by the play of supply and demand fluctuating around an objective social value. For this to happen, the wage worker must be deprived of access to the means of production as well as to the means of subsistence. But this is not yet the case in the Soviet Union, insofar as the 'right to work' is guaranteed not only by the Constitution but in actual practice. Labour-power (with significant exceptions) is thus not a commodity, and the wage worker is not a wage-earner in the capitalist sense. Pierre Naville's otherwise impressive study of the 'socialist wage' is marred by his failure to distinguish between these two aspects of the concept. See *Le salaire socialiste*, two vols, Paris 1970.

37. This is the basic error made by Castoriadis and others when they claim that the armaments industry has achieved complete autonomy in the USSR. See Cornelius Castoriadis, *Devant la guerre*, Paris 1981.

38. See on this subject Moshe Lewin, *Political Undercurrents in Soviet Economic Debates*, London 1975, pp. 104–106, 116–18.

39. We disregard the impossible 'special case' in which the USSR would so conclusively overtake international capitalism in terms of labour productivity that it would be in a position to free itself from the law of value by 'purely economic' means. But in this event, it would become a land of plenty – in other words, a communist society with, objectively, no room for a new ruling class.

40. See, inter alia, E. Mandel, 'The Laws of Motion of the Soviet Economy', *Critique* No. 12, 1980. We already expressed the same basic viewpoint in the chapter on the Soviet economy in *Marxist Economic Theory*, written in 1960 and first published in 1962.

41. See our polemic with Paul Sweezy in *Monthly Review*, and with Rudolf Bahro on issues arising from his book *The Alternative*. The expression 'bureaucratic state' is meaningless: the state is 'bureaucratic' by definition. It consists of the apparatuses which have been separated off from society. All depends on the class nature of the state and hence of the bureaucracy. There are despotic bureaucracies (those subject to the Asiatic mode of production), slavery-based bureaucracies, feudal and semi-feudal bureaucracies (the latter in absolutist monarchies), bourgeois bureaucracies, workers' bureaucracies, and so on. The Soviet bureaucracy, in our view, is still a workers' bureaucracy, a fact which in no way 'excuses' or mitigates its parasitical features, its tremendous squandering of resources or its crimes.

42. There is an immediately striking and, in sociological terms, extremely significant parallel between, on the one hand, the complicated, hierarchical and ultra-formalized system of officialdom in classical China and, on the other, the nomenklatura in the Soviet bureaucracy. Both, it should be noted, involve a process of selection by examination – in the Soviet case, examinations in Stalinized, dogmatized and corrupted 'Marxism–Leninism'.

43. *La bureaucratie céleste*, Paris 1968, pp. 142, 144–45.

44. Various observers of Soviet daily life – most notably the philosopher and satirist Alexander Zinoviev but also, unfortunately, the revolutionary socialist Hillel Ticktin – asserted that the stability of the Soviet Union was founded on tacit connivance between the bureaucracy and the workers. (Zinoviev, *Homo Sovieticus*, London 1982; Ticktin in *Critique* no. 12, pp. 129, 132–35.) Whatever these authors' intentions, such a line of argument is ultimately an apology for existing conditions, exactly comparable to the notion of a consensus between capitalists and the 'silent majority' in the West. It does, however, have a rational kernel that can be seen in the fierce opposition of Soviet workers to any destabilizing change in their workplace security.

It is true that in the 'private' sectors of 'underground' work, wages may be six or seven times higher than in the state sector, and that therefore there is a common interest between 'black market' entrepreneurs and workers engaged in the informal sector. But this is possible only because such sectors do not weigh significantly in the scales of the economy as a whole. There is no material base for the average wage in the USSR to be six or seven times what it is today. Cf. Marx's remarks on the role of slave-owning production within capitalism: 'Slavery is possible at individual points within the bourgeois system of production . . . only because it does not exist at other points; and appears as an anomaly opposite the bourgeois system itself.' *Grundrisse*, p. 464.

45. Charles Bettelheim (*Class Struggles in the USSR: Second Period 1923-1930*, Brighton 1978) analyses in detail the workers' struggles of the twenties, but he nowhere proves they ended with the resurrection of a *labour market* – that is, with an economic defeat and the conversion of the proletariat into 'free wage-labourers'. What he does show is that there was a major *political defeat* of the Soviet working class – a conclusion which the Soviet Left Opposition, disregarded by Bettelheim, and later the Trotskyist movement have drawn for more than sixty years. This *Soviet Thermidor*, like its namesake in the French Revolution, did not destroy but retained the economic foundation of society created during the revolution.

46. In this context we do not refer to exchange-values or prices, because we are not speaking of the capitalist mode of production alone.

47. Cf. A. Bagdarasov, S. Pervushin, 'Labour Productivity, Reserves for Growth', *Kommunist* 2, 1983. 'A major cause of the poor quantitative and qualitative statistics of economic growth stems from the fact that, rather than a real labour economy on an equivalent basis, there is a trade-off between living labour and dead, objectified labour, in terms of which *each new step towards higher labour productivity based upon greater expenditure on objectified labour* is not offset by savings in expenditure on living labour.'

48. Soviet sources themselves estimate the cost of bureaucracy (that is, category C) at around 30 per cent of national income. (Alexander Zaichenko, in *Moscow News*, 11 June 1989.) In our opinion, this is still an understatement. On the other hand, Soviet sources reckon that the part of wages (including those of administrative personnel) in the net

product of industry declined from 58 per cent in 1928 to 33.4 per cent in 1950, then increased moderately to reach 37.7 per cent in 1987.

49. Gérard Roland has recently published an innovative and stimulating work: *L'Economie politique du système soviétique*, Paris 1989. Unfortunately, his many insights are flawed by a reifying characterization of the Soviet economy as ruled by 'indicator values', that is, the gross output targets set for enterprises. Planning, he argues, and hence also planning by means of gross output indicators, only makes sense if it tends to maximize output. But why? Roland provides only some circular and tautological arguments in support of this statement, which does not stand up to logical scrutiny. For planning implies only that *goals set by those who control the planning process* (or, if one prefers, who control the social surplus product) have to be implemented by economic units. But who actually controls that process, and what goals are set, are questions that can only be answered by concrete analysis, not by a priori assumptions. It does not require much effort to prove empirically that the maximization of output has never been either the goal or the result of bureaucratic planning.

Similar criticisms could be made of Walter Süss's concept of the 'Stalinist mode of production' in his otherwise excellent book *Die Arbeiterklasse als Maschine*, Wiesbaden 1985.

50. Alec Nove has correctly pointed out that, contrary to the legend of Trotsky as the father of 'barracks communism', he actually proposed the introduction of NEP a year earlier than Lenin, only to be defeated by a vote on the Politburo. 'Trotsky, Collectivization and the Five-Year Plan', originally published in Francesca Gori, ed., *Pensiero e azione politica di Lev Trockij*, Florence 1982.

51. In assessing the potential of central planning, we should also remember the remarkable shift of Soviet heavy industry from the Ukraine to the Urals in 1941 – a move completely unforeseen by the German (and Anglo-American) military and political leaders which was one of the key factors helping the USSR to survive Hitler's onslaught.

52. Peter Ruben, 'Was ist Sozialismus?', in the GDR magazine *Initial* No. 2, 1990.

53. M. Gorbachev, 'Die sozialistische Idee und die revolutionäre Umgestaltung', *Der Spiegel-Dokument*, January 1990. A classical defence of the thesis of market socialism as the only possible framework for workers' self-management is Selucki, 'Marxism and Self-Management', in J. Vanek, ed., *Self-Management: Economic Liberation of Man*, Harmondsworth 1975. On the Yugoslav experience, see Catherine Samary's excellent book *Le marché contre l'auto-gestion*, Paris 1988.

54. V.I. Lenin, *Sochineniya* (collected works in Russian), vol. 43, p. 403 of the fifth edition. The resolution adopted by the 19th conference of the CPSU explicitly states that since 1924 power has been usurped by the bureaucracy and the soviets have been devoid of all real power. This is a perfect definition of the Soviet Thermidor, virtually identical to Trotsky's formula of a political expropriation of the Soviet proletariat by the bureaucracy.

55. See, among many other sources, David Mandel, *The Petrograd Workers and the Soviet Seizure of Power*, London 1984, which is the standard work on the subject; A. Rabinowitch, *The Bolsheviks Come to Power*, New York 1976 and London 1979; A.M. Pankratova, *Fabrikräte in Russland*, West Berlin 1976; O. Anweiler, *The Soviets: The Russian Workers, Peasants and Soldiers Councils, 1905–1921*, New York 1974; V. Brugmann, *Die russischen Gewerkschaften in Revolution und Bürgerkrieg, 1917–1919*, Frankfurt 1972.

56. In addition to the works mentioned in fn. 55, see Victor Serge, *Year One of the Russian Revolution*, London 1972; E.H. Carr, *The Bolshevik Revolution*, vol. 1, Harmondsworth 1966; and L.N. Kritzmann, *Die heroische Periode der grossen russischen Revolution*, Frankfurt 1971.

57. See Walter Süss, pp. 79–89.

58. According to Süss (pp. 62–65), the average real wage of a worker in April 1928 was a little higher in Moscow than in Vienna or Prague, and only 30 per cent less than in Berlin. By 1929, the illiteracy rate of the Russian working class had declined to 13.9 per cent from 36 per cent in 1918.

59. Trotsky Archives, T 895, quoted in E.H. Carr and R.W. Davies, *Foundations of a Planned Economy 1926–1929*, vol. 1, II, London 1969, p. 494.

60. Süss, pp. 214–33, 162–72, 141–48.

61. Süss (p. 153) quotes Lunacharsky as follows: 'Our economic needs imperiously demand people with a certain specialized formation. It is therefore understandable if, on the part of the Supreme Committee for Vocational–Technical Training, an irritated wave of the hand sometimes brushes aside some of the pedagogues' pleas – in the name of a harmoniously developed man and citizen – for the child's right to all-round and not just specialist knowledge. We understand that the disorganized Russian economy needs specialists. But . . . as socialists, who have defended the worker's rights vis-á-vis the factory under capitalism, we cannot remain silent when we see that in these hard years the new Soviet communist factory shows the same tendency to swallow up the personality.'

62. This statement, of course, needs to be placed in context. As numerous and contradictory 'planning goals' had to be achieved, the practice of judging managerial performance by gross physical output always implied that other goals would not be realized. The whip that was available for use against 'violations of the plan' would therefore crack only under special circumstances.

63. This is one of the basic reasons why the 'modernizing', technocratic wing of the bureaucracy, under Gorbachev, threw its full weight behind perestroika.

64. It is true that under monopoly capitalism, in sectors controlled by a small number of big trusts, this pressure is lessened. But in the late-capitalist phase of monopoly capitalism, with the emergence of the transnational corporation as the main organizational form of Big Business, it is again increased.

65. See Moshe Lewin, pp. 116–17.

66. In practice, of course, managers vary widely in self-consciousness – that is, in the way they see their capacity to run the factory 'efficiently' to meet the challenges of the market and competition.

67. Cf. the telling remark by a Soviet foreman in the building trade: 'There's no way we can force the workers to do overtime.'

68. On the shopfloor situation in the USSR, see David Seppo, 'Conscience ouvrière et alternative socialiste en URSS', *Quatrième Internationale* no. 36, April–July 1990.

69. In his posthumous work *Die illegale Partei*, Otto Bauer notes: 'Every minister of external affairs gives his ambassadors and envoys instructions on how to assess the events of the day in conversations with the diplomats of other states, and on which arguments they should use in intercourse with foreign statesmen. In the professional jargon of diplomacy, it is said that the minister *regulates the speech* of his ambassadors and envoys.' *Werkausgabe*, vol. 4, Vienna 1976, p. 488.

70. Süss, pp. 203f. For the classical analysis of this function of capitalist Taylorism, see Harry Braverman, *Labor and Monopoly Capital*, New York 1974.

71. See, for example, Trotsky, *Literature and Revolution*, University of Michigan Press 1960, p. 185.

72. 'Critique of Hegel's Doctrine of the State', in *Early Writings*, Harmondsworth 1974, pp. 107–109.

73. L.S. Mamut, 'Socio-philosophical Aspects of the Marxist Doctrine of the State', *Voprosi filosofii* no. 2, 1982.

74. 'The Origin of the Family, Private Property and the State', p. 577.

75. Letter to Bebel of 18–28 March 1875, in *Marx– Engels Selected Correspondence*, pp. 275–76.

76. *The State and Revolution*, pp. 50–51.

77. *Sämtliche Werke*, first edition, vol. 22, p. 390.

78. Minutes of the Twelfth Congress of the RCP, quoted in Süss, pp. 102–103. Stalin's 'classical' justification of the survival of the state under socialism – by reference to the threat from abroad (survival of capitalism) and the presence of large numbers of spies, assassins, wreckers, agents and diversionists inside the country – is to be found in his speech to the Eighteenth Congress of the CPSU, in March 1939. Trotsky's no less classical response is his article 'The Bonapartist Philosophy of the State', in *Writings of Leon Trotsky 1938–1939*, New York 1969.

79. *Economic Problems of Socialism in the USSR*, pp. 18–19.

80. Ibid., pp. 7–8.

81. A.I. Malych, 'Fragen der ökonomischen Theorie in Friedrich Engels' *Anti-Dühring*', in *Marx-Engels Jahrbuch 2*, Berlin/GDR 1979, pp. 103–104.

82. *Grundlagen der marxistischen Philosophie* (German translation of a Soviet work), Berlin/GDR 1959, p. 584.

83. L. Abalkin, 'Essor de l'économie politique du socialisme', *Revue Internationale* no. 12, 1986.

84. Ibid.

85. 'The Soviet Economy in Danger', *The Writings of Leon Trotsky 1932*, New York 1973, p. 274.

2

Organization and the Usurpation of Power

1. The Genesis of Workers' Bureaucracy

The problem of bureaucracy within the working-class movement arises from the fact that full-timers and petty-bourgeois intellectuals come to occupy the middle and top functions of a permanent apparatus. As long as the working-class organizations are limited to small groups, there is no apparatus, no full-timers, and so the phenomenon does not present itself. At the most, there is a problem of the relationship with petty-bourgeois intellectuals who come to aid in the formation of the embryonic movement.

However, the development of mass political or trade-union organizations is inconceivable without an apparatus of full-timers and functionaries. At the most basic level, it is impossible to collect, centralize and administer the dues of a million members through purely voluntary labour. Parvus lucidly explained this tendency before the turn of the century:

> Clearly a political party of nearly two million members, which is spread right across the country, has nearly half a hundred deputies in the Reichstag alone, disposes of dozens of newspapers and holds thousands of rallies every year – such a party needs many more agitational forces, a much more numerous and complex mechanism for organization and propaganda. It would be criminal folly to seek to construct such a movement simply out of the self-sacrificing devotion of individual agitators, who with the best will in the world could not put more than their spare time at the party's disposal. So a political middle layer of agitators numbering several hundreds becomes a reality, without which the party at its present size could no longer even exist.[1]

The development of an apparatus transfers into the workers' organizations one of the key characteristics of class society: the social division of labour. Within capitalism this assigns the labour of current production to the working class, while the production and assimilation of culture – as well as all the tasks of accumulation – are the near-monopoly of other social classes and layers. The nature of its labour – physically and emotionally exhausting and, above all, time-absorbing – does not allow the majority of the proletariat to acquire and assimilate scientific knowledge in its most advanced form, or even to engage in continuous political and social activity outside the sphere of production and current material consumption, properly so called. The status of the proletariat under the rule of capital is thus normally one of cultural underdevelopment. Traditionally, this social division of labour has been conceptualized as a separation between manual and intellectual (mental) labour.

With the creation of an apparatus of professional functionaries, whose specialized knowledge is necessary to fill the gaps caused by the cultural underdevelopment of the modern proletariat, there is a risk that working-class organizations will themselves become divided between layers exercising different functions. Specialization can result in a growing monopoly of knowledge, of centralized information. Knowledge is power, and a monopoly of it leads to power over people. Thus, the tendency to bureaucratization can, if not checked, mean a real division between new bosses and the bossed-over mass.

Parvus recognized this danger but, failing to see its material basis, reduced it to a question of routinism:

> It is a proletarian officialdom, some of it particularly marked as such through its receipt of deputies' allowances, but an officialdom more poorly recompensed than any other in the world, and overloaded with work of the most diverse, most multiform kind that reaches and indeed exceeds the limits of what is humanly possible. . . .
>
> But precisely because this political middle layer is so dependent, it reflects most accurately the general political condition. It reacts immediately if pressure is exerted on it from above or from below. But if neither is forthcoming, a *routine* soon sets in.[2]

The main tendency that Parvus misses here is the one towards autonomization of the layer of proletarian functionaries – that is, incipient bureaucrats. But these are potential dangers; there is nothing inevitable in them. Powerful counter-tendencies can and do operate.

Collective organizations of the working class are also vehicles for the partial self-emancipation of individuals.[3] From the very beginning, workers created these organizations not only to defend themselves against the ruthless exactions of bourgeois society and to improve their working and living conditions, but also to educate themselves and raise their general level of culture. This struggle to wrest an element of human dignity was a feature of the young labour movement that struck all objective observers.[4] Nor did it disappear – on the contrary – with the conversion of small self-defence groupings into mass organizations.

Working-class cultural organizations involving thousands, later tens or hundreds of thousands, developed side by side with mass trade unions and parties, while newspapers, pamphlets and – in a more limited way – books were read by ever increasing numbers of workers. A whole counter-culture took shape, both as a vehicle of class independence from the bourgeoisie and as a means of individual cultural emancipation.[5] Henriette Roland-Holst, in her pamphlet on the political mass strike, perfectly summed up this aspect of self-organization:

> The proletarian organization only assembles people of the same position, with the same interests and goals. They gather on a voluntary basis in the organization, conscious of the fact that they need each other. Its power lies in the spirit of sacrifice and the enthusiasm, in the love of the masses; they have nothing else on which to base themselves. Precisely for this reason they are indestructible. Their form can be destroyed, but the consciousness of a common destiny, a unity of purpose, cannot be taken away from the masses. . . .
>
> All the power and all the self-confidence of the modern proletariat is based upon organization. It gives to it what weapons gave the feudal nobility, what money gives the bourgeoisie, capacity to resist, pride and dignity. An unorganized worker is the weakest creature on earth; he trembles before each threat; the feeling of dependence all too often saps his moral foundation, makes him cowardly and servile.
>
> The organization educates the proletariat not only for the class struggle but for social life in its totality. In the organization it learns *how to govern itself*.[6]

Rosa Luxemburg, expanding Marx's concept of the 'moral-historical' component of wages, went on to coin the formula of the 'cultural-social minimum' standard of living:

> The main function of the trade unions is that for the first time, through the expansion of workers' needs and their moral development, they set up the cultural–social subsistence minimum in place of the physical subsistence minimum – that is, they produce a certain cultural–social standard of living of workers beneath which wages cannot fall without immediately calling forth a coalition struggle, a movement of resistance. Here too lies the great economic significance of social democracy: through the intellectual and political arousal of the broad masses of workers, it raises their cultural level and hence their economic needs.[7]

Even more important than this cultural progression is the conquest of self-confidence for parts of the class and for the individuals of which it is composed. Successful class struggles tend to convert demoralized, subservient and downtrodden human beings into defiant, militant, self-confident actors, ever more capable of standing up to whoever tries to humiliate or oppress them. This transformation makes itself powerfully felt in the working-class organizations themselves. Thus Bebel, when questioned in the Reichstag about the alleged authoritarianism inside German social democracy, could answer in all sincerity:

the great advantage [we have] is that we know no authorities. If there is some authority in our ranks, it is the authority gained by individuals . . . through their activity, through their capacities, through their self-sacrifice, through their devotion to the cause. There is no other authority in our ranks; we don't know any artificial or imposed authority. Party members who believe to have before them someone who fully represents their interests will naturally assign to him the necessary positions of trust, and so such people come into certain positions of authority. But of how little importance such positions of authority really are, you can see at each of our party congresses. If we have done things which are not to someone's liking, Liebknecht and myself must tolerate being questioned and attacked there by even the last one of our comrades, if I may use this term – in a way that does not happen in any other party. . . . How could we try to be tyrannical towards any comrade? We would set off a real uproar. We have clear programmatic principles on this matter, and clearly expressed organizational norms [statutes] that we have to apply as do all members. Whoever would act in contradiction with these norms, and try to get something to which he is not entitled, would land himself in big trouble. There is no party in which tyrannical tendencies are opposed in such an energetic way as they are in the social-democratic party, which in its very essence and inner nature is a thoroughly democratic party *and must be if it is to achieve its goals*.[8]

At the end of the same debate, Wilhelm Liebknecht could affirm with the same sincerity that the strength of social democracy lay in the fact that 'the leaders are nothing but simple soldiers, *who have to march with the broad mass* on each and every occasion.'[9]

In other words, the embryonic tendencies to bureaucratization arising out of the development of a professional apparatus could be stopped through the rising level of culture, self-confidence and self-assertion of the membership, provided that internal democracy (the 'norms' to which Bebel refers) was respected and the organization remained functional to the socialist goal. There is a further important condition: namely, the conscious endeavour of socialist leaders to combat incipient bureaucratization by fighting for and successfully applying adequate organizational and political safeguards.

Ever since they first emerged as a political tendency, beginning with Marx and Engels themselves, Marxists have been perfectly aware of the danger that working-class organizations might undergo a process of bureaucratization, even after the overthrow of capitalism. In *The Civil War in France*, Marx outlined the measures guaranteeing that the 'commune-state' would be fundamentally different from the bourgeois state – essentially, the broadest possible transparency of all proceedings, the free, democratic election of all officials by the rank and file, the instant recallability of all delegates, and the limitation of their income to that of a worker with average skills. And he added: 'The Commune made that catchword of bourgeois revolutions, cheap government, a reality, by destroying the two greatest sources of expenditure – the standing army and state functionarism.'[10]

In the introduction that he wrote for this pamphlet by Marx, Engels stated quite explicitly:

> From the very outset the Commune was compelled to recognize that the working class, once come to power, could not go on managing with the old state machine; that in order not to lose again its only just conquered supremacy, this working class must, on the one hand, do away with all the old repressive machinery previously used against itself, and, on the other, *safeguard itself against its own deputies and officials*, by declaring them all, without exception, subject to recall at any moment.[11]

On this basis, Lenin was able to draw the following conclusion:

> In socialist society the 'sort of parliament' consisting of workers' deputies will, of course, 'draw up the working regulations and supervise the management' of the 'apparatus' – *but* this apparatus will *not* be 'bureaucratic'. The workers, having conquered political power, will smash the old bureaucratic apparatus, they will shatter it to its very foundations, they will destroy it to the very roots; and they will replace it by a new one, consisting of the very same workers and office employees, *against* whose transformation into bureaucrats the measures will at once be taken which were specified in detail by Marx and Engels.[12]

After the October Revolution, Lenin added another measure on which we would insist even more today as central to a successful struggle against bureaucratization: that is, the radical shortening of the working day. Lenin's formula was: 6 hours work + 4 hours of administrative activities, so that *all* should be able to engage in both and no social division of labour should emerge inside workers' organizations, including the soviets. The equivalent today would be: 4 hours work + 4 hours of (self-)administration.

In the early years of this century, Karl Kautsky published a remarkable work, *The Origins of Christianity*, in the preface of which he raised the possibility that the working-class movement and the workers' state might undergo a process of bureaucratization similar to that which the Catholic Church experienced after its transformation into a party of the ruling establishment in the fourth century A.D., under Constantine the Great.[13] Of course, he realized that the analogy could not be stretched too far, but he saw it as a suggestive way of posing a real problem facing the socialist movement.

Kautsky's own answers are certainly full of interest, going beyond Marx's exclusive focus on institutional safeguards and pointing towards those later produced by Trotsky. Kautsky argued that the parallel would be perfectly tenable if the historical conditions under which the working class came to power resembled those under which the Church had triumphed – a time marked by stagnation and decline of the productive forces. But, in reality, the conditions of the workers' conquest of power would today be the exact opposite. For socialism means a tremendous development of productive forces, which lays the foundation for the withering away of the division of labour and a revolutionary rise in the cultural level of the masses. A victory of the bureaucracy was therefore historically inconceivable.

In the light of subsequent experience, however, two objections leap to mind. What if the working class is forced to take power under conditions of sharp decline of the productive forces, as was the case in Russia?[14] What if it is left isolated in a culturally backward country as a result of the failure of revolution to spread?[15] And what if a deep process of bureaucratization has already gripped working-class mass organizations, either preventing the conquest of power (and condemning society to the 'parallel decline of both contending classes' that Engels saw as an explanation for the demise of ancient civilization) or making it occur under extremely unfavourable subjective conditions?[16]

Whereas Lenin directed his attention to the political opportunism of right-wing tendencies within international social democracy,[17] Trotsky already insisted in 1905–6 on the *social* conservatism underlying this trend.[18] Rosa Luxemburg linked this conservatism more explicitly to the phenomenon of bureaucratization, especially of the trade unions:

> The specialization of professional activity as trade-union leaders, as well as the naturally restricted horizon which is bound up with disconnected economic struggles in a peaceful period, leads only too easily, amongst trade-union officials, to bureaucratism and a certain narrowness of outlook. . . .
>
> Fulsome flattery and boundless optimism are considered to be the duty of every 'friend of the trade-union movement'. . . .
>
> In close connection with these theoretical tendencies is a revolution in the

relations of leaders and rank and file. In place of the collective direction by unpaid colleagues through local committees, moved by pure idealism, the initiative and power of making decisions devolves upon trade-union specialists, so to speak, and the more passive virtue of discipline upon the mass of members. This dark side of officialdom also assuredly conceals considerable dangers for the party, as from the latest innovation, the institution of local party secretariats, it can quite easily result, if the social-democratic mass is not careful, that these secretariats may remain mere organs for carrying out decisions, and not be regarded in any way as the appointed bearers of the initiative and of the direction of local party life.[19]

In this way one of Bebel's three safeguards against bureaucratization of the mass organizations – namely, internal democracy, full independence and freedom of criticism of the membership – became seriously undermined.

On the basis of the more advanced experience of the Italian class struggle of 1919, Gramsci went still further in identifying the trade-union bureaucracy as a distinct social layer, even using the term 'caste' that Trotsky would later apply to the Soviet bureaucracy.

The selection of trade-union leaders has never been made on the basis of industrial competence, but rather simply on the basis of juridical, bureaucratic and demagogic competence. And the more the organizations expanded, the more frequently they intervened in the class struggle and the more massive and widespread their activity became, the more they found it necessary to reduce their headquarters to a purely administrative and accounting centre; the more technical and industrial capacities became redundant and bureaucratic, commercial capacities came to predominate. Thus a veritable caste of trade-union officials and journalists came into existence, with a group psychology of their own absolutely at odds with that of the workers. This eventually came to occupy the same position vis-à-vis the working masses as the governing bureaucracy vis-à-vis the parliamentary State: it is the bureaucracy that rules and governs.[20]

2. Organizational Fetishism

The growth of a new division of labour between apparatus and membership almost inescapably gives birth, at the level of mentalities (ideology), to phenomena of organizational fetishism. Given the extreme division of labour prevailing in bourgeois society in general, the fact that people are imprisoned in a tiny sector of activity tends to find expression in a consideration of this activity as an end in itself. This is particularly true of those who identify with an apparatus, who live permanently within it and draw their livelihood from it: in other words, the full-timers, the potential bureaucrats.

This process feeds on another source of social conservatism within the mass organizations: the dialectic of partial conquests. The famous sentence in the *Communist Manifesto* which states that the proletariat has nothing to lose but its chains is true in an immediate sense only for the destitute, unorganized workers of the mid-nineteenth century. While it remains *historically* valid, the organized proletariat of today does have something to lose *conjuncturally* – namely, the economic, social and political gains that its long struggle has wrested from the ruling class. It learns from experience that it can lose these conquests as a result of deliberate actions by the bourgeoisie. The pros and cons of every struggle must now be carefully weighed within the mass organizations and the working class as a whole, even more among unorganized than among organized workers. For, instead of achieving something new, it is always possible that it will result in the loss of what has already been won.

It should be stressed that the dialectic of partial conquests reflects real problems and not a logical contradiction that can be resolved simply through correct argument. Nor is it simply a question of 'betrayal by the leadership' – which would lead us straight into a conspiracy theory of history.

Nevertheless, we can see here the fundamental roots of bureaucratic conservatism, already found in the social-democratic movement before the First World War and in the Soviet Union even before the Stalinist era. The reason why we use the term 'conservatism' – and regard it as harmful to the interests of the proletariat and therefore of socialism – is that this mentality refuses to wage and support more advanced struggles, assuming a priori that any revolutionary leap forward, whether on a national or international level, will jeopardize the gains of the working class.

The dialectic of partial conquests, linked to the phenomenon of fetishization characteristic for a society of generalized commodity production and extreme division of labour, is inherent in the development of the working-class movement in the stage of historical decline of capitalism and transition to a socialist society. However, its operation tends to undermine the second of Bebel's safeguards against bureaucratization: the dedication of the mass organizations to the socialist goal. What organizational fetishism really means is that the party or trade union becomes more and more a goal in itself, so that working-class emancipation is identified with defence and consolidation of 'the organization', itself increasingly defined in terms of its apparatus. Bernstein's famous formula 'The movement is everything, the goal is nothing', which he launched during the Revisionist controversy at the turn of the century, has remained the clearest statement of this mentality.[21]

The ideological expression of this process is a multi-dimensional phenomenon, much more than a trick, an exercise in conscious treachery or deception of the workers. In fact, the emergence of 'false conscious-ness' involved a strong element of *self*-deception. At least the first generation of leaders of bureaucratized mass organizations genuinely believed that they were working for socialism, or defending the revolu-tion, when they identified defence of the apparatus with the struggle for these lofty goals. Deliberate treachery and duplicity crept in later – and even then they remained combined with self-deception.

The SPD leader Gustav Noske gave one of the clearest demonstrations of this organizational fetishism when he visited Brussels after the arrival of the German occupation army in 1914. 'Why are you so hostile to German occupation?' he asked the Belgian Socialist Party leader Anseele. 'Our organization is stronger in Germany than in Belgium. It enjoys universal suffrage. If Belgium is incorporated into Germany, the organization will become stronger. Universal suffrage will be granted. The workers will be strengthened.'[22] All the political, economic, social, cultural and national aspects of annexation were thus either ignored or subordinated to the key question of 'the organization'. There was no understanding of the fact that a working class deprived of some of its key democratic rights, like national self-determination, perhaps even the franchise, would be much weaker and not much stronger than before; no understanding of the fact that Noske's monstrous statement made of him a spokesman for German imperialism. No: he really did believe that 'strengthening the organization' was the alpha and the omega of socialist wisdom.

Much worse was to follow. After Hitler had become head of govern-ment, the trade-union leaders desperately tried to save 'the organization' through despicable ideological and political concessions to the Nazis. Claiming that they welcomed and wished to participate in the 'national rebirth', they even joined the Nazi-led demonstration on 1 May 1933 which perverted the workers' day of struggle into a common 'celebration of German labour', with employers, workers and Nazi butchers all 'uniting' around Nazi slogans.[23] In return for this capitulation, the Nazis dissolved the unions the very next day, occupied their offices and confiscated their assets. The workers had become so disoriented and demoralized by the social-democratic (and Stalinist) bureaucrats that no serious resistance was offered to this destruction of more than half a century of painstaking effort. Organizational fetishism had led to the ruin of the organization.

When Stalin made his famous pronouncement of 1927: 'The cadres decide everything', he provided the key to the existence and self-consciousness of the bureaucracy. A ruling bureaucracy can perfectly well coexist with all manner of combinations of planning and market mechanisms (although not with generalized market economy, that is, capitalism). But it cannot maintain itself if the rule of the cadres – that is, of the apparatus – is fundamentally questioned and overthrown.

Organizational fetishism implies not only identification of the goal with the means, but also subordination of the goal to the means. This is evident enough in the case of the Stalinized Communist movement, where the struggle for revolution outside the USSR, the strengthening of the rights and power of the Soviet working class, were subordinated to defence of the bureaucratic apparatus of the CPSU and the Soviet state. However, a similar logic may operate, sometimes in quite extreme forms, in any working-class mass organization. Take the following example.

Trade unions accumulate money as a potential strike fund to make more effective their members' struggle for wages and other immediate material interests. This is perfectly natural and legitimate. The trade-union apparatus then invests this money in a savings institution to make it grow by a modest interest, and as long as it remains semi-liquid there again seems nothing wrong in the operation. More money will be available to finance a long strike. However, if the investment should lose this semi-liquidity, the decision on whether to call a strike – or at least on when to call it – will no longer depend exclusively on the will and objective needs of the majority of members, or on an objective analysis of the relationship of forces with the employers. The tying up of the strike fund will influence the outcome in a way that has nothing to do with the workers' fundamental interests or with the initial goals and functions of the trade unions.

Now, all pressures of the dialectic of partial conquests notwithstanding, class-conscious workers will at least periodically tend to oppose such a perversion of their union's aims. Hence the drive by the incipient bureaucracy gradually to eliminate workers' power and workers' democracy within the mass organizations created for self-emancipation of the class. Only in this way is it possible to transform them into organizations which more and more push that goal into the background. But at the same time, the usurpation of decision-making power transforms the incipient bureaucracy into a fully fledged bureaucracy. A new social layer finally takes shape: *the working-class bureaucracy*.

Here it is necessary to combine the arguments of Kautsky, Bebel, Luxemburg, Trotsky or Gramsci on how to counter the trend towards bureaucratization – although the experience since their times has shown that this is by no means easy. Already in 1906 Rosa Luxemburg could see this process unfolding in the German trade-union movement:

> The concentration of all the threads of the movement in the hands of a trade-union functionary (generally sent there from outside of the town) makes the capacity to judge regarding trade-union matters into a professional speciality. The mass of members are degraded to the status of a mass incapable of judgement, whose main duty becomes that of 'discipline', i.e., of passive obedience. . . . Inside the trade unions the relation of ruling body to lowly mass exists to a much greater degree.
> One consequence of this conception is the argument with which every theoretical criticism of the prospects and possibilities of trade-union practice is tabooed, and which alleges that it represents a danger to the pious trade-union sentiment of the masses. From this the point of view has been developed that it is only by blind, childlike faith in the efficacy of the trade-union struggle that the working masses can be won and held for the organization . . . the upside-down theory of the incapacity of the masses for criticism and decision. 'The faith of the people must be maintained' – that is the fundamental principle, acting upon which many trade-union officials stamp as attempts on the life of the movement all criticism of the objective inadequacy of trade unionism.[24]

One is forcefully struck here by the parallel between the rationalizations of the trade-union and the Soviet bureaucracy: most of Rosa Luxemburg's formulations could apply to both with scarcely a word being changed.

However, the usurpation of power provokes resistance on the part of workers and is therefore inseparable from repression, reprisals, threats or actual expulsions, splits and deep divisions of the labour movement. In times of acute crisis, this may even involve denunciations to the bourgeois authorities, sackings from work, the provision of cover for police repression or even the murder of comrades.[25] The record of German social democracy in this respect is but a tragic, if milder, preview of the history of Stalinism.

Why then does the usurpation of power by privileged bureaucracies endure for such a long time within the mass organizations and states created by the working class? Why is it still predominant today, at least in the major countries of the world? The reason must be sought in the dialectical interaction between objective developments and the 'subjective factor'. When the bureaucratic apparatuses take advantage of a temporary decline in workers' activity to strengthen their hold over institutions of the working class, they help to bring on defeats of the labour movement that further cultivate disorientation, disarray, scepticism and demoralization within that class. The emergence of new hopes, a new self-assurance, new perspectives to inspire higher forms of activity – all this becomes more difficult for all but a limited minority of the working class.[26] And this reinforces still further the process of bureaucratization itself.[27]

Workers are not stupid. They notice what is going on. They see that organizations which they have created and defended with great effort and sacrifice are turning against them on critical matters of their day-to-day existence. So they feel cheated. The question arises in their mind: 'Was it all really worth the trouble?' Their answer is not a clear-cut 'No'. They continue partially to identify with these organizations, especially when they are under attack by the class enemy.[28] From time to time sections of workers exert pressure to recover some of the decision-making power within these institutions.[29] But their basic attitude remains sceptical. You can't go on being cheated, two, three or four times in succession, without drawing some negative conclusions. You don't want to be cheated a fifth time.

The relative passivity of workers within the mass organizations – which largely results from the bureaucracy's practice and policies – offers that apparatus an additional element of self-justification. 'You see,' they argue, 'the workers are passive. They are backward. If we didn't do the job for them, the union or the party or the "socialist state" would collapse.'[30] The sophistry involved here soon becomes apparent when the workers do become active, even hyper-active, especially in a mass strike or pre-revolutionary explosion. Then the bureaucrats, far from letting this activity unfold, do everything in their power to apply the brakes. They divide the working class, they collaborate with the class enemy to end or even to repress the struggle, revealing their basically conservative, counter-revolutionary nature in all its glory. And yet it is only through such an experience, through a new cycle of social tensions and class struggles ultimately rooted in a crisis of economic and political structures, that the whole dialectic of bureaucratic usurpation and workers' passivity can be overcome.

3. Bureaucratic Privileges

For any adherent of the materialist interpretation of history, it is obvious that the appearance of a new social layer – the bureaucracy of workers' mass organizations – cannot be divorced from its specific material interests. The mentality of the bureaucratic leaders involves growing conservatism towards the existing social order. But it also involves a deepening wish to preserve a privileged social position, with all the advantages, power and authority that their status bestows upon them. In

70

the first organizations of the working class, the trade unions and social-democratic mass parties, two distinct processes were at work.

First, to leave the place of production and become a full-timer – especially in conditions of a twelve-hour day, total lack of social security, etc. – unquestionably represented for a worker a certain degree of individual social promotion. It would be wrong to equate this with *embourgeoisement* or the creation of a privileged social layer. The early secretaries of such organizations lived in modest material circumstances, and often spent a considerable part of their life in prison. But all the same, from a social point of view, they lived better than the rest of the workers at that time.

Second, at a psychological level, it is infinitely more satisfying for socialist or communist militants to spend all their time fighting for their ideas than to be tied to mechanical work in a factory – especially when they know that the fruits of their labour will only serve to enrich the class enemy.

Now, the phenomenon of individual social promotion undoubtedly contains the potential seeds of bureaucratization. Those who occupy full-time positions quite simply want to carry on occupying them. They will defend their status against anybody who wishes to establish a rota system instead, whereby each member of the organization would at some time fill these posts. Social privileges are not very tangible at the beginning, but they become considerable once the organization gains a position of strength within capitalist society.

Moreover, it now becomes necessary to select municipal councillors, parliamentary deputies and trade-union secretaries who are capable of directly negotiating with the bosses – and thus, to some extent, of coexisting with them. Newspaper editors have to be appointed, as well as managers of all kinds of other activities through which the labour movement intervenes in society.

This again produces a genuinely dialectical, and not merely trivial, contradiction. For example, when the labour movement sets up a newspaper, it faces the real dilemma of whether to apply Marx's rule that a full-timer's salary should not exceed that of a skilled worker. The most politically conscious militants will accept the logic of this position, but many talented journalists who are able to earn a lot more elsewhere will be continually tempted to take up the more lucrative option. So long as they are not sufficiently committed, they will be in danger of assimilating to the bourgeois milieu and thus being lost to the workers' movement.

Similarly, in towns administered by the labour movement, a strict application of Marx's rule would in most cases lead to the elimination of public architects, engineers, doctors and others whose political consciousness is insufficiently developed, but who might be better qualified from a professional point of view. Again there is no easy answer. If mediocrity becomes the norm in public employment, without material advantages, it too can become a breeding-ground for conformism and obedience.

In a society where capitalist norms and values are dominant, it is impossible to build a perfect system of socialist human relations – even within the workers' movement. This might just be viable for a nucleus of highly conscious revolutionaries. But a large workers' movement is objectively more integrated into bourgeois society, and communist principles are much more difficult to practise within it. Consequently there is always a danger that specific barriers to bureaucratization will become progressively weakened.

In the phase of history characterized by capitalist decline, the dialectic of partial conquests assumes its fully developed form of conscious integration into bourgeois society, together with the logic and politics of class collaboration. All obstacles to bureaucratization disappear within the reformist or neo-reformist mass organizations. The social-democratic leaders no longer give part of their parliamentary salary to the organization – indeed, party and union functionaries come to represent a client layer of the bourgeoisie within the working class, the labour lieutenants of capital, to repeat the formula of the American socialist Daniel De Leon. Bureaucratic deformation advances by leaps and bounds towards bureaucratic degeneration.

4. The Labour Bureaucracy in Power

A similar three-stage process can be found at work in the Soviet state. At first there are only privileges of authority and political advantage stemming from a monopoly in the exercise of power. Then follow socio-economic privileges of a material and cultural nature. Finally, complete degeneration sets in. The party/state bureaucracies fuse with the bureaucratic administrators of the economy to form a hardened and immovable social layer (Trotsky called it a caste), which uses its monopoly of power to maintain and extend its material–social position. The fact that the labour bureaucracy now exercises state power multiplies tenfold all the anti-working-class, conservative and parasitic features already visible in the trade-union and party bureaucracies of the mass workers' movement.

Much has recently come to light about the growth of the bureaucratic apparatus, the extent of its privileges and its near-absolute power in Soviet Russia since the early twenties.[31] The apparatus of full-time functionaries in the Communist Party soared from barely 700 in 1919 to

15,300 in 1922 and more than 100,000 some years later. Whereas the initial 700 were elected by the rank and file, the 15,300 were appointed by the centre and welded into a clientele structure owing allegiance, and their own job security, to the Party Secretariat and its general secretary, J.V. Stalin.

Illegally violating the principle of the 'party maximum', Stalin began to distribute hierarchically differentiated monetary and non-monetary advantages to members of the apparatus, whose total remuneration had reached ten times the average worker's wage by 1923–24.[32] From the thirties on, these material privileges grew and became institutionalized in a monstrous way – bloated incomes, special shops, weekend houses (*dachas*), private rooms in hospitals, special education camouflaged as 'schools for the gifted', reserved access to foreign travel, and so on. Whatever the myths spread by Maoists and neo-Maoists in China and elsewhere, the sum total of privilege was certainly greater under Stalin than under Khrushchev. Boris Yeltsin, in his recently published auto-biography, devotes several pages to the life-style of the top nomenkla-tura. Here are just a few significant extracts:

> Obsequiousness and obedience are rewarded in turn by privileges: special hospitals; special sanatoria; the excellent Central Committee canteen; the equally excellent service for home delivery of groceries and other goods; the Kremlin-line closed telephone system; the free transportation. The higher one climbs up the professional ladder, the more there are comforts that surround one, and the harder and more painful it is to lose them. . . . It has all been carefully devised: a section chief does not have a personal car, but he has the right to order one from the Central Committee car pool for himself and his immediate staff. The deputy head of a department already has his personal Volga car, while the head has another Volga, fitted with a car phone.
>
> But if you have climbed your way to the top of the establishment pyramid, then it's 'full communism'. . . . Even at my level as a candidate member of the Politburo, my domestic staff consisted of three cooks, three waitresses, a housemaid, and a gardener with his own team of under-gardeners. . . . And, surprisingly, all this luxury was incapable of producing either comfort or convenience. What warmth can there be in a marble-lined house? . . .
>
> The dacha had its own cinema, and every Friday, Saturday and Sunday a projectionist would arrive, complete with a selection of films. As for medical treatment, the medicines and equipment are all imported, and all of them the last word in scientific research and technology. The wards of the 'Kremlin hospital care' are huge suites, again surrounded by luxury: porcelain, crystal, carpets and chandeliers. . . .
>
> The 'Kremlin ration', a special allocation of normally unobtainable prod-ucts, is paid for by the uppermost echelon at half its cost price, and consists of the highest quality foods. In Moscow, a total of some 40,000 people enjoy the privilege of receiving these special rations.[33]

Similarly, in the GDR, while the country was starved of foreign currency for the import of vital spare parts, ten million marks (more than $5 million at the official exchange rate) was set aside annually just for the importing of luxury goods for twenty-three Politburo members. The practice in Poland, not to speak of Ceausescu's Romania, was much worse.

Of course, we should never forget that such privileges are really trifling in comparison with the wealth of top monopolists and top gangsters in capitalist countries. Here we have billionaires: there we have mere millionaires, or people owning even less than the equivalent of a million dollars. Nevertheless, from a psychological point of view, these differences in structure and power hardly modify the indignation and sense of betrayal felt by working people in the post-capitalist societies. As Angelica Babanova pointed out long ago, it is one thing when a capitalist who never claimed to defend social equality and justice cynically enjoys luxury amidst mass deprivation. It is quite another thing when people claiming to be socialists or communists no less cynically draw comforts, be they minor or major, amidst much greater penury.[34]

This brings us on to an important historical distinction between the Soviet bureaucracy and capitalist ruling classes. During the period of the bourgeoisie's rise to power, it was already an economically and culturally privileged and self-confident class, aggressively asserting its ideological hegemony over society while still being politically oppressed. It could therefore, in the aftermath of victorious revolutions, capture with relative ease the absolutist state apparatus and remodel it in its own interests. It could create a special corps of state functionaries subordinated to it by the all-pervading power of money and wealth. In other words, to use Kautsky's formulation, it could rule without governing directly.

After a victorious socialist revolution, the working class finds itself in an entirely different situation. It has no experience of how to rule. It does not have ideological hegemony in society. It is culturally less developed than the former ruling classes, whose influence it continues to endure for a long period. It cannot use the bourgeois state apparatus for purposes of self-emancipation. When isolated in one or a few countries – particularly if these are relatively backward – it constantly suffers the 'consumerist', technological and cultural pressure of the world market, in the first place of the leading industrial nations of the world.

There is no way in which the working class can rule without governing. It has to exercise power simultaneously within enterprise and branch, municipality and region, as well as at the aggregate levels of the state and the national economy, if it is to 'rule' in any real and direct sense of the word: to take the key decisions about economic, social and cultural priorities in the allocation of scarce resources. Thus, the functional division of the proletariat, between those who 'professionally exercise power' and the mass of the class, sets in motion a social process which suppresses the direct collective rule of the class as such.

It is well known that, under the conditions obtaining in Russia at the end of the Civil War, a whole series of unfavourable circumstances sharply speeded up that process. In terms of concrete mechanisms, however, it was the rise of an autonomous apparatus – appointed, controlled and centralized from above, and intent on maintaining its stability of tenure – which was the way in which the working class as such ceased to exercise power in Soviet Russia. Here is how Rakovsky describes this bureaucratic usurpation:

> Certain functions, formerly exercised by the party as a whole, by the whole class, have now become the attributes of power – that is, of only a certain number of persons in the party and in this class. . . .
>
> The function has modified the organism itself: that is to say, the psychology of those who are charged with the diverse tasks of direction in the administration of the economy and the state, has changed to such a point that not only objectively but subjectively, not only materially but also morally, they have ceased to be part of this very same working class. Thus, for example, a factory director playing the satrap in spite of the fact that he is a communist, in spite of his proletarian origin, in spite of the fact that he was a factory worker a few years ago, will not become in the eyes of the workers the epitome of the best qualities of the proletariat.[35]

With hindsight, one cannot stress enough the lucidity of the October 1923 *Declaration of the 46* – the first Left Opposition's analysis of the historical regression then taking place:

> The Party is to a considerable extent ceasing to be that living independent collectivity which sensitively seizes living reality because it is bound to this reality with a thousand threads. Instead of this we observe the ever increasing, and now scarcely concealed, division of the party between a secretarial hierarchy and 'quiet folk', between professional party officials recruited from above and the general mass of the party which does not participate in its common life.
>
> This is a fact which is known to every member of the Party. Party members who are dissatisfied with this or that decision of the central committee or even of a provincial committee, who have this or that doubt on their minds, who privately note this or that error, irregularity or disorder, are afraid to speak about it at Party meetings and are even afraid to speak about it in conversation unless the partner in conversation is thoroughly reliable from the point of view of 'discretion'. Free discussion within the party has practically vanished. The public opinion of the party is stifled.
>
> Nowadays it is not the Party, nor its broad masses, who promote and choose

members of the provincial committees and of the Central Committee of the RCP. On the contrary: the secretarial hierarchy of the Party to an ever greater extent recruits the membership of conferences and congresses, which are becoming to an ever greater extent the executive assemblies of the hierarchy.

The regime established within the Party is completely intolerable. It destroys the independence of the Party, replacing the party by a recruited bureaucratic apparatus which acts without objection in normal times [cf. the 'routine' in Parvus's formula], and which threatens to become completely ineffective in the face of the serious events now impending.[36]

All this is now by and large recognized and repeated by Gorbachev and his followers, but sixty to sixty-five years late. Grigorii Volodazov, for example, writes:

Mature, developed Stalinism, as it was in the mid thirties, is the ideology of the bureaucratic elite. . . . It is an infallible expression of the objective interests of the bureaucratic layer. . . . Noting a powerful surge of military–communist and bureaucratic commandist tendencies, Lenin anxiously wrote in the early twenties that if we were to go under, it would be the fault of the bureaucracy. He was seriously reflecting on the dangers of 'Thermidor'.[37]

The cumulative result of the bureaucracy's usurpation of power, and of the workers' atomization and depoliticization, is the terrible discredit into which communism, Marxism and socialism are thrown among the masses. It is not so much that the masses continue to be passive – indeed, they eventually awaken and act more boldly. But they do so with a qualitatively lower level of political consciousness, and with deep hostility to a party that is identified with the privileged bureaucracy. As the opposition predicted long ago, instead of guaranteeing the 'leading role of the Party', the bureaucratic regime produced a loss of credibility and removed any possibility of leadership by the Party.[38]

It is sometimes said that the exercise of power after the expropriation of the capitalists is fundamentally a question of economics, and that the bureaucracy rules to the extent that it controls the social surplus product. But to make this the main focus is to miss the point. Under capitalism, the bourgeois class rules by essentially economic means: that is why it can rule under a regime of restricted franchise as much as under universal suffrage, under parliamentary social-democratic governments as well as military or fascist dictatorships. Pre-capitalist ruling classes, by contrast, exercised power essentially through extra-economic rather than economic compulsion, and this is true also of the Soviet bureaucracy. But this extra-economic compulsion can operate only if it coincides with the atomization and passivity of the working masses. If these challenge the bureaucracy's control on the political level, its control over the social

76

surplus product dissolves like dew in the sunlight. The rule of the bourgeoisie is compatible with widespread (if limited) democratic rights of the masses. The bureaucracy's rule is incompatible with a broad extension of those rights.

Thus the problem of power in a post-capitalist society is essentially political in nature. It involves *the key question of socialist democracy, of decisive control by the toiling masses over the state, of forms of decision-making in which the autonomy of the apparatus is decisively broken, its dimensions radically reduced, its elective character imposed against bureaucratic resistance.*

The main alternative to our materialist explanation of the rise and role of the Soviet bureaucracy is an idealist–moralistic account in terms of 'errors', 'deviations', 'misconduct', 'personal thirst for power', 'lack of communist morality', 'bad habits', 'factionalism', 'cliquism', 'a wrong leadership style', and so on. This is even true of Lukács, for example, at least before the last period of his life. He begins his analysis of the Twentieth Congress of the CPSU with an outright rejection of the 'personality cult' as an explanation of Stalinism, taking instead the first timid steps towards a social and materialist viewpoint: 'My initial, almost immediate, reaction at the Twentieth Congress was directed beyond the person, against the organization, against the bureaucratic apparatus which produced the personality cult and which then adhered to it as a permanent and expanding reproduction.'[39]

However, the deviation towards historical idealism follows immediately. Instead of explaining the autonomy of the apparatus in terms of a *conflict of social interests*, using the method of historical materialism, Lukács accounts for Stalin's enormous crimes by referring to his mistaken ideas: 'I have not yet got fully to grips with the subject, but these passing and fragmented observations are enough to show you that with Stalin, *it was certainly not a question of isolated, occasional mistakes*, as for a long time many wished to believe. It was much more a question of *a system of mistaken perceptions* which developed over a period of time.'[40]

In other words, the bureaucracy did not actively work to institutionalize the 'personality cult' – and its monopoly of power – in the service of material interests that confronted it with the working class as an alien social force. No, Stalin's 'mistaken ideas' (which emerged in the special situation of the Soviet Union in the thirties) produced the total and arbitrary authority of the bureaucracy.

Jean-Paul Sartre, when he was in his apologetic phase towards Stalinism, also used idealist or fetishistic formulations: 'From the moment the USSR, encircled and alone, undertook its gigantic effort at industrialization, Marxism [?] found itself unable to bear the shock of these new struggles, the practical necessities and the mistakes which are always

77

inseparable from them.'[41] The USSR in general and in the abstract? Not a concrete society structured by social classes and layers with conflicting interests? What were these 'practical necessities'? Forced collectivization of agriculture, perhaps? And what 'Marxism' suffered the results of these necessities? Stalin's 'Marxism'?

The other side of the coin of Lukács's idealist theses is the 'objectivist' explanation à la Ellenstein, which attributes the Stalin phenomenon to the historical circumstances of the time. Again this leaves out of account the specific social nature of the bureaucracy, and the effects of Stalinist policy on the circumstances in question.[42] Only the revolutionary Marxist analysis brings fully into play the dialectic of the objective and the subjective in the concrete historical process that produced Stalinism.

5. The Bureaucratic Theory of Labour

Just as we have seen the consolidation of the bureaucracy's power express itself in a distinctive view of the state and commodity production, so does its existence as a separate social layer find reflection in a characteristic deformation of the Marxist theory of labour.

Some years ago an interesting debate developed in the GDR about the seemingly abstract philosophical question of the basic nature of labour. According to the official Party ideologues, labour is 'telos-directed praxis' – that is, activity with a given goal. It is true that Marx says as much in the first chapter of Volume One of *Capital*, and to deny this dimension of labour would be to fall back into a mechanically materialist conception. But as early as *The German Ideology*, and in their later writings, Marx and Engels also stress the fact that labour materially produces both human survival (subsistence) and the human species itself.[43] Indeed, we should understand the Marxist concept of labour as a dialectical combination, a contradictory unity, of both the material and the purposive component of human activity, of both production and communication, each determining and depending upon the other.

Once this indissoluble relation is clarified, a further question immediately arises. Who fixes the goals of labour, the 'telos' of production? When Marx says that even in the worst architect's head, the image of what he wants to construct exists before it is materially realized, the example obviously presupposes *private individual labour*. Nobody could seriously argue that the final skyscraper, not to say the final aeroplane, lives in the head of each individual worker directly or indirectly involved in its production. Very often he or she does not even know to what final product their labour is actually contributing. Very often they are just a link in a complex chain of living and dead labour – of workers and machines – whose final product is comprehended only by a tiny group of scientists, designers, planners and technocrats.

Every advance in the objective socialization of labour – that is, mass production and large-scale industry – is accompanied by a parallel advance in the technical division of labour within the factory and the economy as a whole, which separates conception from actual production. Social forces other than the direct producers determine the goals of production.

Socialism does not necessarily imply the total disappearance of the *technical* division of labour (although, as we shall see in the final chapter, its reduction through a radical revolution in technology is necessary for reasons of both human and natural ecology). But what socialism certainly does imply is the withering away of the *social* division of labour between those who fix and those who accomplish the goals of production, between administrators and producers, between bosses and the bossed-over. And yet, if we follow through the logic of their position, this is precisely what is denied by the official ideologues of the bureaucracy, who continue to reduce creative activity to 'intellectual labour', separate and apart from material activity or manual labour.[44] Such a view assumes that the 'thinkers', 'planners', 'administrators' or 'bureaucrats' operate and exist separately from the direct producers – or, as Harald Boehme puts it, that 'the activity of functionaries' is 'above labour'.[45] So the neo-Hegelian, neo-Lukácsian concept of labour as exclusively goal-oriented, separate and apart from its material–sensuous content, implies a perpetuation of the social division of labour under socialism; it is a typical self-justification of the bureaucracy.

Boehme also correctly points to the connection between this one-sided concept of labour and the bureaucratic ideology of commodity production under 'socialism'. For the theoretical separation of department I and department II as existing independently of each other implies that under state ownership of the means of production, or even under higher forms of social ownership, a force distinct from the direct producers represents the state, the community, the 'collective producer', society in its totality. Otherwise, 'exchange' between the two departments (that is, the survival of commodity production) makes no sense. You don't exchange with yourself.

Once again, then, the existence of the bureaucracy as a separate social layer is justified by its ideologues as corresponding to 'objective economic laws', as necessary and useful. But when the bureaucracy assumes that the division of the social product between departments I and II continues to have a value form and leads to exchange, it takes for granted that the direct producers will accept their subordinate place in the social division of labour – in spite of their material interests being opposed to those of the bureaucrats. There is no empirical evidence of the long-term validity of that assumption, to say the least.[46]

The bureaucracy simply cannot conceive that in a classless society the mass of the direct producers (including, of course, scientists, inventors or technicians, insofar as these remain distinct professions within the labour force necessary for continuous production) could freely and democratically determine both the goals and the organization of the labour process. And yet, that is the meaning of the concept of planned (articulated) workers' self-management plus socialist democracy. That is ultimately what the withering away of commodity production, the social division of labour and the state are all about.

Even independent research in East European countries can sometimes harbour some curious silences in this regard. Thus the Hungarian Ferenc Tökei is a sophisticated Marxist historian. But in his fundamental work on the theory of social forms – essentially an extensive comment on Marx's *Grundrisse* devoted to pre-capitalist formations – he tries in a rather scholastic manner to reduce all of humankind's prehistory and history to a dialectical inter-relationship between labour, property and the individual.[47] He completely leaves out the function of the state, and does not even mention Marx's own specific reference to it in his original plan of *Capital*.

With the beginning of glasnost, however, a number of Soviet authors, following the lead of Butenko, have acknowledged the nature of the bureaucracy as a social layer with specific interests,[48] and everything indicates that this is now a widespread view in the USSR.

6. Bureaucratic Power and Control over Labour

The specific nature of the Soviet bureaucracy becomes much clearer in the light of its relationship to labour and the control over labour. The Hungarian András Hegedüs, an ex-Stalinist prime minister, has produced a remarkable analysis of this problem:

> In my view, relationships of domination and subordination under socialism arise directly from differences in the position occupied in the division of labour, and from the fact that the bureaucratic relation as an essential relation has survived in socialist society (although it plays a role essentially different from that under capitalism), principally because further growth and survival of a hierarchically structured administrative apparatus is a social necessity.[49]

We have already expressed our views on the limits of this 'social necessity'. Hegedüs also pays insufficient attention to the social and political consequences of the bureaucracy's material privileges. But he goes on to make an interesting point that ties in with Boehme's argument to which we have already referred:

> If we identify the position in the division of labour as the most important independent variable in socialist society, this must not be identified with occupations. The position occupied in the social division of labour is in fact a definite type of relation of production, which is never simply a characteristic of individual work, but always includes essential relationships to other persons and to society. . . .
>
> There are various types of work within the social division of labour defined in accordance with the degree to which they allow control over one's own work and that of others.
>
> The number of non-manual workers has grown both absolutely and relatively, and has done so particularly fast in the past ten years. The present figure is on average 29.3 non-manual workers for every 100 manual workers.
>
> Such a division is, however, only a rough and ready one, and does not satisfy anyone making a close study of the social structure of the socialist society, since neither of the two groups can be called a homogeneous stratum. . . .
>
> Non-manual workers in the statistical sense should, in my view, be listed in at least five groups for sociological purposes:
>
> 1. Those in executive positions who not only exercise a relatively high degree of control over the work of others but also control their own . . .
>
> 2. Those in executive positions who do control the work of others, but whose work takes place largely within hierarchical and standardized systems . . .
>
> 3. Those doing primarily intellectual work who do not control the work of others but do control their own . . . These include doctors, teachers and lawyers.
>
> 4. Those doing primarily intellectual work who do not control either the work of others or their own . . .
>
> 5. Those who do work that requires attention but not intellectual activity of a higher kind, who could control neither their own work nor that of others, such as stock accountants, clerks or research aides.[50]

Table 2 summarizes this social division of labour in the bureaucratized societies in transition between capitalism and socialism.

As the East German philosopher Peter Feist has pointed out, there is also another dimension to the problem of control over labour. Labour represents activity in the most general sense of the word, which is a fundamental physical–psychological need of human beings.[51] Passivity or non-activity, on the other hand, is a source of deep frustration: it involves a feeling of personal uselessness. Moreover, the less labour, or activity in general, appears as self-controlled and meaningful in the eyes of those who perform it, the more frustration grows. Under bureaucratic management of the socialized (statized) economy, this frustration inevitably

Table 2 Social Division of Labour

Social layer	Control over own labour	Control over labour of others
Top bureaucrats & leading scientists, artists, etc.	Yes	Yes
Middle bureaucrats & intellectuals	Yes	No
Petty bureaucrats, foremen, etc.	No	Yes
Ordinary workers & peasants	No	No

pervades nearly all layers of society.[52] Frustration with work feeds an escape into consumerism, itself consciously spurred by the bureaucracy as a lesser evil compared with self-management. But as the mismanaged economy cannot satisfy consumer needs, a vicious circle sets in which sooner or later must lead to explosions of anger.

Harry Braverman rightly insisted on the importance of the capitalists' control of the labour process as an essential condition for the functioning of the capitalist mode of production,[53] while André Gorz has stressed that this necessity of control – rather than the quest for ever greater profits – is the main reason for the massive fragmentation of labour in twentieth-century capitalism.[54] Other authors have even gone so far as to coin the formula 'political relations of production'. A control pyramid comprising time-keepers, foremen, quality controllers, factory security and other personnel enforce these constant attempts to subordinate labour not only to the machinery but also to the human agents of capital. The separation between labour and knowledge – which is one of the characteristics of class society, reaching its peak under capitalism – is expressed in a network of institutions confining labour to mechanical and repetitive functions.

Now, in all his major writings, from *The German Ideology* through the *Grundrisse* to *Capital*, Marx specifically maintained that in a classless society the mass of producers *control their own labour*. There is no separation between those who design and administrate and those who apply labour to direct production. The social division of labour disappears: 'Universally developed individuals, whose social relations, as their own communal [*gemeinschaftlich*] relations, are hence also subordinated to their own communal control . . .'[55]

Marx did not envisage a complete disappearance of all forms of the occupational division of labour – that would be utopian except in a highly robotized society. But he drew a clear distinction between this and the *social* division of labour, which is incompatible with the rule of the freely associated producers.[56] He did not deal with the question of control over labour in the period of transition between capitalism and socialism. But here again his thinking clearly goes in the same direction. Once they have freed themselves from the rule of capital, the producers have to become, and are capable of becoming, their own masters, including at the workplace.[57]

7. The Structure of the Bureaucracy

We have discussed in a previous section the general importance of privileges in the formation of a bureaucracy in workers' states. We now need to look more closely at the social structure that this entails.

In a typically demagogic manner Yegor Ligachev, the spokesman for the more conservative wing of the Soviet bureaucracy, has denied the whole problem of privilege by arguing that the average income of Party and state functionaries is slightly below that of a worker with average skills: 200–250 rubles a month. Formally speaking, he is right. There are eighteen million functionaries in the Soviet Union, and obviously each of them cannot earn ten times more than an ordinary worker. In the USA too, there are not eighteen million families who earn ten times as much as a fully employed skilled industrial worker. Nevertheless, Ligachev knows perfectly well that the numerous workers and intellectuals who denounce bureaucratic privileges are referring not to petty functionaries but to the nomenklatura. It is this elite, numbering some 300,000 to 400,000 people, whose monetary and other benefits certainly outstrip the average worker's income by ten times and more.

Should we therefore restrict the concept of the bureaucracy to its top layer, the nomenklatura? By no means. It would be wrong both analytically and in functional terms not to include in this category the middle ranks of Party, state and trade-union functionaries, as well as officers in the police and army. The nomenklatura would be unable to rule a modern industrialized and urbanized society like the USSR, Czechoslovakia, Poland, Yugoslavia or Hungary – even a vast backward country like the People's Republic of China – with a just a few hundred thousand people. It needs intermediary instruments for keeping the social fabric together, and by and large it is the middle layers of the bureaucracy, some two million people, who serve this function.

In bourgeois society this role is played by the middle classes, including the so-called 'new middle classes' which, from a strictly scientific point of view, constitute the upper part of the proletariat, not owning enough property to be free of the economic compulsion to sell their labour power. Among all these layers, the acquisition, defence and ideology of private property are of absolutely crucial significance, as anyone not blinded by ignorance or self-deception is forced to admit.

In the Soviet Union, things stand rather differently. Of course, the trend towards personal enrichment has not disappeared: indeed, it has steadily been gathering momentum since the establishment of the Stalinist dictatorship. But it would be wrong to assume that a person is driven to become a minor Party, state or trade-union functionary by the urge to acquire private property and monetary wealth. The modest privileges attaching to their position are nearly always outside the purely monetary sphere, the big exception being the bureaucracy of the distribution system with its links to local and regional mafias. In general, the most significant benefits involve access to certain goods and services, career security, a quiet life, the satisfaction of bossing other people around, and so on.

Moreover, just as no bureaucracy can rule a mass trade union without the mediation of at least part of its membership, so the Stalinist bureaucracy cannot rule the bureaucratized workers' states without the mediation of a minority of the working class. When we say 'mediation', we do not necessarily mean open or conscious 'collaboration', although this does exist. Nor is it possible to draw up general patterns for all these societies. The Romanian bureaucracy under Ceausescu, for example, was certainly more divorced from the working class than its counterpart in the GDR, while the Czechoslovak bureaucracy had greater links with the masses during the Prague Spring than under Novotny or Jakes. In Yugoslavia the national liberation struggle, the post-war revolutionary upheavals, the successful resistance to Stalin and the self-management experiment meant that for a long time the Party's relations with the working class were deeper than in any other East European country.

What can be expressed as a general rule is that none of these parties is widely considered to be an instrument for the defence of workers' interests.[58] They are seen as state parties, as tools of the 'new masters', and that is what they are in reality. It does not follow, however, that the divorce with the workers is complete. The place of these parties within society, including the factory, makes such a situation an objective impossibility. For the Party is not composed only of managers and foremen: it includes in its ranks a large number of functionaries whom the workers have to use in order to gain redress for their grievances, to overcome delays with sickness benefits or pensions, to secure a place in a trade-union holiday home, and so on. It also includes millions of direct producers – some seven to eight million in the USSR, and a similar proportion in Eastern Europe – the great majority of whom did not join out of fear or straightforward careerism. It would be ludicrous to present these workers as mere stooges or henchmen of the CP bureaucracy.

Thus the ruling Communist Parties reflect a more complex and dialectical social relationship than that which exists between exploitative employers and exploited wage-earners. This difference, and the specific nature of the bureaucracies of the workers' states, are also evident in the relatively high degree of vertical mobility that traditionally obtained.[59]

In capitalist countries, particularly under monopoly capitalism, the evolution of social structures is generally determined by the growing centralization of capital and proletarianization of labour. To be sure, these tendencies do not operate in a linear or mechanical way – especially in periods of expansion, not insignificant counter-tendencies are also at work. But in the long run, the part of dependent (wage) labour in the active population is increasing, while the party of independent petty entrepreneurs is declining. The fraction of small and medium bourgeois who have 'made it' – that is, become big capitalists – is also diminishing historically. As for those who reach the very top, who become dollar billionaires and remain there for several generations, they have been reduced to a handful since the end of the nineteenth century.

In the Soviet Union, by contrast, a worker with above-average intelligence and initiative can still become a middle-layer bureaucrat. Indeed, the bureaucracy will make a big effort to absorb such people into its ranks, especially if they also show a mildly critical spirit. The middle layers of the bureaucracy are rapidly growing, not declining.[60] A young, rather poor local bureaucrat can still become a key member of the nomenklatura, if he combines the above qualities with particular tactical skill and lack of scruples, ingratiates himself with those who count at local, regional and national level, and lives up to expectations in a series of crisis situations. After all, that is how Mikhail Gorbachev rose to the summit of the hierarchy.

It is true that nowadays hardly any sons and daughters of manual workers are to be found among the top layers of the nomenklatura. But on the other hand, only a minority of these are sons and daughters of former high bureaucrats. Not a single member of the Politburo or the Council of Ministers is the offspring of a former member of the Politburo or the Council of Ministers. The difference with bourgeois society is certainly striking.

Nevertheless, a further characteristic of the Soviet bureaucracy needs to be borne in mind if we are to grasp its nature and dynamic. For it is not a 'pure' labour bureaucracy but one which, from the beginning, was also intertwined with non-proletarian petty-bourgeois and even bourgeois layers, as well as with remnants of Tsarist officialdom. As E.H. Carr puts it, 'the management of industry was passing back into the hands of former bourgeois managers and specialists, and a higher proportion of these were acquiring the dignity and security of party membership.'[61] Lenin strongly emphasized the element of continuity with the past in some of his last writings, and Trotsky would later write:

> The army of the Soviet Thermidor was recruited essentially from the remnants of the former ruling parties and their ideological representatives. The former landed gentry, capitalists, lawyers, their sons – that is, those of them that had not run abroad – were taken into the state machine, and quite a few even into the Party. A far greater number of those admitted into the State and Party machinery were formerly members of the petty-bourgeois parties – Mensheviks and SRs. To these must be added a tremendous number of pure and simple philistines who had cowered on the sidelines during the stormy epoch of the Revolution and the Civil War and who, convinced at last of the stability of the Soviet government, dedicated themselves with singular passion to the noble task of securing soft and permanent berths.[62]

In the long run, however, Trotsky insisted in the *Transitional Programme*, the relationship of forces inside the bureaucracy would shift:

> The revolutionary elements within the bureaucracy [would only be] a small minority. The . . . counter-revolutionary elements, growing uninterruptedly, express with ever greater consistency the interests of world imperialism. These candidates for the role of compradors consider, not without reason, that the new ruling layer can insure their positions of privilege only through rejection of nationalization, collectivization and monopoly of foreign trade in the name of the assimilation of 'Western civilization', i.e., capitalism. Between these two poles, there are intermediate, diffused Menshevik–SR– liberal tendencies which gravitate towards bourgeois democracy.[63]

Written more than fifty years ago, these lines present a truly prophetic picture of what has begun to occur in the USSR.

If we turn now to the contemporary functional differentiation within the Soviet bureaucracy, it is possible to break down its ranks into the following categories: (a) the state bureaucracy, including the central economic administrations; (b) the military bureaucracy; (c) the police bureaucracy; (d) the bureaucracy of the mass organizations of youth, women, and so on; (e) the 'cultural' bureaucracy; (f) the trade-union bureaucracy and (g) the Party bureaucracy. The last of these exercises a degree of ultimate control over all the others, but less than is generally assumed. It may be seen as the iron ring holding the barrel together.

The 'compartmentalization' – some use the term 'feudalization' – of the bureaucracy has asserted itself to an ever greater extent. In each of the above branches, 'internal promotion' is the rule. Intervention by the Party bureaucracy can still make and unmake careers, but it does so within established hierarchies and hardly ever through the catapulting of outsiders into the posts of generals, top planners, association secretaries, trade union bosses, and so on. Needless to say, each part of the nomenklatura 'looks after its own', sometimes with major political consequences.[64]

Tatiana Zaslavskaia has proposed another criterion for sub-dividing the bureaucracy by level of education and relationship to change.[65] Among the twelve 'key social groups' that she enumerates, four can be considered as part of the bureaucracy: economic managers, leading cadres in trade, high functionaries in the Party and state, and politicians. The 'cultural and educational intelligentsia' and 'small entrepreneurs' are analysed as groups apart. Zaslavskaia adds some considerations on differences in attitude according to age group, and makes the point – confirmed by recent experience in the GDR – that the managerial bureaucracy is divided between supporters and opponents of perestroika in accordance with its level of competence and capacity for change. While her conclusions are interesting, they do not justify any theoretical downgrading of the key structural differentiation.

8. The Schizophrenic Self-consciousness of the Bureaucracy

It is clear from our discussion so far that the bureaucracy has not been able to sever all links with the working class, while continuing to behave as a parasitical, wasteful, treacherous, oppressive and materially privileged layer of that class. In the same way, it has not been able to sever all its links with the theory of Marx and Lenin, while debasing that critical, emancipatory set of ideas and methods of investigation into a series of wildly varying dogmas. Its essential approach to the Marxist tradition is one of scholastic quote-culling, whose sole purpose is to justify existing social and political structures in the states that it rules, and the various, often contradictory, policies that it successively applies. The bureaucracy thereby instrumentalizes science into a handmaiden of conjunctural policies and the interests defended by them.

All this being said, it is still from Marx, Engels and Lenin that the dogmas are culled, albeit sometimes with a strong element of distortion or even falsification, and not from luminaries of the Stalin, Khrushchev or Brezhnev type.[66] That cannot be accidental, nor can its results be altogether unforeseen.

In Chapter 1 we indicated a crucial aspect of the bureaucracy's ideology: the combination of state and commodity fetishism. A further essential dimension is its incapacity to achieve self-awareness and open self-affirmation, to formulate with any consistency a world-view that can truly be called its own. This weakness, which is in striking contrast with the behaviour of all ruling classes throughout history, provides fresh confirmation that the bureaucracy is not in fact a ruling class. One can hardly imagine Sieyès proclaiming: 'What is the Third Estate? It doesn't exist.'[67] Nor can one visualize Southern slaveowners in the ante-bellum USA denying that the 'peculiar institution' exists, or European aristocrats claiming that there is no hereditary nobility endowed with special rights. Yet that is precisely the kind of thing that the nomenklatura has been saying about itself for more than half a century.

This ideological self-denial is evidently a huge exercise in mystification. It is full of explosive contradictions. It flies in the face of what anyone with a modicum of perception and intelligence notices day after day in real life. It therefore invites massive doubts and intellectual rejection. It can be foisted on a recalcitrant society only by means of institutionalized lies, which again invite massive rejection.[68] A high degree of repression is required to sustain it, not only or even mainly against intellectuals but also against workers. The crime of voicing 'bad thoughts' ('slander of the Soviet-socialist order', 'anti-socialist propaganda', etc.) had to be put in the penal code and punished by harsh sentences of confinement in prison or labour camp.[69] The bureaucracy's efforts to deny its own existence led it to deny social reality as such, with an effective strangling of all social science.

The fact that this whole operation occurs not in a vacuum but within a framework still pregnant with references to Marxism makes it susceptible to explosive pressures. The effects of bureaucratic dictatorship tend to discredit Marxism as a 'state religion' in the eyes of the broad masses, but so long as the works of Marx, Engels and Lenin remain widely available, there will always be some who draw from them analytical tools to explain the mystery of the bureaucracy, how it was born, what it means, how it can be overcome. For the bureaucracy critical Marxist thought is like a hydra. You can cut off head after head, but new ones will always spring forth again.

This is the price the bureaucracy has to pay for its continuing reference to Marxism. It has found no way out since the first days of the Soviet Thermidor. Moreover, when the apologetic distortion of social science reaches a certain threshold, it begins to have objective consequences which turn it from a prop of the dictatorship into a time-bomb against it. Mystification becomes self-mystification. The bureaucracy is less and less able to see or comprehend processes of social change that are taking place right under its nose. It does not know its own country any more.[70]

But since this reduces its capacity for defending its rule, it has to loosen the iron grip on social science. This is one of the reasons for Gorbachev's glasnost.

Now, precisely because Marxism remains the official ideology, the revival of social sciences cannot be purely empirical or pragmatic, as the 'modernizing' wing of the bureaucracy would like it to be, but becomes increasingly intertwined with a revival of critical Marxist thought and analysis. In the Soviet Union today a discussion is unfolding on the bureaucracy as a social phenomenon – as distinct from the problem of bureaucratic habits and mentality – which is much more profound than the debate of the twenties. Though only two years old, it already equals in depth and sophistication the fifty-year theoretical tradition in the West, if it does not actually outstrip it.

Nor is this the whole of the story. As the renaissance of Marxist and other critical social thought is combined with new social movements and mass actions contesting the existing order, it generates a deep and permanent crisis of identity of the bureaucracy. Particularly when they are faced with working-class contestation, a number of bureaucrats have to ask some taxing questions: Who are we? Communists or just members of a party that calls itself Communist? What is our main allegiance – to the Party, or to the working class, emancipation and Marxism?[71] If the Party now admits that it is not always right, have we or have we not to decide for ourselves, with our own individual conscience, what is right and what is wrong in a given situation? Are we really free to debate all this? Inside formal Party structures as well as outside them? Only with Party members or also with other workers and critical intellectuals?

Thus all the key questions posed during the onset of bureaucratization and stifling of workers' democracy are beginning to come to the surface, in the heads of at least part of the bureaucracy and its ideologues. And not just in their heads. For the generation of Stalinist and post-Stalinist bureaucrats, ideologues and fellow-travellers, a terrible guilt is starting to burn in their hearts. They were guilty of monstrous crimes, or of a systematic cover-up for them – not a few of which were committed against their own Party comrades. The mark of Cain stares out from their foreheads.

Yesterday, everything was explained away as necessary and unavoidable, a lesser evil or an unfortunate mistake.[72] Today the heinous crimes, contrary to any interest of the working class and socialism, are called by their right name. Only the most cynical or morally base seek to deny or minimize their guilt.[73]

It is significant that those who were confronted with the largest working-class revolt in Eastern Europe have also developed some of the frankest recognitions of guilt and of the need for self-criticism: we are referring to the Hungarian Stalinists. Already before the beginning of the 1956 revolution, Imre Nagy, who was an honest communist, wrote a reappraisal of the whole Rákosi period in which he identified the existence of the CP bureaucracy as a key element in that party's degeneration:

> The predominance of the apparatus and the eclipse of the elected organs, with a resulting increase in administrative methods in Party leadership, is nothing new in the life of our Party. It was typical of the pre-June methods of Party leadership. We were unable to alter this, which was particularly bad because the Soviet comrades, and especially Comrade Khrushchev, on many occasions called our attention to the danger: to the fact that the apparatus is leading us and is overpowering the Party. [The 'Soviet comrades' forgot to mention, however, that this had already happened in the USSR as early as 1923 – EM.] The growing pressure, terrorism, and browbeating in the field of intra-Party democracy and criticism and self-criticism, is closely related to the predominant role assumed by the apparatus and the increasing use of administrative devices in the internal life of the Party. . . .
>
> The charge of factionalism stems from distorted views concerning the rules of the internal life of the Party. Every political statement of the Party members looks like factionalism to persons who deny the fundamental right of Party members to discuss Party problems and to debate and exchange opinions; who believe that Party members may discuss Party life, political, economic, cultural or international questions only in the presence of the Party Secretary or under the surveillance of members of the apparatus; who feel that discussions must be conducted according to specific rules or from a predetermined point of view and within a limited scope – in other words, only under the conditions that the 'left-wing' extremists and the Party bureaucracy are willing to tolerate.[74]

Imre Nagy did not hesitate to call things by their name. What Stalinism had created in Hungary was a real degeneration of the workers' state:

> The degeneration of power is seriously endangering the fate of socialism and the democratic basis of our social system. Power is increasingly being torn away from the people and turned sharply against them. The People's Democracy as a type of dictatorship of the proletariat, in which the power is exercised by the working class and depends on the partnership of the two large working groups – the workers and the peasantry – is obviously being replaced by a Party dictatorship which does not rely on the Party membership, but relies on a personal dictatorship and attempts to make the Party apparatus, and through it the Party membership, a mere tool of this dictatorship. Its power is not permeated by the spirit of socialism or democratism but by a Bonapartist spirit of minority dictatorship. Its aims are not determined by Marxism, the teachings of scientific socialism, but by autocratic views that are maintained at any cost and by any means.[75]

Anticipating debates that would be conducted on a broad scale in the USSR and China thirty years later, and echoing what the Left Opposition in the CPSU had stated as early as 1923, Nagy correctly established the connections between a given set of ethical–moral standards – we would say, rather, ethical–political standards – and the struggle against bureaucratic degeneration of workers' power. For the bureaucracy's consolidation of material privileges, together with the material pressure, not to say repression, brought to bear on the Party membership and the broad masses, create a social atmosphere of all-pervading cynicism in which corruption becomes rife:

> It is not compatible with public morality to have in positions of leadership the directors and organizers of mass lawsuits [that is, the show-trials – EM], or those responsible for the torturing and killing of innocent people, or organizers of international provocations, or economic saboteurs, or squanderers of public property who, through the abuse of power, either have committed serious crimes against the people or are forcing others to commit these crimes. The public, the Party, and the state organs must be cleansed of these elements.
>
> There is a type of material dependence that forces men to relinquish their individualities and their convictions, which is not compatible with morality in public life. Unfortunately, this has assumed mass proportions here and must be considered virtually a disease of our society. Excessive centralization of the economic and political structure is the inevitable concomitant of personal dictatorship. What sort of political morality is there in a public life where contrary opinions are not only suppressed but punished with actual deprivation of livelihood; where those who express contrary opinions are expelled from society with shameful disregard for the human and civil rights set down in the Constitution; where those who are opposed in principle to the ruling political trend are barred from their professions? . . .
>
> This is not socialist morality. Rather it is modern Machiavellianism. This all-powerful material dependence, this anxiety for bread, is killing the most noble human virtues, virtues that should most especially be developed in a socialist society: courage, resolution, sincerity and frankness, consistency of principle, and strength. In their place, the leaders have made virtues of self-abasement, cowardice, hypocrisy, lack of principle, and lies. The degeneration and corruption of public life and the deterioration of character that takes place in society as a result thereof are among the most serious manifestations of the moral–ethical crisis that is taking place before our eyes. . . . Falsehood and careerism are spreading dangerously in our public life and are deeply affecting human morality and honour; distrust is gaining ground; and an atmosphere of suspicion and revenge is banishing the fundamental feature of socialist morality, humanism; in its stead, cold inhumanity is appearing in our public life. It is a shocking picture that the moral situation of our social life reveals.[76]

The identity crisis of bureaucrats who have not cut all their proletarian ties was expressed in the clearest possible way by the Budapest police chief Sandor Kopacsi, a former worker and son of a worker who went over to the side of the revolution in October 1956 and became a particular *bête noire* of the KGB. He narrowly escaped the death sentence inflicted upon Imre Nagy.[77] When interrogated after his arrest about his identity and profession, he did not know what to say:

> I opened my mouth. Then, to my great astonishment I realized that I no longer knew. The police chief of Budapest? No. A young metalworker roaming the woods of the north? No. The devoted son of my father? The adored father of my daughter? A spy in the pay of Allen Dulles? A follower of Khrushchev and Imre Nagy? Or, indeed, of Janos Kadar? An empty snail-shell? A snowflake, brother to the one that had just landed on my forehead.[78]

Three well-known writers in the GDR gave literary expression to this schizophrenia. The most pathetic case is the former Minister of Culture, Johannes R. Becher, who allowed himself to be drawn into a provocation against his life-long friend Lukács, which served to get another friend, Janka, as well as Wolfgang Harich, sentenced to long terms of imprisonment. In a scandalously servile letter to the Central Committee of the SED, he explained how he had adored Stalin and sincerely written poems to his glory, and how he had been shaken by Khrushchev's revelations at the Twentieth Congress of the CPSU – but without drawing any negative conclusions about 'unconditional Party discipline'.[79] At the same time, however, he secretly wrote a series of intense poems condemning those writers who denounced their own comrades to the police and murdered them with a few lines. The poem ends with the suicide of one such informer: 'After that you can no longer live as a human being. And he shot himself with the hunting-rifle.'[80]

The second case is the novelist Stephan Hermlin who, when confronted by an interviewer after the Twentieth Congress, declared that he had not known that the Moscow Trials were based on fabrications, but that even if he had he still would not have denounced them, as this would have helped the enemies of the USSR, the only bulwark against Hitler. Later, Hermlin recognized that only the truth is revolutionary, and that it has at all costs to be spoken, if possible inside the Party, even at the risk of expulsion.[81]

The most striking example of schizophrenia is that of the most talented German Stalinist writer, Bertolt Brecht. In his terrible play *Die Massnahme* he tried to justify in advance, as it were, the murder of innocent comrades. Many years later, he did not publicly voice his criticism of the brutal crushing of the East German workers' revolt of 17 June 1953. Yet simultaneously, he wrote a famous sarcastic entry in his diary: 'If the people do not follow the Party's correct line, the Party has the right to dissolve the people.' And a secret poem labelled Stalin as the *'verdienter Mörder des Volkes'* (distinguished murderer of the people).[82] It should be added that he did publish an unmistakably anti-Stalinist play *Galileo*, by far his best, which offered a defence of freedom of thought and science while its hero manoeuvres with principles in order to stay alive in a climate of repression.

9. Is the Bureaucratization of Mass Workers' Parties Inevitable?

Since the latter part of the nineteenth century, two distinct traditions have raised the question of whether the bureaucratization of mass working-class parties is inevitable. On the one hand, Robert Michels, inspired by Mosca and Pareto's 'circulation of elites' theory, posited an 'iron law' of oligarchy affecting all parties.[83] On the other hand, anarchists developed a similar idea right from the time of Bakunin's fight within the First International, and this was to some extent taken up by various Left Oppositionists within social democracy (such as the German Johann Most, who later went over to anarchism). Both of these traditions stressed the inevitably 'authoritarian' character of party leaders, as did the KAPD and 'council communists' around Pannekoek and Gorter after the First World War.[84] But then the roads diverged. While at least one wing of the anarchists (the anarcho-syndicalists), as well as the 'council communists', stressed the decisive importance of mass action and organization, the Pareto–Michels school proclaimed the intrinsic incapacity of the working-class masses to achieve their own emancipation.[85]

Here we are indeed *in media re*. If one asserts the inevitability of bureaucratic degeneration of mass workers' parties, then one posits at the same time that mass activity and self-organization will inevitably decline, or at least remain at a permanently low level. Evidently, much more is at stake than the problem of bureaucratization. The whole fate of the modern proletariat, nay the whole fate of humanity, is in question. For, without self-emancipation of the working class, no socialism is possible. In the best of cases, only a reform of capitalism would remain as a way to a better society. But in the long run, capitalism produces one disaster after another. Mere reforms of capitalism did not prevent Hitler from taking power or block the path to Auschwitz and Hiroshima; nor will they remove similar dangers tomorrow. If that is all there is, then there is no escape from barbarism or outright self-destruction.[86]

The historical record clearly shows that to focus on the specificity of 'parties', as the anarchists and council communists do, is really to evade the issue.[87] Trade unions, including those led by anarcho-syndicalists, are prone to even more rapid bureaucratization in conditions of declining mass activity. The same is true of soviet-type bodies. In fact, revolutionary parties often resist the tendency longest, partly because most of their membership has a higher level of continuous activity, and partly because it is usually more aware of the dangers.

In the last analysis, the problem can be correctly posed and solved only if the simplistic counterposition of 'black' (bureaucratization) and 'white' (workers' self-rule) is replaced by a dialectical understanding of contradictory and combined *processes*. An incipient trend towards bureaucratization of working-class mass organizations is indeed unavoidable, as are periodic declines in mass activity. But periodic surges in the level of mass activity are equally unavoidable products of the inner contradictions of capitalism and bourgeois society: they more than once have taken on the form of revolutionary action.

The more this process unfolds, the more the trend towards bureaucratization can be checked and its previous results reversed. Outstanding examples in the course of the twentieth century are: Russia 1917–19; Germany 1917–20; Italy 1917–21; Spain 1934–May 1937; Belgium 1956–62; Italy 1969–73; Czechoslovakia 1968–69; Chile 1970–73; Portugal 1974–75; Poland 1980–81; Brazil 1985–90; and, in a more limited way, France 1934–37, the USA 1934–39, and Argentina 1973.[88] A similar process has been gathering pace in the USSR over the past few years.

Thus, the real task for socialists or communists who pursue the goal of workers' self-emancipation is to organize themselves and propagate their ideas and aims inside the working class; to participate with the greatest commitment, loyalty and lucidity in all its struggles and those of all the exploited and oppressed; and to act in such a way as to stimulate the self-activity and self-organization of the class as such, or at least of major parts of it. History has shown that this is a formidable, but also a possible, undertaking.

Another real and not 'logical' contradiction underlies the cycles of mass activity. On the one hand, wage-workers cannot survive in capitalist society without selling their labour power. They cannot start to emancipate themselves without trying to sell the only commodity they possess at a higher price. In doing so, and in using money wages to buy commodities, they become a key element in the reproduction of the capitalist mode of production – that is, in their own exploitation. This cannot but have certain effects on their consciousness.[89] And it is obviously no answer to suggest that workers should withdraw their energies from the struggle for higher wages. A pauperized working class, as Marx saw, would be far too demoralized to be capable of overthrowing capitalism.

On the other hand, wage-workers are also producers who suffer the yoke of capitalist exploitation and oppression at the workplace. From its earliest days, the labour movement fought not only to protect and increase real wages but also to shorten the working week and to establish some form of control over the labour process. By acting in this way, workers do not help to reproduce capitalism: they challenge it objectively and – more and more – consciously. As militant consumers of commodities, workers can be integrated into bourgeois society. As producers militantly disputing the amount of surplus labour extracted from them, and even the mechanics and human structure of surplus extraction, they cannot be integrated into bourgeois society. They undermine its very foundations.

This dual position of the working class is reflected in different forms of actual (not ideal or idealized) consciousness. A number of theorists have written in this regard of a contradiction between workers' everyday consciousness and class consciousness in the traditional, higher sense of the term – a consciousness of the common, collective interests of all members of the class as such.[90] Lenin's distinction between trade-unionist class consciousness and socialist class consciousness is also pertinent here.[91] And we have added a third, intermediate level with obvious historical importance: namely, political class consciousness that is not yet socialist but expresses an understanding of the need for workers to organize and vote independently of the capitalists and their parties.[92]

Another line of analysis, first advanced by Hendrik De Man and most articulately by Rudolf Hilferding, centres on a distinction between 'general' and 'particular' interests in the field of ideas. In this view, class consciousness does not simply substitute the former for the latter. It also goes beyond immediate material interests (including those of the working class) to develop a set of ideas necessary for the freeing of the productive forces from the fetters of existing relations of production.[93] These ideas, originating with intellectuals and the dialectic of ideologies, may even clash with the material interests of the majority of the class.[94]

Once launched on this road De Man, the older Sorel or Hilferding raised the question of why most workers so often dismiss correct ideas. Apart from the pressure of bourgeois ideology, what is the irrational source of their motivations in passions, myths, instinctual drives, the desire for 'values' higher than material interests, and so on?[95]

The basic difference between these two approaches – which are not, of course, completely separate from each other and could be combined to a certain degree – can be stated quite briefly. According to one approach, the main obstacle to higher levels of class consciousness lies in the workers' immediate self-interest as they themselves perceive it in everyday life. For the other, the resistance to higher consciousness occurs in spite of this perceived immediate self-interest. In our view, the first school is by and large correct, although valuable insights can be drawn from the 'psychological' current.

Many theoreticians see these obstacles as confirmation that the bureaucratization of working-class mass organizations is inevitable; that the working class has the organizations and leaders that it deserves. In Otto Bauer's fatalistic interpretation of historical materialism, for example, history could not have moved in any other way. If things went wrong, in Russia as in Central Europe, this was because objective conditions did not allow the mass upsurge to become sufficiently powerful.[96] In other words: the deficiencies of the proletariat were the root cause of bureaucratization.

The trouble with this reasoning is that, in trying to prove too much, it proves very little. If the masses always have the leadership they deserve, how can one explain that in many situations a number of rival leaderships and parties combat one another within the labour movement? Why should the relationship of forces between these tendencies vary so strongly, sometimes in the course of a few months? Why should countries with virtually identical objective conditions display such a great discrepancy in the degree of workers' democracy within the labour movement?

To conclude: the real contradictions in consciousness can only be solved in practice, through developments in the real movement of the class. Advanced forms of mass activity and organization, and the parallel conquest of higher levels of class consciousness, will tend to transform mass actions into direct challenges to the bourgeois order. But the building of vanguard parties is an essential, if not sufficient, component of this progress towards self-emancipation of the working class.

To reject all centralized workers' organization on the grounds that it can become bureaucratized – or, worse, to reject all organization outside the individual workplace – is to propose a cure worse than the sickness itself.[97] However its proponents may see it, such a relapse into primitivism denies the very possibility of workers' self-emancipation, which can be achieved only at the level of society in its totality. Some at least of the anti-organization theorists logically end their particular trajectory by integrating themselves into bourgeois society.

NOTES

1. Parvus, *Die Gewerkschaften und die Sozialdemokratie*, Dresden 1896, pp. 65–66.
2. Ibid., p. 66.
3. For reasons of ideological prejudice, this is rarely understood by liberals and conservatives alike, who tend to oppose collective organization to individual emancipation. (Stalinists generally defend an analogous position.) They do not seem to grasp that 'the mass' is composed of individuals defending themselves and striving for their rights as

individuals. The only difference with members of the ruling class is that because of their economic weakness, institutionalized by bourgeois society, they cannot achieve a minimum of counter-power and dignity through purely individual endeavours, but only through collective organization and action. Their goal remains free or freer development of their personality. But the liberals and neo-conservative bourgeoisie, who tend to deny them that right of self-assertion they so loudly claim for themselves, can see only a 'faceless mob' in which each of its components has been rendered 'faceless' by the beholder himself.

4. See Marx's famous remarks in the 'Inaugural Address of the International Working Men's Association', in Marx, *The First International and After*, Harmondsworth 1974.

5. The Socialist Encyclopedia published by the French socialists just before the First World War gives impressive figures in this respect. In many European countries, tens or even hundreds of thousands of people belonged to workers' theatre and music groups, sports and gymnastic associations, and so on. In Cuba the cigar-workers union forced the bosses to hire someone to select books of an educational and political value and to read them aloud during working hours. In Finland, on the eve of the First World War, the quite left-wing social-democratic party compelled Parliament to print volume one of *Capital* in Finnish at the state's expense.

6. Henriette Roland-Holst, *Algemeene Werkstaking en Sociaaldemocratie*, Rotterdam 1906, pp. 111–12. Emphasis added.

7. Rosa Luxemburg, 'Einführung in die Nationalökonomie', in *Gesammelte Werke*, vol. 5, Berlin/GDR 1975, p. 763.

8. August Bebel, *Der sozialdemokratische 'Zukunftsstaat', Verhandlungen des Deutschen Reichstags am 31. Januar, 3., 4., 6. und 7. Februar 1893*, Berlin 1893, p. 11. Emphasis added. This 127-page pamphlet sold more than a hundred thousand copies.

9. Ibid., p. 125. Emphasis added.

10. 'The Civil War in France', in *The First International and After*, p. 212.

11. *The Civil War in France*, Peking 1966, p. 15. Emphasis added.

12. *The State and Revolution*, Peking 1965, p. 131. Emphasis added.

13. Karl Kautsky, *The Origins of Christianity*, London 1917. Although this was the first time that the problem of bureaucratization had been posed so clearly by a Marxist, the method of historical comparison was not the fruit of Kautsky's theoretical labours alone. Engels, in his introduction to Marx's *Class Struggles in France* (Moscow 1960, pp. 25–26), compared the persecution suffered by the working-class movement to that of another movement of the oppressed sixteen hundred years earlier. In spite of harsh repression at the hands of the ruling classes, Christianity had gone from strength to strength until it reached all social classes and ended in being victorious.

14. Bukharin wrongly generalized from these exceptional circumstances of the Russian Revolution in his book *The Economics of the Transition Period* (English translation as Part Two of *The Politics and Economics of the Transition Period*, London 1979). There is no law in contemporary history that the conquest of power by the working class is always and everywhere accompanied by a steep fall of the productive forces.

15. After 1917 Lenin was obsessed by the relative cultural backwardness of the Russian working class. Under more favourable circumstances, however, the Cuban Revolution succeeded within one generation in spectacularly raising the cultural level of the masses.

16. This was by and large the case of the Yugoslav, Chinese and Vietnamese revolutions, all led by strongly bureaucratized parties.

17. See, in particular, *One Step Forward, Two Steps Back* (1904).

18. See L.D. Trotsky, *Results and Prospects*, London 1962.

19. 'The Mass Strike, the Political Party and the Trade Unions', in *Rosa Luxemburg Speaks*, ed. Mary-Alice Waters, New York 1970, pp. 214–16. Translation modified.

20. Antonio Gramsci, 'Trade Unions and the Dictatorship', *Ordine Nuovo*, 25 October 1919, reproduced in Gramsci, *Selections from Political Writings 1910–1920*, ed. Quintin Hoare, London 1977, pp. 105–106.

21. See E. Bernstein, *Die Voraussetzungen des Sozialismus und die Aufgaben der*

Sozialdemokratie, Berlin 1899. Abridged English translation: *Evolutionary Socialism*, New York 1961.

22. Quoted from Gilles/Ooms/Delandsheere, *Cinquante mois d'Occupation Allemande*, vol. 3, Brussels 1919, pp. 395–96.

23. See Erich Mathias, *Das Ende der Parteien 1933*, Dusseldorf 1979, pp. 177–80; Wolfgang Abendroth, *Die deutschen Gewerkschaften*, Heidelberg 1954, p. 34. The social-democrat leaders, prisoners of a pathetic belief in 'legality' and 'maintaining the organization at all costs', even voted for Hitler's foreign policy in the Reichstag session of 17 June 1933, the last they were allowed to attend.

24. 'Massenstreik, Partei und Gewerkschaften', first edition, in *Gesammelte Werke*, vol. 2, Berlin/GDR 1972, p. 165. English translation modified from *Selected Political Writings*, ed. Dick Howard, New York 1971, p. 264, and *Rosa Luxemburg Speaks*, p. 216. The text continues with a powerful paragraph: 'In contradistinction to social democracy, which bases its influence on the . . . critical attitude of the masses to all factors and stages of their own class struggle, the influence and power of the trade unions are founded upon the theory of the incapacity of the masses for criticism and decision.'

25. Examples of denunciation were provided by the SPD leadership almost immediately after 4 August 1914. In his disgusting memoirs, Noske tries to cover up for the murder of Rosa Luxemburg and Karl Liebknecht.

26. One sad, even tragic aspect of this contradiction can be seen in the large-scale withdrawal from political or trade-union activity of tens of thousands of critical worker-cadres, active strike leaders, and so on, during the last forty years in Europe. Even when they are laid off with the complicity of the bureaucrats, or expelled from the union, or both, they stubbornly continue to fight for a certain time. But in the absence of a strong vanguard organization to make that fight effective in the longer term, the great majority eventually call it a day, and the rebuilding of a genuine socialist mass vanguard becomes correspondingly more difficult.

27. Thus, in the *Transitional Programme* Trotsky suggests that a generation of militants who have suffered great defeats will not easily involve themselves again in socialist politics, and that the task will normally be taken up by a new, younger generation.

28. This occurred not only during the rise of fascism in the thirties but also in the 1970s and 1980s – for example, the impressive display of mass mourning and mass solidarity after the murder of Swedish Social-Democrat leader Olaf Palme.

29. We deal further with this phenomenon in Chapter 5 below.

30. We shall deal below with the Bauer–Hilferding version of this argument.

31. The term 'totalitarian power', which even Trotsky occasionally used, implies a degree of total, unshakable control over society that did not exist under either Hitler or Stalin. Significantly, even at the height of the dictatorship in the USSR, popular wisdom had it that '*blat*' or 'connections' are 'stronger than Stalin' – which was quite true and reflected the growing internal compartmentalization of the bureaucracy. In his sadly mistaken dystopia *Nineteen Eighty-Four*, George Orwell went so far as to predict that in a 'totalitarian' society, the bulk of its citizens would gladly accept their wretched fate. The evolution of the USSR precisely since 1984, not to speak of Eastern Europe, has spectacularly contradicted this literary projection.

The kernel of truth in the concept of 'totalitarianism' is that, under both the fascist and the Stalinist regime, the dictatorial control and suppression of basic liberties reached a qualitatively higher level than under other regimes, including Bonapartist ones, however repressive. In this sense, the USSR today is obviously no longer such a 'totalitarian' dictatorship.

32. See the report given by Alex Podshekoldin, of the Institute of Marxism–Leninism of the Central Committee of the CPSU, to the Trotsky Symposium held in Wuppertal in March 1990. According to E.H. Carr (*The Interregnum 1923–1924*, London 1969, pp. 49f.), the maximum salary for industrial managers in January 1923 was 1,500 rubles a month, or more than thirty or sixty times the minimum wage and 20–22 times the average. The 'party maximum', which had been introduced by Lenin, stipulated that no member of the Communist Party, including Politburo and top government figures, should be paid more than a skilled worker. Officially the principle was only abolished in 1930.

33. B. Yeltsin, *Against the Grain*, London 1990, pp. 127–29, 111. Yeltsin has been branded a traitor by the nomenklatura caste because of his frank revelations.

34. See the pertinent reflections in Angelica Balabanov, *My Life as a Rebel*, London 1938.

35. Christian Rakovsky, 'The Professional Dangers of Power' (6 August 1928), in *Selected Writings on Opposition in the USSR 1923–1930*, ed. Gus Fagan, London 1980, pp. 126, 160. Rakovsky recalls that on the eve of the French Thermidor, Robespierre began to replace the judges and commissioners of the *sections* of Paris, who until then had been elected, by people nominated from the top. He himself designated the presidents of the revolutionary committees and even began to substitute functionaries for all the leaders of the Commune. This killed off mass initiative, already in a weakened state as a result of economic misery and Robespierre's repression of the extreme left. The victory of Thermidor was greatly facilitated by the resulting passivity of the Parisian masses.

36. *Documents of the 1923 Opposition*, London 1975, pp. 7–8.

37. G. Volodazov, 'The Roots and Essence of Stalinism', *Oktyabr*, No. 6/1989.

38. 'The results have been illegal movements which draw members of the Party outside the limits of the Party, and a divorce of the Party from the toiling masses.' Ibid., p. 8. See also Rakovsky: 'I think of the masses as reduced to penury, or semi-pauperized, who, thanks to the derisory subsidies given out by the state, are on the border of pauperism, theft and prostitution. . . . They are beginning to consider Soviet power, and that part of the working class working in industry, with hostility. They are especially becoming the enemies of the functionaries of the soviets, of the party and of the trade unions. They can sometimes be heard speaking of the summits of the working class as the "new nobility".' ('The Professional Dangers of Power', p. 130.)

39. Georg Lukács, Letter to Carocci, p. 658.

40. Ibid., p. 674.

41. Jean-Paul Sartre, *The Problem of Method*, London 1963, p. 22. Sartre (on p. 23) accuses the Trotskyists of an unscientific 'apriorism', 'parallel' to that of Stalin, when they interpreted the Soviet intervention in Hungary in 1956 as an act of 'aggression against the democracy of Workers' Councils', without bothering to study the facts. We would point out that while many Trotskyist publications gave a long and detailed report of 'the facts', Sartre glides over the whole affair in a couple of sentences. But, more important, the first problem is not to analyse the details of the activities of the workers' councils, and the various tendencies that arose in their midst. Before that, it is necessary to resolve whether the struggle in Hungary concerned *different social forces with conflicting social interests*. To do otherwise would be like trying to determine the significance of the Paris Commune or the Russian Revolution without even referring to the underlying class struggles.

42. Jean Ellenstein, *The Stalin Phenomenon*, London 1975.

43. See especially the famous section 'The Part Played by Labour in the Transition from Ape to Man' (1876), in Friedrich Engels, *Dialectics of Nature*, Moscow 1964, pp. 172–186.

44. See, among other sources, G. Redlow, *Materialismus und Dialektik. Zu einem unakzeptablen philosophischen Konzept*, DZfPh, 9, 1981, pp. 1032f.; and W. Eichorn, *Ueber Dialektik in der Geschichtsfassung*, DZfPh, 2, 1982. We here use the concept of 'manual labour' as embracing all the direct producers, including those who work with technologies indispensable to the final output.

45. See Harald Boehme, 'Sozialistische Reproduktion und Revisionismus – Zum Fall Peter Ruben', in Damerow, Furth and Lefevre, *Arbeit und Philosophie – Symposium über philosophische Probleme des Arbeitsbegriffs*, Bochum 1983.

46. In an interview with the Belgian daily *Le Soir* (27 July 1989), a Ukrainian miner commented as follows on the miners' strike of that month in the USSR: '*Question*: Do you accuse the bureaucrats of these misdemeanours? *Answer*: Yes, that's right. But after all, they do the same as us: they defend themselves. Put yourself in their place. You think you're protected till retirement age, and then some guys pop up and ask for your ministry or department to be done away with. Are they going to stand by and watch the end of a structure they've spent decades patiently building up for themselves? Never! Do you know how much this class has grown? First they thought of themselves. Then they found a place

for their sons, then their brothers and cousins, then their friends, the guy who helped your wife's nephew to get into university. . . . So one, two, three ministry departments were set up. Meanwhile we had to break our backs working. Now we're saying: that's enough.'

47. Ferenz Tökei, *Zur Theorie der Gesellschaftsformen*, Budapest 1977.

48. A. Butenko, 'The Contradictions in the Development of Socialism as a Social Order', *Voprosi Filosofii* No. 10, 1982. See also the article by this journal's chief editor, V.S. Semionov, 'The Problem of Contradictions under Socialism', in ibid., No. 7, 1982. Of more recent contributions, we shall mention just two: L. Batkine, 'Sombre optimisme', in J.N. Afanassiev, ed., *La Seule Voie*, Paris 1989; and Tatiana Zaslavskaia, *Die Gorbatschow-Strategie*, Vienna 1989.

49. Hegedüs, *The Structure of Socialist Society, I: Theoretical Problems*, London 1977, p. 52. The Hungarian text dates from 1966. Hegedüs elaborated this idea in a series of articles, 'The Bureaucratic Relation under Socialism', which appeared in the journals *Magyar Tudoma*, April 1966, *Kortars* No. 8, 1966, *Kozgazdasagi Szemle* Nos. 7–8, 1966. These have been translated for us by friends.

50. *The Structure of Socialist Society*, pp. 49–51.

51. 'Zum Bewegungsverlauf dialektischer Widersprüche in der sozialistischen Gesellschaft', unpublished thesis, 1988.

52. See the appendix to M. Vozlensky, *The Nomenklatura*, London 1984, 'One Day in the Life of Ivan Ivanovich', which has become a classic sociological text on this question.

53. *Labor and Monopoly Capital*. Braverman's main weakness is his overemphasis on workers' original skills and their destruction under capitalism. In reality, the deskilling of labour has been intertwined with an opposite process of reskilling since the Industrial Revolution.

54. André Gorz, 'Technique, techniciens et lutte de classe', in Gorz, ed., *Critique de la division du travail*, Paris 1973.

55. *Grundrisse*, p. 162. See also p. 708: 'Real wealth is the developed productive power of all individuals.' Marx contrasts the separation of science and labour under capitalism with their unification under the rule of the freely associated producers.

56. In *Capital*, moreover, Marx states that large-scale industry 'makes the recognition of variation of labour and hence of the fitness of the worker for the maximum number of different kinds of labour into a question of life and death. This possibility of varying labour must become a general law of social production, and the existing relations must be adapted to permit its realization in practice.' Volume One, p. 618. The quotations in this and the previous footnote may be found in Ali Rattansi's interesting work *Marx and the Division of Labour*, London 1982.

57. See the footnote in *Capital* Volume One (p. 449): 'A philistine English periodical, the *Spectator* . . . finds that the main defect in the Rochdale cooperative experiments is this: "They showed that associations of workmen could manage shops, mills and almost all forms of industry with success, and they immediately improved the conditions of the men, but then they did not leave a clear place for masters." *Quelle horreur!*'

58. Many opinion surveys in the USSR have confirmed that this is the view of the vast majority of workers. A significant minority, however, still thinks otherwise.

59. Various successor parties to the Stalinist or post-Stalinist CPs retain some degree of hearing among the broad mass of voters and in the working class. In Bulgaria, Romania and Yugoslavia, this seems to be substantially greater than in the ex-GDR and Czechoslovakia, but nowhere, with the possible (but probably not definitive) exception of Poland, have these formations become marginal.

60. Rudolf Bahro's *The Alternative in Eastern Europe*, London 1977, provides convincing first-hand evidence of this trend in the GDR. Since NEP, the Soviet bureaucracy has followed a systematic policy of cooptation under the name *vydvizenie* ('advancement' or 'vertical mobility'). See Walter Süss, pp. 93f.

61. *The Interregnum*, p. 49.

62. L. Trotsky, *Stalin*, New York 1941, pp. 404–405.

63. *The Transitional Programme for Socialist Revolution*, New York 1973, p. 103.

64. Thus, immediately after Stalin's death, Marshal Zhukov led a drive to free military victims of the purges, including four Red Army officers who had figured in the first

mass revolt inside the gulag, at Chaisky. This was one crucial factor in the downfall of Beria and the dismantlement of the total power of the secret police. See the article in *Trud*, 30 December 1989.

65. *Die Gorbatschow-Strategie*, pp. 286–93.

66. It should be noted, however, that during the period of Stalin's dictatorship, his works were much more widely printed and circulated than those of Lenin.

67. Sieyès's famous call 'What is the Third Estate? Nothing. What does it want to be? Everything' was issued in his pamphlet *What Is the Third Estate?* which became the bourgeoisie's key manifesto at the beginning of the French Revolution in 1789.

68. Cf. Zaslavskaia, p. 162; Gorbachev, *Perestroika*, London 1987.

69. Indictment and repression for 'forbidden thoughts' are also practised by social-democratic and trade-union bureaucrats, usually (but not always) in milder forms. Not long ago, the left wing of the CFDT hospital workers union were driven out as 'black sheep' [sic], on the basis of a few quotes from Trotsky and the publication of the LCR, the French section of the Fourth International. The real reason for the expulsions was that these militant unionists had supported a victorious nation-wide strike, led by elected committees, which involved nearly all wage-earners in this sector but which the bureaucrats refused to recognize.

70. A most pathetic example is the Czechoslovak CP leader Jakes, who early in 1989 calmly stated in an interview with the German weekly *Die Zeit*: Why should we give the floor to these dissidents, to this Václav Havel? They have the support of less than one per cent of the population. Less than a year later, Havel was elected president of Czechoslovakia with the support of the overwhelming majority of the Czechoslovak people.

71. One is reminded of the terrible question that a Soviet author was asked by his son: 'Father, are you a Party member or are you a communist?'

72. Deng Xiaoping is reported to have said of Pol Pot: 'I don't understand why some people want to remove Pol Pot. It is true that he made some mistakes in the past . . . ' (Quoted in Ben Kiernan, *How Pol Pot Came to Power*, vol. 2, University of Wollongong.) More than a million people killed are supposed to be a 'mistake' . . .

73. According to official Soviet sources, between 1930 and 1953, 3,778,234 persons were victims of 'unjustified reprisals' in the USSR. A total of 768,089, the great majority Communists, were shot. For a particularly moving self-criticism, which cannot fail to impress every objective reader, see Ernst Fischer's autobiography, *An Opposing Man*, London 1974. Togliatti did not have the courage to make such a self-criticism, even though (or should we say because?) his responsibility for the purges in the Comintern was much greater.

74. Imre Nagy, *Imre Nagy on Communism*, New York 1957, pp. 289–90.

75. Ibid., p. 50.

76. Ibid., pp. 55–56.

77. At Nagy's trial, Kopacsi was called upon to testify and to explain that Nagy's manuscript, originally entitled *Morality and Ethics*, had influenced his political choice.

78. Sandor Kopacsi, *In the Name of the Working Class*, London 1989, p. 253.

79. Reprinted in the GDR literary magazine *Sinn und Form*, March–April 1990.

80. In *Sinn und Form*, p. 342.

81. Ibid., pp. 315–16. Hermlin also drew the important distinction between 'party discipline' and 'blind obedience'.

82. In Heiner Müller, *Wolokolamsker Chaussee I–V*, Berliner Ensemble 1989, p. 3.

83. R. Michels, *Political Parties*, New York 1962, originally published in 1913 as *Zur Soziologie des Parteiwesens*.

84. As many writers have followed Marx in pointing out, authoritarianism and leadership cults generally flourish even more strongly in anarchist and ultra-left sects than they do in mass parties, not including extreme Stalinist organizations. This is quite logical, for only mass activity and mass democracy are an effective antidote to authoritarian tendencies.

The notion that workers' councils could survive in periods of steep decline of mass activity has been refuted by historical experience. To withdraw from mass unions and from the building of vanguard parties in order to create tiny, unrepresentative 'councils' or 'unions' does not solve any of the problems posed by the contradiction between the need for collective self-emancipation of the working class as such, and the incipient bureaucratization of its mass organizations.

85. See Michels, ch. 2. We shall return to this question in the final chapter.

86. See Chapter 5 below. Trotsky already formulated this dilemma in 1939, though he concentrated it in too restricted a time-span.

87. For a discussion and bibliography of the council communists, see Serge Bricianer, *Pannekoek and the Workers' Councils*, St Louis 1978.

88. Nelson Lichtenstein (*Labor's War at Home: The CIO in World War II*, Cambridge 1982) gives an interesting account of the re-bureaucratization of American industrial unionism after 1939. Adolfo Gilly ('La anomalía argentina', *Cuadernos del Sur* no. 4, October–December 1985) describes the brief but explosive de-bureaucratization of the Argentina labour movement at plant level in 1973.

89. Old-age pensions are a particularly clear example in this respect. Without them, major sectors of the working class are vulnerable to the utmost misery and destitution. But once state pensions have been secured, workers from a certain age tend to lose at least some of their militancy. This is the core of truth in the otherwise trite remark that no one remains a radical militant after the age of fifty or fifty-five.

90. See especially Reinhard Kannonier, *Zentralismus oder Demokratie. Zur Organisationsfrage in der Arbeiterbewegung*, Vienna 1983, pp. 21–27.

91. See section three of *What Is To Be Done?*, Moscow 1968.

92. See E. Mandel, 'The Leninist Theory of Organization', in R. Blackburn, ed., *Revolution and Class Struggle: A Reader in Marxist Politics*, London 1977. While class consciousness can be seen as a concentration of lived experience, especially of struggle, the discontinuous character of that experience for the majority of workers justifies the building of political vanguard organizations that embody that process of concentration. They function, so to speak, as the collective memory of lessons of class struggle.

93. R. Hilferding, 'Das historische Problem' (first published posthumously in September 1940), in Cora Stephan, ed., *Zwischen den Stühlen oder über die Unvereinbarkeit von Theorie und Praxis*, West Berlin 1982, pp. 311f.

94. The apologetic character of this theory should not be overlooked. In the name of 'political priorities', it attempts to justify, at least objectively, social-democratic government policies that conflict with material interests of the working class. We shall return to this question in the next chapter.

95. The classical starting-point for this line of thought was Hendrik De Man, 'Zur Psychologie des Sozialismus', Jena 1927. We shall look in the next chapter at certain of Wilhelm Reich's views on politics and psychology.

96. Otto Bauer, 'Die illegale Partei'.

97. Lenin's theory of organization does not involve a conspiracy to impose leaders on recalcitrant workers, but is based on the need to centralize workers' experiences, to overcome the inevitable narrowness of outlook deriving from the experience of life and struggle in just one factory, occupation or – we can add today – country. See E. Mandel, *The Leninist Theory of Organization*.

Substitutionism and Realpolitik: The Politics of Labour Bureaucracies

1. The Roots of Substitutionism

As we saw in the last chapter, the appearance of a new social division of labour in the working-class movement leads to reified thinking and a reversal of the means/goals dialectic among at least some of its professional functionaries. To underpin that fetishism of the organization, a whole series of axioms are put forward, some openly proclaimed, others only tacitly introduced for at least a long period of time. They form a more or less coherent corpus of prejudices and sophisms on which the bureaucratic leaders base their actions, and which they seek to impose on the membership as general norms.

These axioms are fewer in the trade-union and social-democratic bureaucracies than in their Stalinist or post-Stalinist counterparts, but they are no less real. They may be reduced to the following seven:

(a) The strengthening of the traditional mass organizations (trade unions and social-democratic parties) is an absolute precondition for the emancipation of the working class.

(b) This can be achieved only through respect for legality ('the rules of the game') under all conditions, with elections, parliamentary activity and collective bargaining with the employers as the chosen instruments, occasionally backed up by legal strike action.[1]

(c) Mass organization of the working class has to be essentially dualistic. Political activities, for all intents and purposes, are reserved for a party geared to elections, while the trade unions have to confine themselves to collective bargaining with the employers over wages and work conditions.

(d) The absolute priority of achieving good election results ('electoralism') and of respecting (bourgeois) legality implies a basically positive attitude to the (bourgeois) state. Acceptance of 'state interests' entails acceptance of 'national interests' over and above working-class interests. Hence the preparednesss to back the police and the army, to endorse 'national defence', and to support external wars including those fought to maintain colonies.

(e) Unity and discipline, if necessary enforced through reprisals against alleged transgressors, are absolutely vital for the strengthening of the working-class organization.

(f) Leadership authority is crucial to the strengthening of the organization and must be maintained at all costs, including the use of sanctions and expulsions against those who undermine it by 'personal denigration' (or who sin against the 'socialist fraternity', as it is sometimes called).

(g) Any practice, including mass activity, which threatens or even questions these rules is to be thwarted by all means necessary, even if this produces deep splits inside the working class. Examples of such activity are political mass strikes, open challenges to the legal rules established by the bourgeois state, and the setting up of workers' or people's councils.

This set of principles gradually hardened in the years before the First World War, crossing the point of no return in August 1914 when the majority leaderships of most social-democratic parties and nearly all trade unions rallied to the policy of class collaboration with the bourgeoisie in the name of national defence.[2] Traditional 'centrists' in these organizations mounted a rather ineffective challenge between 1917 and 1923, and still later in Austria. But by the late twenties the seven precepts commanded widespread acceptance, and that has been the case ever since.

When we turn to the Stalinist faction of, first, the Russian Communist Party and then the Communist International, we find a much thicker web of axioms that was gradually imposed in the twenties and reached 'full maturity' in the mid thirties. Khrushchev's report at the Twentieth Congress called some of the secondary aspects into question. But the essential core of the dogma reigned supreme among Stalinist and post-Stalinist parties (with the partial exception of the Yugoslav Communist Party) for more than half a century, until the second phase of glasnost in the USSR in the late eighties. This formidable straitjacket, which was imposed on honest communists, genuine dupes, uneducated workers, fellow-travellers and cynical accomplices, was made up of the following components.

(a) Social revolution and even social progress hinge upon the assertion of the working class's leading role in society. The working class can only achieve this through the leading role of the Communist Party.

(b) The dictatorship of the proletariat, established after the victory of the socialist revolution, can therefore be exercised only through the rule of the Communist Party.

(c) Under the dictatorship of the proletariat, the state and the party fuse to a great extent – some think completely, although this was never stated unequivocally.

(d) The Communist Party is always right, because it embodies the scientific truth of 'Marxism–Leninism' and expresses the collective experience of the working class.

(e) Only the Communist Party represents the working class. Indeed 'Marxism–Leninism' implies the single-party principle under the dictatorship of the proletariat. Where other parties are legally admitted, they are representatives of 'progressive' non-working-class social forces, and are allowed to operate only within 'national fronts' tightly controlled by the Communists.

(f) All other parties claiming to be working-class, socialist or even revolutionary therefore represent alien class forces that have infiltrated the labour movement in order to split, weaken and eventually defeat it. They have to be mercilessly crushed if the working class is to march forward.[3]

(g) In order to exercise its leading role in the state and society, the Communist Party must maintain its unity at all costs, in the first place by imposing 'iron discipline' on all its members and leaders. Under no conditions can internal differences on matters of policy be made public.

(h) As Communist parties in power (and some before then) count a large number of members, any publicization within the party of policy differences will inevitably leak outside, gravely threatening the party's unity and authority and thereby undermining its leading role and the dictatorship of the proletariat itself. Therefore, all minorities on leading bodies must defend majority positions within lower bodies against their own convictions – that is, they must act unanimously not only in public or in the class struggle but even inside the party.

(i) Hence there can be no question of a right to form tendencies in the Communist Party around different platforms. That would be tantamount to 'factionalism'. All factions or tendencies are potential 'second parties' – that is, agencies of the class enemy – and have to be crushed in the same way as counter-revolutionary organizations. The expression of differences should be restricted to the day-to-day policy-making bodies (the Politburo).[4] All members of the day-to-day leadership are duty-bound, even in pre-conference periods, to express only the opinions of the majority leadership before the membership.[5]

(j) Besides, all differences of opinion within the leadership objectively (and, more often than not, subjectively) express 'alien class interests'. To accord freedom of expression to minorities within the Party, not to say inside the working class or broader society, would be to grant freedom of expression to the class enemy.

(k) Ruling Communist parties operate in an extremely hostile international environment, with constant attempts by imperialism to send spies, saboteurs, wreckers, agents and the like into the 'socialist countries' and the Communist parties.[6] Utmost vigilance and secrecy, as well as constant growth of police methods in the party and society, are demanded to thwart these efforts.[7]

(l) The leading role of the party entails, in all circumstances, upholding the authority and unity of the central leadership, with a strong tendency to form a cult around its supreme figure. To question this is to weaken the dictatorship of the proletariat.

(m) Total loyalty to the Party means total loyalty to the Party leadership. A good Communist should avoid all critical thought, displaying blind obedience in every situation.

(n) As all ideological, cultural, artistic and scientific activities are highly political in the building of socialism, they should be handled from the point of view of the overall interests of the Party (*partiinost*, to use the Russian phrase). Any critical spirit in the arts would threaten the Party's authority and the dictatorship of the proletariat. Mao's widow, Jiang Qing, went so far as to say that if the 'capitalist line' prevailed in the theatre, the restoration of capitalism would be inevitable. After the Hungarian Revolution of 1956, the Stalinist leaders of the East German SED maintained that if a clear break was not made with the 'revisionist' ideas of Georg Lukács, counter-revolution would triumph. And in the Stalinist reaction to the Prague Spring of 1968, an unequivocal condemnation of Kafka became a crucial task in preventing counter-revolution.

(o) 'Cadres decide everything. These cadres can only be removed through a civil war.' These famous words of Stalin's seem quite logical in the light of the preceding theses, for only 'the cadres' are capable of exercising the dictatorship of the proletariat, which can in turn only be overthrown by a social counter-revolution.

(p) The main task of the international working class is to defend 'the socialist fortress'. 'Proletarian internationalism' = defence of the Soviet Union. Defence of the Soviet Union = unconditional support for all current policies of the Soviet government. Any other attitude 'objectively' assists imperialism, the class enemy. After the conquest of power by other Communist parties, this dogma inevitably led to splits within the so-called 'world Communist movement' as the defence of other 'fortresses' – especially China, after the Mao–Khrushchev break, then, in a farcical way, Albania and/or North Korea – came to replace for some the defence of the USSR.

The ultimate result of this nightmarish logic is massive repression of communists and workers on the grounds that they are dominated, or 'objectively driven', by bourgeois ideology. Repression of the workers 'in reality' means repression of the bourgeoisie. So the axiom 'the party = the working class' leads to the conclusion that under certain circumstances 'the actually existing working class = the bourgeoisie'.

The bloody mass purges in the USSR between 1934 and 1939, reaching a peak at the infamous Moscow Trials, became the touchstone of the loyalty towards the Kremlin of CP leaders and fellow-travellers. To endorse them meant to accept the whole chain of dogmas, and the moral depravity to which it led.

To what extent can the leading spokespersons and fellow-travellers of the Stalinized Communist parties be regarded as dupes? Did they genuinely believe that the purge victims of 1934–39 or 1949–53 were counter-revolutionary traitors and imperialist police agents? Were they accomplices who covered up for the crimes and slanders with the rationalization that the only choice was Stalin or Hitler after 1933, Stalin or US imperialism after 1945? Or were the two attitudes mixed together? All we can do is take each individual case and consider what he or she said afterwards.

In the best of cases, we can conclude that they showed a lack of political judgement, of the most lamentable kind. In all other cases, we have to assume a lack of character and of elementary proletarian, or humanist, morality – that is, of commitment to the emancipation of all the exploited and oppressed. We shall return later in this chapter to some of the psychological dimensions of the formation of a Stalinist. For the moment let us just take four instances from the published literature of reactions to the repression in the Soviet Union and Eastern Europe.

The French Communist Party journalist and ideologue Dominique Desanti has explained how she came to write an infamous pamphlet *Masques et Visages de Tito et des Siens*. Her motivation was self-doubt, fear of succumbing to what Lukács once called the 'naturally Trotskyist' (that is, oppositional) inclination of all intellectuals, a desire to maintain her identity with 'the Party' at all costs. And in the last analysis, there was the familiar two-camp logic: since the class enemy is utilizing the Tito–Rajk–Kostov affairs to discredit Stalin and the USSR for its own foul purposes, we have unconditionally to defend Stalin and the USSR.[8]

More naive and more simple is the account of the Dutch CP leader, and later oppositionist, Henk Gortzak. He believed all the charges at the Moscow Trials because people in Holland in whose integrity he had faith (as he had in Stalin and other Soviet leaders) assured him that they were well founded. He was only 'astonished' that people like Trotsky, whose revolutionary past was undeniable, could have fallen so low.[9]

In his nauseating apology for Stalin, the British CP leader J.T. Murphy justified the purges as an expression of the struggle of revolution against counter-revolution, arguing quite incredibly that the show trials had been directed against persons whose 'guilt' was already proven and that their purpose had therefore been one of political propaganda. In similar vein, leading intellectuals like D.N. Pritt, Romain Rolland or Lion Feuchtwanger, and liberal journalists like Walter Duranty, publicly defended the Moscow Trials, often against their own inner convictions.[10]

Rudolf Herrnstadt, the only talented theoretician in the top leadership of the East German SED, gave pathetic expression to most of this Stalinist reasoning. Herrnstadt was chief editor of the Party's central organ, *Neues Deutschland*, and the author of most of the Politburo's political documents in the 1952–53 period. After the workers' uprising of 17 June 1953 Ulbricht, on the advice of the Kremlin, made him and Stasi chief Wilhelm Zaisser into scapegoats for the events, probably because Herrnstadt had waged a systematic campaign on the Politburo against Ulbricht's dictatorial tendencies. Over the next month a 'Herrnstadt–Zaisser faction', with a 'social-democratic capitulationist platform' linked to Beria, was invented by Ulbricht and his henchmen, with no basis in reality.

And yet, at the decisive meeting of the Central Committee on 24–25 July 1953, Herrnstadt himself voted for the slanderous resolution condemning him and Zaisser. 'It was inconceivable for me even to think of voting against the Plenum,' he wrote. To have told the truth 'would have carried the risk of weakening the Soviet Union'. He further explained to Hermann Matern, chief inquisitor of the Party apparatus: 'In my life I've carried out every task the Party has given me. If the Party were to tell me: "Jump in the water and don't ask questions", I would jump. If the Party said that we needed a "Herrnstadt–Zaisser case" after the 17th of July, I would accept that.' When his closest collaborators protested against the slanders, he reminded them: 'We've been singing together: "The Party is always right." We can't change that.'

Herrnstadt's widow correctly summarized his attitude as follows: 'For the accused in the Herrnstadt–Zaisser "case", Party discipline played a special but not the most fatal role. Strongly marked by years of the anti-fascist resistance struggle, both had always subordinated themselves to the interests of the Party. To break with the organization, even with substantial justification, was impossible for them. It would have meant that three decades of personal activity had become meaningless.'[11]

In local units of the Communist parties, an atmosphere of hysterical fear against 'imperialist plotters' had to be maintained in order to justify such purges in its ranks. Typical examples are to be found in the famous Smolensk archives, first analysed by Merle Fainsod and then by Nicolas Werth.[12] Here is just one example from the secretary's report to the Party cell of the regional tribunal: 'The reporter states that the capitalist countries, feeling the victory of socialism to be near, have but one solution: to send spies and saboteurs into our country to sabotage our economic strength and to destroy the dictatorship of the proletariat which has established socialism on one-sixth of the earth. It is not by accident, as Comrade Stalin said at the February Plenum, as the genius he is, that each capitalist country sends the greatest number of saboteurs to our Soviet land, more than to any other country.'[13]

The political premises of substitutionism led in practice, at the end of the Second World War, to the imposition of Kremlin-type regimes in Eastern Europe (bar Yugoslavia) by military-police pressure from above, against a recalcitrant if not outrightly hostile population.[14] All subsequent events, including the collapse or near-collapse of these regimes in 1989, flow from this initial condition. They prove the impossibility of 'building socialism' against the wishes of a majority of the toiling masses.

2. The Marxist Refutation of the Ideology and Practice of Substitutionism

Marxists consider all those axioms and all that 'logic' without exception to be theoretically unfounded, politically ruinous adaptations to bureaucratic interests. Evidently they should not be seen as the origin of the bureaucratic dictatorship: it is not because leaders of the Stalinist faction wanted to apply their version of 'Marxism–Leninism' that the dictatorship was erected in the USSR and later extended to Eastern Europe.[15] Only *post festum*, some time after the Soviet Thermidor, did it refer to this corpus of ideas as a 'theorization' of its monopoly of power. We might say that a number of wrong-headed, 'Zinovievist' concepts about the Party, circulating after Lenin's death, made Stalin's victory easier. But in no sense did they cause it.

Social classes are not homogeneous: particular layers have different historical backgrounds, experiences and educations. So they have generally tended to form not one but several parties. A multi-party system corresponds to the reality of class. Its elimination implies political repression of at least part of the working class and not just of other social classes.

It is true that a vanguard party can best represent the historical interests of the working class, as well as fighting in a more consistent way for its immediate interests.[16] But that potential will be fulfilled only if the party is solidly implanted in the working class, centralizes the real experiences of key sectors of the class, and criticially reviews its own programme and principles through scientific analysis of an ever-changing reality. This is impossible without freedom of enquiry and discussion within both the party and society at large.[17] No party, no group of leaders, and certainly no individual person are infallible. All inevitably commit errors. The only advantage of a vanguard party – if it really is such – is that it makes fewer mistakes and corrects them more smoothly and more rapidly, all the time relying on the stimulus of internal and public democracy.[18] Not servility towards the 'leadership' but a capacity for critical thought, for independent judgement on policies and political controversies, is a key condition for being 'a good socialist or communist'.[19] Tendency rights within the party and the right to free public debate are the necessary corollaries of a multi-party system.

Perhaps the most important point is that the building of socialism is a historically new experience, whose 'rules' or 'laws' cannot be read off from any textbook. Society and social experience become a vast laboratory in which various projects and policies in all social fields have to be debated in the broadest democratic conditions and put to the test.[20] Especially in economic planning, political democracy – the possibility of choosing between different platforms – is essential if society is to achieve greater efficiency and reduce waste and disproportions.

Emancipation of the working class means self-emancipation and self-rule,[21] and these entail the direct exercise of power by elected organs of the mass of workers – that is, a strict separation between party and state.

The vanguard party attempts to win a leading role within the state organs of workers' power, not by resorting to administrative or repressive methods but by convincing a majority of the correctness of its proposals. All restrictions on workers' self-government are counterproductive, produce demoralization and depoliticization of the working class, and make the building of socialism immensely more difficult, if not impossible.

Similarly, the struggle against the internal and external class enemy will be the more successful, the more the working class is united in action in that fight, the more it is politically aware and active. Again, a multi-party system and full political rights for the masses are a sine qua non for the construction of such a united class front.[22]

The Marxist vision of the dialectical inter-relationship between workers' self-organization and the vanguard party is at the antipode of the Stalinist concept of a monolithic single party.[23] Progress towards socialism, a classless society, cannot be imposed upon the actually existing workers against their will; in the long run such methods of rule only aid and comfort the class enemy. They are expressions of alien class forces, of the privileged workers' bureaucracy. Rosa Luxemburg, resolutely placing herself in the tradition of Marx and Engels, had the last word to say on these matters: 'But with the repression of political life in the land as a whole, life in the soviets must also become more and more crippled. Without general elections, without unrestricted freedom of press and assembly, without a free struggle of opinion, life dies out in every public institution, becomes a mere semblance of life, in which only the bureaucracy remains as the active element.'[24]

Practice is the final arbiter of the truth of cognition. The decisive criterion for judging party decisions and policies – and thus ultimately the character of the party itself – is their practical results for the class struggle. This is especially true in the wildly fluctuating conditions of pre-revolutionary and revolutionary upheavals. As Lenin himself stated:

> In a revolutionary epoch like the present, all theoretical errors and deviations of the Party are most ruthlessly criticized by experience itself, which enlightens and educates the working class with unprecedented rapidity. At such a time, the duty of every Social Democrat is to strive to ensure that the ideological struggle within the Party on questions of theory and tactics is conducted as openly, widely and freely as possible, but that on no account does it disturb or hamper the unity of revolutionary action of the Social-Democratic proletariat.[25]

For their part, Marx and Engels frequently expressed the inner cohesion of the struggle for socialism, the self-emancipation of the actually existing working class, and workers' democracy. We shall limit ourselves to just a few quotations.

Commenting on the draft statutes drawn up by the Lassalleans for the unions under their control, Marx wrote to Schweitzer in 1868:

> Centralist organization, though very useful for secret societies and sectarian movements, goes against the nature of trade unions. Even if it were desirable, I state outright that it is impossible – it would not be possible, and least of all in Germany. Here, where the worker's life is regulated from childhood by bureaucracy and he himself believes in the authorities, in the bodies appointed over him, he must be taught before all else to walk by himself.[26]

Regarding the American labour movement, Engels wrote in 1886:

> It is much more important that the movement should spread out, develop harmoniously, strike root and as far as possible embrace the entire American proletariat, than that it should from the beginning set out and advance on the basis of a completely correct theoretical line. There is no better way to clarity of theoretical knowledge than by learning from one's own mistakes, 'becoming clever through misfortunes'. And for a whole great class there is no other way. . . . The main thing to achieve is that the working class acts *as a class*.[27]

Clearest of all is the following passage by Engels from 1890:

> The Party is so large that absolute freedom of debate within it is a necessity. Many new elements have come to it in the last few years who are still quite raw and green, not at all to be assimilated and cultivated. . . . The largest party in the country cannot exist without every hue finding voice within it, and even *the appearance* of Schweitzer-style dictatorship must be avoided.[28]

More generally, any strategy that transfers the basic mechanisms of social progress to organs of indirect, representative democracy has demobilizing, and in the long run depoliticizing, effects on the broad masses. As their self-reliance and self-confidence are sapped, and as they come to depend on the capitalists to 'deliver the goods' and on the state to redistribute the 'fruits of growth', their attachment to democratic processes is put under increasing strain.

3. Is Lenin the Source of Substitutionism?

For decades bourgeois ideologues, social democrats and anarchists have sought to hold Lenin responsible for substitutionism, for the concept of the monolithic party, and for Stalinism. Today this charge is also increasingly heard in the post-Stalinist Communist parties of both East and West, and even in the Soviet Union itself.[29] What truth, if any, lies behind it?

As a matter of fact, the charge of substitutionism was first levelled against Lenin by Axelrod, Martov, Trotsky and Rosa Luxemburg in the early years of this century, when the faction fight between Bolsheviks and Mensheviks was gathering pace in the aftermath of the Second Congress of the Russian Social-Democratic Labour Party. In his pamphlet *Our Political Tasks*, Trotsky coined the famous sentence: 'These methods lead, as we shall yet see, to this: the party organization is substituted for the party, the Central Committee is substituted for the party organization, and finally a "dictator" is substituted for the Central Committee.'[30]

Such polemics did a grave injustice to Lenin. His initial struggle with the Mensheviks centred on the problem of how to tighten party organization *in conditions of illegality*, so that it could maintain and extend the political autonomy of the working class vis-à-vis the bourgeoisie. No general pattern was put forward for a situation where mass activity was legal. It is true that in *What Is To Be Done?* Lenin sometimes bent the stick too far in one direction, as he himself would recognize in 1908. In fact, the previous year, in a preface to a re-publication of that pamphlet, he had clearly stated:

> Basically, of course, their success [that is, of revolutionary organizations] was due to the fact that the working class, whose best representatives built the Social-Democratic Party, for objective economic reasons possesses a greater capacity for organization than any other class in capitalist society. Without this condition an organization of professional revolutionaries would be nothing more than a plaything, an adventure, a mere signboard. *What Is To Be Done?* repeatedly emphasizes this, pointing out that the organization it advocates has no meaning apart from its connection with the 'genuinely revolutionary class that is spontaneously rising to struggle'.

Reviewing the lessons of 1905 in the same preface, he adds:

> Despite the split, the Social-Democratic Party earlier than any of the other parties was able to take advantage of the temporary spell of freedom to build a legal organization with an ideal democratic structure, an electoral structure, and representation at congresses according to the number of the organized members.[31]

During the 1905 Revolution itself, Lenin expressed himself still more forthrightly, coming close to the formulations of the mature Trotsky of the thirties:

It seems to me that Comrade Radin is wrong in raising the question . . . : the Soviet of Workers' Deputies or the Party? I think that . . . the decision must certainly be: *both* the Soviet of Workers' Deputies *and* the Party. . . . It seems to me that the Soviet of Workers' Deputies, as an organization representing all occupations, should strive to include deputies from *all* industrial and professional and office workers, domestic servants, farm labourers, etc., from *all* who want and are able to fight in common for a better life for the whole working people, from *all* who would have at least an elementary degree of political honesty, from all but the Black Hundreds . . . politically, the Soviet of Workers' Deputies should be regarded as the embryo of a *provisional revolutionary government*.[32]

In opposition to Bolshevik 'committee members', Lenin unequivocally asserted:

The principle of democratic centralism and autonomy for local Party organizations implies universal and *full freedom to criticize* so long as this does not disturb the unity of *a definite action*. . . . We were all agreed on the principles of democratic centralism, guarantees for the rights of all minorities and for all loyal opposition, on the autonomy of every Party organization, on recognition that all Party functionaries must be elected, accountable to the Party and subject to recall.[33]

This is a very far cry from Stalin's 'The cadres can only be removed through civil war'! Nor did Lenin hesitate to dot the i's: 'Criticism within the limits of the *principles* of the Party Programme must be quite free . . . not only at Party meetings, but also at public meetings.'[34]

Lenin was so remote from any substitutionist concept of working-class emancipation that his main work on these questions, *State and Revolution*, has nothing to say about any 'leading role of the Party'. The same is true of the first Soviet Constitution – that of the Federal Socialist Republic of Soviet Russia – which served as a model for the 1923–24 Constitution of the USSR. The idea that every worker, every housewife – not only Party members or cadres – should 'decide everything' runs through all of Lenin's writings in the period between 1917 and 1919.[35]

Similarly, the statutes and organizational principles of the Bolsheviks, adopted in November–December 1905, do not bear out the notion of a fundamental continuity between Lenin and Stalin:

The RSDLP must be organized according to the principle of democratic centralism.

All Party members must take part in the election of Party institutions. All Party institutions are elected for a [specific] period, are subject to recall and obligated to account for their actions both periodically and at any time upon demand of the organization which elected them.

Decisions of the guiding collectives are binding on the members of those organizations of which the collective is the organ.

Actions affecting the organization as a whole (that is, congresses, reorganizations) must be decided upon by all of the members of the organization. Decisions of lower-level organizations are not to be implemented if they contradict decisions of higher organizations.[36]

Recognizing as indispensable the principle of democratic centralism, the conference considers the broad implementation of the election principle necessary; and, while granting elected centres full power in matters of ideological and practical leadership, they are at the same time subject to recall, their actions are given broad publicity, and they are to be strictly accountable for these activities.[37]

In 1906 Lenin even suggested the institutionalization of a membership referendum on key political questions. But compare all this with the 'official' statement of the Stalinist position:

In order to function properly and to guide the masses systematically, the Party must be organized on the principle of *centralism*, having one set of rules and uniform Party discipline, one leading organ – the Party Congress, and in the intervals between congresses – the Central Committee of the Party; the minority must submit to the majority, the various organizations must submit to the centre, and lower organizations to higher organizations. Failing these conditions, the party of the working class cannot be a real party and cannot carry out its tasks in guiding the class.[38]

When democratic centralism is invoked in the Stalinist text, it is restricted to the election of leading bodies by the membership.[39] In contradiction with the whole experience of the Bolshevik Party, the ban on tendencies and factions, on platforms differing from that of the leadership majority, is presented by Stalinists and post-Stalinists as an organizational *principle*. The principles of criticism and self-criticism – the very essence of internal democracy – are completely subordinated to defence of the authority and unity of the Party leadership, regardless of the effects of its policies on the class struggle: 'The Party could not accept that, under cover of freedom of criticism, ideas are expressed whose aim is to discredit and weaken the Party leadership, to undermine the principles of the Party spirit.'[40] Lenin's principles of accountability and recallability of all Party functionaries, of freedom of criticism and discussion inside and outside the Party, of autonomy of local bodies, of the right to constitute alternative platforms – all these have completely disappeared.

It is refreshing to note that the unfolding debate in the Soviet Union on the origins of Stalinism, and on the relevance of organizational norms to bureaucratic dictatorship, has posed the basic difference between democratic and bureaucratic centralism. For instance, Leon Onikov, who has responsibility for the Central Committee apparatus, states:

[At the Seventeenth Congress] four points explaining democratic centralism according to Stalin were inserted into the Party statutes. . . . First, he legitimized his own conception of this principle whereby centralism took precedence over democracy. Secondly, he secured the consecration of this principle so as to rule out the necessity of flexibly varying the relationship between democracy and centralism in light of the obviously ever-changing situation. Between the 17th and 26th Congresses . . . the Stalinist interpretation of democratic centralism was made everlasting. . . . After the 17th Congress the Party took over entirely the functions of state administration and economic management. Having been fixed in the Party statutes, the sense of Stalin's dispositions on democratic centralism were mechanically extended to the activities of the soviets and management bodies. The definitive victory of bureaucratic centralism was marked by a bloody landmark: 1937.[41]

Or, even more clearly:

Up till now, the Party has applied the norms and principles proclaimed by Stalin: first, with regard to its organizational structure, where the absolute power of the apparatus goes together with a total lack of rights for the majority of militants; secondly, with regard to the qualities expected of a Communist in our time – conformist, compliant, disinclined to show any independence in ideas or actions, without initiative or civic courage, incapable of bold action. The result: a party which is prisoner of the system it has itself created; a system which, as soon as the party's administrative functions are taken away from it, proves incapable of functioning in a normal way.[42]

In other words, far from guaranteeing 'the leading role of the party', bureaucratic centralism and the rule of an all-powerful unelected and uncontrolled apparatus make the party a total prisoner of the bureaucracy, unable to exercise any 'leading role' in the true sense of the term. Lenin had already noted this in 1922, and the Left Opposition took it up in October 1923.[43]

For his part, A.P. Butenko realizes that the ideological conceptions prevailing in the USSR before the Twenty-seventh Party Congress, including those to do with 'democratic centralism', 'tended towards a theoretical motivation and intellectual defence of bureaucratic centralism . . . – a natural product of the everyday activity of the bureaucracy . . . the sum of its constant positions which are bound up with the essence of its professional and social aspirations, that complex of ideas beyond which its everyday activity does not normally move.'[44]

4. 1920–1921: The Dark Years of Lenin and Trotsky

At the end of the Civil War, economic conditions in Russia were nothing short of catastrophic. Industrial output had declined to 18 per cent of its level in 1914 and 24 per cent of that of 1917.[45] The industrial proletariat was down from a total of 3 million in 1917 to 1,243,000 in 1921–22.[46] It is true that the number of employees, especially civil servants, rose steeply, and that by the middle of 1920 trade-union membership had increased to more than 5 million from 700,000 in 1917.[47] However, the total urban population declined by more than thirty per cent.[48] Hunger, disease, epidemics were rampant. Misery and a resulting demoralization bore down heavily on the working class.

Under these circumstances, the Bolshevik leadership decided to turn from war communism to the New Economic Policy (NEP) permitting a partial reintroduction of market relations. Industrial and especially agricultural output soon showed a definite upward trend, as did the number of workers.[49] However, this retreat on the economic front was accompanied by a political turn that brought the banning of all political parties and groupings outside the Russian Communist Party (RCP), and soon thereafter a ban on factions inside the RCP.

There was something paradoxical in these measures. Whereas the government had previously tried to maintain a maximum of democracy compatible with war conditions,[50] it reversed this course once the war had been won. There is no doubt in our mind that this was a tragic mistake on the part of Lenin and the entire Bolshevik Central Committee. Trotsky, who was no exception in this respect, wrote towards the end of his life in a clearly self-critical vein: 'The prohibition of oppositional parties brought after it the prohibition of factions. The prohibition of factions ended in a prohibition to think otherwise than the infallible leaders. The police-manufactured monolithism of the Party resulted in a bureaucratic impunity which has become the source of all kinds of wantonness and corruption.'[51]

Victor Serge sharply noted the same trend in his *Year One of the Russian Revolution*: 'With the disappearance of political debates between parties representing different social interests through the various shades of their opinion, soviet institutions, beginning with the local soviets and ending with the VTsIK and the Council of People's Commissars, manned solely by Communists, now function in a vacuum: since all the decisions are taken by the Party, all they can do is give them the official rubber-stamp.'[52]

At the root of this turn lay two assumptions, one completely wrong and one partially wrong (that is, conjuncturally correct but wrong from a long-term point of view). The straightforward misjudgement was to conclude that, despite victory in the Civil War, the economic context of famine and then the consequences of NEP would actually make the danger of counter-revolution greater than before. This position had more than a trace of 'economism' with its underestimation of the relative autonomy of the political factor in history and the class struggle – which is strange, to say the least, since the whole tradition of Lenin and the Bolshevik Party pointed in the other direction. Not only with the benefit of hindsight but even at the time itself, it should have been apparent that the kulaks, dispersed all over Russia, without so much as an embryo of political centralization, would not constitute a weightier threat to soviet power than the armies of Kolchak, Wrangel, Denikin or Pilsudski supported by French imperialism.

At first sight the second argument stood on stronger ground. The end of war brought a relaxation, a desire for a quieter life, among the masses, including the worker-Bolsheviks. Moreover, the working class had been drastically reduced and *déclassé* as a result of war, plummeting production, and the absorption of its best elements into the army and the state apparatus. The masses, then, would become politically more passive, less ready to rise up from one day to the next against a counter-revolutionary menace. The defence of the revolution had to rely more than ever upon the class-conscious Party cadre, which in turn had to rely more than before upon specialized apparatuses.[53]

The description of the situation in Soviet Russia on the eve of NEP was no doubt broadly accurate, but the analysis left out the key structural question of where things were going, or could go. And what would be the effects of the measures restricting soviet and inner-party democracy? In reality, the social collapse was rapidly checked after the introduction of NEP. The number of wage-earners reached and then surpassed the level of 1916. Real wages rose. Cultural life flourished. Skills grew numerically and qualitatively. Material conditions were thus created for much stronger working-class involvement in the direct exercise of power. By 1924, and still more by 1927, it would have been quite inappropriate to describe the Russian working class as objectively *déclassé*. The early twenties' trend towards political passivity could have been put into reverse.

Such a political revival, however, could not occur in the climate of growing restrictions and apparatus rule; it absolutely required a radical extension of soviet and inner-party democracy. It is therefore undeniable that the measures taken in 1920–21 by the Bolshevik leadership contributed, through their effects on the level of workers' self-activity, to a consolidation of the process of bureaucratization.

Unfortunately, at that same point in time, Lenin transformed the conjunctural analysis into a wrong general theory. He wrote:

But the dictatorship of the proletariat cannot be exercised through an organization embracing the whole of that class, because in all capitalist countries (and not only over here, in one of the most backward) the proletariat is still so divided, so degraded and so corrupted . . . that an organization taking in the whole proletariat cannot directly exercise proletarian dictatorship. It can be exercised only by the vanguard that has absorbed the revolutionary energy of the class.[54]

Similar formulations can be found in Trotsky's writings of this period – above all in *Terrorism and Communism*, certainly the worst of his books. In a speech to the Second Congress of the Comintern, for example, Trotsky said:

Today we have received a proposal from the Polish government to conclude peace. Who decides such questions? We have the Council of People's Commissars, but it too must be subject to certain control. Whose control? The control of the working class as a formless, chaotic [sic] mass? No. The Central Committee of the party is convened in order to discuss the proposal and to decide whether it ought to be answered. And when we have to conduct war, organize new divisions and find the best elements for them – where do we turn? We turn to the Party. To the Central Committee. And it issues directives to every local committee pertaining to the assignment of the Communists to the front. The same applies to the agrarian question, the question of supplies, and all [!] other questions.[55]

And even worse:

The Workers' Opposition has come out with dangerous slogans. They have made a fetish of democratic principles. They have placed the workers' right to elect representatives above the Party, as it were, as if the Party were not entitled to assert its dictatorship even if that dictatorship temporarily clashed with the passing moods of the workers' democracy. . . . It is necessary to create among us the awareness of the revolutionary historical birthright of the Party.[56] The Party is obliged to maintain its dictatorship, regardless of the temporary wavering in the spontaneous moods of the masses, regardless of the temporary vacillations even in the working class. This awareness is for us the indispensable unifying element. The dictatorship does not base itself at every given moment on the formal principle of workers' democracy, although the workers' democracy is, of course, the only method by which the masses can be drawn more and more into political life.[57]

One is struck by the fact that Trotsky uses the term 'temporary wavering', whereas Lenin speaks of long-term division and corruption of the working class. But to all extents and purposes, Trotsky's affirmation of substitutionism is similar to Lenin's at this time: power is to be exercised by a de facto oligarchy of Party leaders.

Such theoretical justifications falsely generalize from a conjunctural situation. But they are also more ambiguous than it might first appear. For Lenin does not specify whom he means by 'the vanguard' that has 'absorbed the revolutionary energy of the class'. Certainly not the 'Leninist Central Committee', the 'inner core' of the Party leadership. To present a few dozen or even a few hundred individuals as 'the vanguard of the class' would have been quite ludicrous for as educated a Marxist as Lenin. Perhaps he had in mind the Party membership, or its whole proletarian component – some hundreds of thousands of workers. But if they were to 'exercise proletarian dictatorship', broad inner-party and soviet democracy would surely have been necessary. Was he then thinking of a layer between the 'inner core' and the mass membership? There is no evidence of this, and such a concept would anyway have had very little objective basis. Or did he extend the concept of 'vanguard' beyond the Party to include certain intermediate strata – for example, trade-union representatives elected by their fellow-workers? This seems implicit in the text, which continues by referring to 'cogs in a wheel' and 'transmission-belts'.

One thing is clear: Lenin would never have used the term 'class vanguard' to denote the Party apparatus, let alone an appointed, unelected party-cum-state apparatus. From the beginning of 1922 until his death in 1924, he showed every sign of being horrified by that bureaucracy and determined to struggle against it.[58] In his speech to the Eleventh Party Congress on 28 March 1922 he insisted that 'the Party machinery must be separated from the Soviet government machinery'.[59] Eight months later he said in a report to the Fourth Congress of the Comintern:

We took over the old machinery of state, and that was our misfortune. Very often this machinery operates against us. In 1917, after we seized power, the government officials sabotaged us. This frightened us very much and we pleaded: 'Please come back.' They all came back, but that was our misfortune. We now have a vast army of government employees, but lack sufficiently educated forces to exercise real control over them. In practice it often happens that here at the top, where we exercise political power, the machine functions somehow; but down below government employees have arbitrary control and they often exercise it in such a way as to counteract our measures. At the top, we have, I don't know how many, but at all events, I think, no more than a few thousand, at the outside several tens of thousands of our own people. Down below, however, there are hundreds of thousands of old officials whom we got from the tsar and from bourgeois society and who, partly deliberately and partly unwittingly, work against us.[60]

In his final article 'Better Fewer But Better', he complained: 'Our state apparatus is so deplorable, not to say wretched, that we must first think very carefully how to combat its defects . . .'[61] This echoed a well-known passage from his report to the Eleventh Congress:

> If we take Moscow with its 4,700 Communists in responsible positions, and if we take that huge bureaucratic machine, that gigantic heap, we must ask: who is directing whom? I doubt very much whether it can truthfully be said that the Communists are directing that heap. To tell the truth, they are not directing, they are being directed. Something analogous happened here to what we were told in our history lessons when we were children: sometimes one nation conquers another, the nation that conquers is the conqueror and the nation that is vanquished is the conquered nation. This is simple and intelligible to all. But what happens to the culture of these nations? Here things are not so simple. If the conquering nation is more cultured than the vanquished nation, the former imposes its culture upon the latter; but if the opposite is the case, the vanquished nation imposes its culture upon the conqueror. Has not something like this happened in the capital of the RSFSR? Have the 4,700 Communists (nearly a whole army division, and all of them the very best) come under the influence of an alien culture?[62]

In his Testament, Lenin's anxiety reaches its harshest pitch:

> In effect, we took over the old machinery of state from the tsar and the bourgeoisie and . . . now, with the onset of peace and the satisfaction of the minimum requirements against famine, all our work must be directed towards improving the administrative machinery.
>
> I think that a few dozen workers, being members of the CC, can deal better than anybody else with checking, improving and remodelling our state apparatus. The Workers' and Peasants' Inspection on whom this function devolved at the beginning proved unable to cope with it. . . . The workers admitted to the Central Committee should come preferably not from among those who have had long service in Soviet bodies . . . , because those workers have already acquired the very traditions and the very prejudices which it is desirable to combat.
>
> The working-class members of the CC must be mainly workers of a lower stratum than those promoted in the last five years to work in soviet bodies; they must be people closer to being rank-and-file workers and peasants, who, however, do not fall into the category of direct or indirect exploiters.[63]

Some time before, in a private letter, he had been still less restrained and uttered these terrible words: 'All of us are sunk in the rotten bureaucratic swamp of "departments". Great authority, common sense and strong will are necessary for the everyday struggle against this. The departments are shit; decrees are shit.'[64]

When Lenin in his Testament criticized the Workers' and Peasants' Inspection, he also attacked Stalin who was at its head.[65] This marked a turn from his earlier defence of Stalin against Trotsky's criticisms of the Inspection,[66] and from his recommendation to the Eleventh Congress that Stalin should be elected general secretary of the Party. After a number of bitter experiences, his struggle against bureaucracy increasingly focused on a clash with Stalin, which finally came to a head over the Georgian question.[67]

Looking back in his Testament on this last conflict, Lenin used words that he had never before uttered in his life, saying that he was 'deeply guilty in the eyes of the Russian and international proletariat' for not having started earlier the fight with the bureaucratic clique in Georgia led by Stalin and Ordzhonikidze. In the course of this fight, he realized with horror that he had assisted in hatching a monster: the central Party apparatus around Stalin. He desperately tried to clip its wings with an all-out attack at the Thirteenth Party Congress, calling on Trotsky to help.[68]

Lenin summoned me to his room in the Kremlin, spoke of the frightful growth of bureaucratism in our Soviet *apparat* and of the need to find a solution for the problem. He suggested a special commission of the Central Committee and asked me to take an active part in it. I replied:

'Vladimir Ilyich, I am convinced that in the present fight against bureaucratism in the Soviet *apparat* we must not lose sight of what is going on: a very special selection of officials and specialists, Party members and non-partisans, in the Centre and in the provinces, even for district and local Party offices, is taking place on the basis of loyalty to certain dominant Party personalities and ruling groups inside the Central Committee itself. Every time you attack a minor official, you run up against an important Party leader. . . . I could not undertake the work under the present circumstances.'

Lenin was thoughtful for a moment and – I am quoting him literally – said: 'In other words, I am proposing a campaign against bureaucratism in the Soviet *apparat* and you are proposing to extend the fight to include the bureaucratism of the Party's Orgburo?'

I laughed at the very unexpectedness of this, because no such finished formulation of the idea was in my mind at the time. I replied: 'I suppose that's it.'

'Very well, then,' Lenin retorted, 'I propose a bloc.'

'It is a pleasure to form a bloc with a good man,' I said.

It was agreed that Lenin would initiate the proposal for this commission of the Central Committee to fight bureaucratism 'in general' and in the Orgburo in particular. He promised to think over 'further' organizational details of the matter.[69]

Stalin, with the (conscious or unconscious) help of Lenin's secretaries and the complicity of all Party leaders except Trotsky, succeeded in defusing Lenin's bombshell for the Twelfth Congress. When the delegates eventually met in May 1924, Lenin had been in the Red Square mausoleum for four months. His letter to the Congress was presented as being a result of his illness and not 'the real Lenin'.[70] All the heads of the main delegations lined up in favour of suppressing his Testament. We can say that Lenin died literally a prisoner of the Stalin machine, denied the possibility of acting as a political leader – or even a political person – inside the Party.

In his last months, Lenin never satisfactorily worked out who could lead the fight against the bureaucracy. Certainly not the Party apparatus, which was itself deeply bureaucratized; nor the Central Committee, which he wanted to be expanded into a body of several hundred workers still in production, not full-time functionaries. The Bolshevik worker-members? The broader mass of workers? He examined the problem from all sides but could not find a definite answer.

Bukharin refused to appeal to the Party members against the leadership; that became his undoing. Trotsky hesitated between 1923 and 1927, sometimes addressing a direct call to the membership, sometimes restricting the fight to leadership bodies. Only after 1927 did his position become one of clearly and consistently appealing to the whole conscious proletariat, and there can be no doubt today that the depth of the Thermidorean reaction left no other course. The only question is whether it should have been adopted as early as 1923.

Those writers who see Lenin's mistakes of 1921 as decisive in the victory of the Stalin faction fatally underestimate the shift in the social relationship of forces that had occurred in Soviet Russia. Neither Lenin nor Trotsky nor any faction of the Party could have achieved a political reactivation of the mass of the Russian working class in 1923 – and without that, the bureaucratic stranglehold over society could not have been broken as it can today. Only if the Party as a whole had mobilized against the bureaucracy would there have been a chance of success. This is how Trotsky later viewed the question:

Numerous critics, publicists, correspondents, historians, biographers and sundry amateur sociologists have lectured the Left Opposition from time to time on the errors of its ways, saying that the strategy of the Left Opposition was not feasible from the point of view of the struggle for power. However, the very approach to the question was incorrect. The Left Opposition could not achieve power, and did not hope even to do so – certainly not its most thoughtful leaders. A struggle for power by the Left Opposition, by a revolutionary Marxist organization, was conceivable only under the conditions of a revolutionary upsurge. . . . But during the early twenties and later, there was no revolutionary upsurge in Russia, quite the contrary.[71]

These lines refute in advance Viktor Danilov's otherwise excellent survey of the 1922–23 faction fight in the CPSU, in which he writes: 'The struggle against personal power must always also be the struggle for power (although not, of course, personal power).'[72] A proletarian revolutionary can only struggle for the power of his or her class on the basis of its active mobilization. Otherwise, the 'struggle for power' is either a doomed putschism or, worse, a prisoner of alien class forces, in this case the bureaucracy.

Did the substitutionist formulas of Lenin and Trotsky in 1920–21, in spite of their subsequent struggle against the bureaucracy, help the development of the general ideology that wrecked the Bolshevik Party? To a certain degree undoubtedly – but much less than is often assumed. For the Party leaders and cadres had a choice between the positions expressed in 1920–21 and those of 1922–23, which after all were in line with the Bolshevik tradition up till 1919. Many Old Bolsheviks joined the Opposition in 1923. Bukharin at least hesitated until the beginning of 1923. So the balance-sheet is that the majority of cadres took wrong decisions for reasons of their own, not because they had been misled by Lenin.

In fact, new light has been shed on Lenin's attitude by archive material that has recently been discovered, published or popularized for the first time. It seems that, on the basic questions of workers' democracy, Lenin was still unsure at the time of the Tenth Congress. It is well known that, in opposition to the neophyte Ryazanov, he defended the right of members to form tendencies and to have congress delegates elected on the basis of different platforms, while still speaking out in favour of banning factions. Similarly, he wanted to include the representatives of opposition tendencies and banned factions in the Central Committee. When Shlyapnikov expressed his fear of repression, Lenin answered that the Workers' Opposition platform had been published in 250,000 copies and discussed throughout the Party.

Furthermore, according to Andrei Sorokin, Lenin is supposed to have stated in a previously unpublished part of a speech to the same congress:

Every emergence of the kulaks and the development of petty-bourgeois relations evidently give rise to corresponding political parties. . . . The choice before us is not whether or not to allow these parties to grow – they are inevitably engendered by petty-bourgeois economic relations. The only choice before us, and a limited one at that, is between the forms of concentration and coordination of these parties' activities.

It seems at this point, says Sorokin, that Lenin is about to take another step and recognize the objective need for a multi-party system as a form of 'concentration' of the political forces:

He emphasized then and there, however, that the Mensheviks and Socialist-Revolutionaries – the Russian socialist parties less radical than the Bolsheviks – should only be allowed to tackle economic issues, in the co-ops, and provided there is 'systematic influence and control' over them by the communists. . . . But in his last years Lenin persistently gave thought to changing the Soviet state's political system. In a draft plan written early in 1922 for an article to be called 'Notes of a Publicist', he talks repeatedly of 'the Mensheviks and their legalization'.[73]

The real tragedy of the Russian Revolution at that moment in history is that the leading cadre of the Bolshevik Party did eventually understand the danger of Stalinist Bonapartism and despotism[74] – *but not together and not at the same time*, rather later than sooner, when it could no longer be stopped from reaching the extremes of the mid to late thirties. Essentially this delay was due to a lack of understanding of a new social phenomenon, the rise to power of the privileged bureaucracy in a workers' state. Nearly all that cadre paid dearly for the delay with their lives.

4. Substitutionism in Other Marxist Currents

We have already stressed that reformist social democracy clearly evolved substitutionist ideologies long before Lenin and Trotsky took their fatal leap in 1920–21. It is also important to realize that such a deviation was by no means a monopoly of the Bolsheviks in the Marxist camp properly so called, to which the latter-day social democrats no longer belong. It was also present in the thinking of two of the main West European Marxists, Otto Bauer and Antonio Gramsci.

The seeds of substitutionism can already be found in Otto Bauer's early writings on the Russian Revolution, which at the same time show an insight surpassed only by Rosa Luxemburg into the dangers of bureaucratization.[75] But the clearest formulations of substitutionist ideas come after the defeats of 1933 and 1934, especially in his last major book, *Die illegale Partei*,[76] and his lectures on political economy at the Vienna Workers' University.

Starting, like Lenin in *What Is To Be Done?*, from party-organizational problems arising out of conditions of illegality (security, secrecy, conspiracy, etc.), Bauer theorizes a form of democratic centralism without any autonomy for local organizations or broad democratic processes, but without such an excess of authoritarianism as would threaten to end in 'personal dictatorship'.[77] In his analysis of the transition from capitalism to socialism, however, Bauer goes much further. He is conscious of the danger that the management of state industry will become bureaucratized, and he criticizes the excessive power of factory managers in the USSR.[78] But he insists on the need for a duality of functions inside the 'socialist factory': on the one hand the producers, on the other the administrators. 'Industrial democracy' should only take the form of co-management not self-management. If the workers alone were to manage the factories, this would inevitably give rise to 'factory egoism' (corporatism) and exacerbate the inner divisions, competition and contradictions within the working class.[79] Economic administration is a necessary instrument for the 'arbitration' of divergent interests in the working class.

Given this apology for labour bureaucracy very similar to the classical bourgeois apology for bureaucracy in general, a number of further things are bound to follow. Strikes have to be banned, to begin with. The workers 'must understand' the requirements of efficient factory administration.[80] Indeed, now 'it is stupid to be indignant about the despotism prevailing in Russian factories.'[81] And there is even a partial apology for Stalin's terror and the Moscow Trials.[82] We have come a long way from the denunciation of the dangers of bureaucracy in 1918–20. 'Industrial efficiency' (micro-economic, at that) must take precedence over all else.

Without going quite as far as Otto Bauer, Gramsci in his *Prison Notebooks* also falls back into forms of substitutionism, blatantly contradicting the positions he developed earlier in *Ordine Nuovo*. Thus, he considers that all political parties also 'carry out a policing function', and that this is directed not only against reactionary classes but even against the backward part of the masses.[83] Gramsci establishes a link between a 'war of position' (similar to Kautsky's *Ermattungsstrategie*) and substitutionism:

> The war of position demands enormous sacrifices by infinite masses of people. So an unprecedented concentration of hegemony [of power] is necessary, and hence a more 'interventionist' government, which will take the offensive more openly against the oppositionists and organize permanently the 'impossibility' of internal disintegration – with controls of every kind, political, administrative, etc., reinforcement of the hegemonic 'positions' of the dominant group, etc.[84]

In the thought of both Otto Bauer and Gramsci, a temporary retreat of the mass movement is translated into a strategy which rules out the possibility of new upsurges, and hence of broad self-activity and self-organization of the masses in their own immediate interests. The party, if not a small group of party leaders, dictates to a refractory proletariat what is historically 'necessary' and 'inevitable'.

At bottom lies an idealist rather than a materialist concept of the party, all the more surprising in the case of Bauer who was one of the first to denounce just such a deformation. It is interesting to note that whereas Bauer slides into substitutionism through his tendency to crude, mechanical determinism, Gramsci is led astray by his voluntarist proclamation of the identity of theory and practice, in which the potential and real contradictions between the two are denied.[85]

5. Realpolitik and Substitutionism

The conceptions of Kautsky, Bauer and Gramsci that we have just been discussing touch the very essence of opportunist realpolitik. It is this which, so to speak, unites social-democratic and Stalinist (or neo-Stalinist) substitutionism.

Of course, the problem of modifying power relations in society, of conquering 'portions of power', lies at the heart of politics in general. Conservative policies tend to maintain these relations, revolutionary policies to overturn them. Reformist policies tend to modify them partially, without any fundamental change.

Whether such change is possible or not, in the short to medium term, crucially determines political choices. That is why politics has so often been described as the art (or science-cum-art) of the possible. But several contradictions in this trite formula immediately leap to mind. Are the boundaries between the possible and the not-possible really so rigid? Can the impossible be transformed into the possible through conscious revolutionary mass activity? Some possibles may be growing today without having broken through to complete clarity. What appears impossible in the short run may very well become possible in the long run – for instance, the Second International's campaign for the eight-hour day, or mass agitation for universal suffrage.[86]

Furthermore, it may be the case that opportunist realpolitik, while immediately successful in its own terms, actually reduces long-term possibilities of radical change that might have grown with a different set of practices. Or mass actions that do not at once bear fruit may have positive long-term effects in terms of mass consciousness.

These considerations, and many others, certainly do not imply a full answer to the basic problem confronting the labour movement, to which Kautsky, Bauer and Gramsci addressed themselves at specific historical moments: namely, what form should socialist class politics take under conditions that are objectively non-revolutionary? But at least they reveal the pitfalls of opportunist, not to say vulgar, realpolitik. An exaggerated emphasis on what seems immediately possible and desirable can blind one to longer-term effects and contradictions.[87]

When acts of realpolitik go against what broad sections of the masses feel to be their interests, they have to be imposed against their will. In fact, since realpolitik implies a high degree of defence of the status quo – which is exploitative and oppressive for broad masses – this contradiction is well nigh inevitable. Certain practices of substitutionism, if not substitutionism pure and simple, are therefore inextricably linked to opportunist realpolitik.

Realpolitik should by no means be confused with the struggle for reforms. It is perfectly possible to combine resolute struggle for immediately realizable reforms with systematic anti-capitalist education and propaganda. What is impossible, at least with any credibility, is to combine such education and propaganda with consensus policies – that is, with defence of the establishment and power-sharing with the ruling class.[88]

The struggle for reforms and the struggle for the final goal of radical social transformation are evidently related to each in a dialectical manner. This entails that sectarian abstention from, or even rejection of, immediate struggles is as detrimental to the socialist cause as is opportunist realpolitik. Without the conquest of partial reforms, the toilers risk becoming a mass of demoralized paupers, perhaps capable of periodic hunger revolts but not of a serious challenge to the existing order. Without the experience of broad mass struggles, the toilers are unable to reach the levels of self-organization and consciousness that are indispensable for a successful fight for a new society. And unless socialists participate in such struggles, trying to win political hegemony within them, they will be incapable of seriously influencing the historical process.

Precisely for all these reasons, the temptations of realpolitik are real temptations; the contradictions of partial conquests, analysed in the previous chapter, are real contradictions. In order to avoid the twin pitfalls of opportunism and sectarianism, it is necessary to assimilate the historical lessons of concrete class struggles, and to enrich them through critical examination of current experiences.

The last word on these matters can again be given to Karl Marx. In 1865 he wrote to his friend Ludwig Kugelmann:

I think that Schweitzer and the others have honest intentions, but they are *'realistic politicians'*. They want to accommodate themselves to *existing* circumstances and refuse to leave this privilege of 'realistic politics' to the exclusive use of Messrs Miquel et Comp. . . . They know that the workers' press and the workers' movement in Prussia (and therefore in the rest of Germany) exist solely by the grace of the police. So they want to take things as they are, and not irritate the government, etc., just like our 'republican' realistic politicians, who are willing to 'put up with' a Hohenzollern *emperor*. But since I am not a 'realistic politician' I together with Engels have found it necessary to give notice to the *Sozial-Demokrat* in a public statement (which you will probably soon see in one paper or another) of our intention to quit.[89]

6. The Psychological Dimension of Substitutionism

In Chapters 2 and 3, we have often referred to psychological aspects of the process of bureaucratization of the workers' mass organizations. The substitution of the apparatus for the working class as the object of self-evident loyalty also involves determinations at the level of individual psychology. A 'campist' view of the world, the seductiveness of being part of a power structure, guilt feelings of petty-bourgeois intellectuals towards 'the party embodying the working class' may all enter into a character structure that is easily manipulable by professional bureaucrats. Vittorio Vidali, the future Stalinist murderer of POUMists, Trotskyists and anarchists in Spain, once gave chilling expression to these half-hidden motivations in a letter which declared his devotion to the Party and willingness to become an 'iron revolutionary' and 'executioner of justice'.

> And if, during the first days, I had some small, brief disillusionments in touching reality, I later felt that it was due to the petty-bourgeois atmosphere that still had not disappeared from my soul. [sic] . . . But then, even this voice from the past . . . disappeared, torn away by larger horizons. And I saw the Red soldiers marching with their rebellious songs, with proud, intelligent faces, and the armed youth and the children who discuss politics. I like serious men. A new society, great, magnificent, raises its superb towers above the old and decrepit. . . .
>
> A Marxist has got to be a cold rationalizer. A Leninist must aim straight to his own goal . . . Write for our newspaper . . . Sacrifice your point of view for that of the Party. . . . Deserve the love of the comrades; it is not that difficult. In a few months you will see that all [sic] doors will open.[90]

After a few years, 'you' will have prisons full not of bourgeois or imperialist spies but of ordinary workers and peasants.[91] After a few years, 'you' will be busy murdering your own comrades.

We can conclude that bureaucratic organizational regimes, not to mention bureaucratic dictatorships, unleash *a process of negative selection* in which persons lacking character, will-power, independence of judgement and capacity to resist pressure, or even displaying servility and conformism tinged with base motivations, will inevitably come to the fore.[92] But whatever the psychological mechanisms involved, the processes of bureaucratization and Stalinization are fundamentally a social phenomenon. Sado-masochistic individuals are present in society in all historical periods. There were certainly no fewer of them in Russia in 1917 or 1918 than in 1929 or 1937. If they came to hold key positions of power in the later rather than the earlier periods, this was because the correlation of social forces had undergone a fundamental change. Certain character-types occupy the proscenium in a time of revolutionary upsurge and generalized mass activity; others thrust themselves forward only in a context of mass passivity when counter-revolution has triumphed. It was not 'bad' personalities which made possible the degeneration of the CPSU and the USSR, but rather bureaucratic degeneration which fed a systematic 'negative selection' of leaders.

When he was still a Marxist, Wilhelm Reich groped towards an answer to the question: why do people end up acting in complete contradiction with ideas, values and norms that they originally accepted? Why do parts of the working class agree to conform to the interests of their worst enemies? More coherently and deeply than Reich, Bernfeld also addressed these problems in an attempted combination of Marxism and psychoanalysis.

With regard to the broad masses, such phenomena cannot be explained by – indeed, directly contradict – the social or material interests of those concerned. As for the leaders, while material privileges do play a role in the acceptance of substitutionist theories and practices, the gradual nature of the ideological transformation confirms that it cannot be simply reduced to these material interests.

Bernfeld and Reich suggest three kinds of answer. First, they point to the machine-like aspect of many forms of mass behaviour. This is inculcated by the power and discipline of hierarchical organizations like armies, with all the risks that a refusal to obey would entail for the individual. But it also fulfils a primitive need for individuals eager to identify with 'the leader' (the father?) – which is supposed to hark back to the very origins of our species. Such processes, however, involve a deep identity-disturbance in individuals, who cannot see themselves operating outside a tightly organized structure. It is not *raison de parti* or 'party reason' but *party being*, existing only in and through the party, which reflects this fear of facing the hostile world.

Psychoanalysts consider bureaucrats to be governed by compulsion neurosis which, in its incipient form, is present in countless individuals. But the bureaucratic regime (system) *institutionalizes* that compulsion. It externalizes the internal pathology by translating it into formal rules that one is compelled to respect unconditionally (Ernst Federn). This upsets the 'normal' balance between non-pathological and pathological motivations of behaviour.

Second, there is an irrational dimension to human behaviour which likewise derives from the earliest phases of hominization of the primates. It implies some form of revolt or individual rejection of rules of social behaviour accompanying the rise of civilization.[93] Rulers or demagogues bent on conquering power (either in mass organizations or in the state) will deliberately play on this irrationalism. And if their opponents are not aware of it and try to respond only with logical argument, they will fail to win over at least some of the people in question.

Third, the struggle to develop class consciousness and class politics involves more than just the struggle for a correct programme or political line. The building of socialist mass organizations, and later of socialism itself, can only succeed if the ever more individualized masses and 'cadres' are able to translate the abstract into the concrete, to identify political generalizations with personal experiences and needs.[94] If this does not happen, or if it remains inadequate, the masses and cadres – including the central leaders – will become more and more frustrated and passive. Then the 'machine', commanding blind obedience, will again be able to close its grip on them.

The above analysis undoubtedly contains a considerable kernel of truth.[95] But like all attempts to explain historical phenomena by individual psychology or, worse, biology, it suffers from a basic flaw. It cannot account for the fact that permanently operating forces lead to different outcomes. History is change, while the irrational components of human behaviour do not change over, at least, thousands of years. The same masses who displayed elements of irrationalism during the rise of Hitler had behaved in a splendidly rational way just ten years earlier, when they broke the Kapp–von Lüttwitz putsch in 1920. The same masses who so abjectly accepted war and carnage in August 1914 would oppose it with equal vehemence in 1917–18, at least in Russia, Germany and Austria.

Such 'mysteries' of individual and collective psychology become intelligible only within the ever-changing framework of historical realities such as mass living conditions, the relationship of forces between and inside the major social classes, the weight of different currents of thought and opinion, and so on. Similarly, only in the interaction of all these forces can an explanation be found for the rise of labour bureaucracies, the consolidation of substitutionist theories and practices, and the personal degeneration of socialist and communist leaders into bureaucrats.

7. Substitutionism and Policy Choices:
The Tragedy of Bukharin and the Old Bolsheviks

During the period when the Stalinist apparatus was consolidating its grip on the Party and the Soviet state, a number of central Old Bolsheviks –

above all, Bukharin, Zinoviev, Kamenev, Rykov and Tomsky – concentrated their attention on what they thought was a leadership struggle over economic and international policies. In doing so, they failed to grasp the key issue of bureaucratic degeneration and played into Stalin's hands. For the General Secretary was essentially interested not in this or that political orientation but in the exercise of total power inside the Party, with the unity and integrity of its full-time apparatus as the number one priority. He was a genuine ideological representative of the bureaucracy, as is clear from the following outburst:

> The opposition headed by Trotsky put forward the slogan of breaking up the Party *apparat* and attempted to transfer the centre of gravity from the struggle against bureaucracy in the State *apparat* to the struggle against 'bureaucracy' in the Party *apparat*. Such utterly baseless criticism and the downright attempt to discredit the Party *apparat* cannot, objectively speaking, lead to anything but the emancipation of the State *apparat* from Party influence.[96]

That the Party could influence and restrain the state bureaucracy through any other means than its own bureaucracy did not even enter Stalin's mind.

Whatever the importance of the issues with which the Old Bolsheviks were obsessed – the tempo of industrialization, the growing weight of the kulaks, the 'price scissors', the relationship with the world market, the immediacy or otherwise of the war danger – it is hard to deny today, with hindsight, that they were all subordinate to the question of who, which group of people, actually exercised power in the USSR. The development of Soviet society and of the CPSU and its policies in the second half of the 1920s serves to confirm the accuracy of this analysis. For it was because the Stalin faction and the bureaucracy held the reins of state power that they were able to move overnight from the NEP to top-speed industrialization and forced collectivization, from growing integration in the world market to a large degree of autarky. And the vagaries of Stalinist and post-Stalinist economic policy, from 1924 to 1953 to 1990, only become comprehensible if we see that their principal motivation was the defence and expansion of bureaucratic privileges and of the power monopoly that sustained them.

It follows from this that Bukharin made a tragic mistake when he allied himself with Stalin, first alongside Zinoviev and Kamenev and then against them – a mistake which finally cost him his life, and for which the working class and the Soviet people paid a tremendous price. Doubtless he took this step because he genuinely believed that the economic policy debate was decisive, and that the line of the Left Opposition was the principal danger. In the event, however, the economic policies conducted by Stalin after 1928, even according to Bukharin's criteria, proved incomparably more devastating than those proposed by the Opposition. And it can clearly be shown that, as early as 1923, the Opposition placed the main emphasis on questions relating to soviet and inner-party democracy.

A Marxist as intelligent and well-trained as Bukharin will inevitably attempt to justify such an error of political judgement by means of theoretical analysis. Thus, in his speeches and writings from the 1923–28 period, his attitude to the danger of bureaucratic degeneration underwent a marked change. Between 1918 and 1922 he had confined himself to the classical viewpoint of Marx and Engels and of Lenin's *State and Revolution*, which entailed a recognition that the working masses might be oppressed by their own officials and that special measures needed to be taken to guard against this. (See Chapters 1 and 2 above.) In a sense, Bukharin may even be said to have provided inspiration for *State and Revolution*, in his article 'Towards a Theory of the Imperialist State', written a year before, in 1916, which advocated the destruction of the bourgeois state.[97] He followed this up with another article that was published in various papers of the socialist left: the Dutch *De Tribune*, the Norwegian *Klassenkampen*, the Bremen periodical *Arbeiterpolitik*, and *Die Jugendinternationale*. At first Lenin attacked these positions as being 'semi-anarchist'. But by April 1917 he had made them fully his own. Up till 1929 the Soviet literature admitted Lenin's ideological debt to Bukharin.

In 1918 Bukharin again took up the same formulae: 'The proletarian dictatorship,' he wrote, 'is not a parliamentary republic . . . but a state along the lines of the Commune, without a police force, without a standing army or professional civil servants.'[98] In his book *The Economics of the Transition Period*, written between 1918 and 1920, he demonstrated the need for self-organization and self-management of the working class, even at a time of massive disruption of the economy.[99] Here, as in the new programme of the Bolshevik Party to which he made a significant contribution, Bukharin devoted considerable attention to trade-union factory management, expressly stating that engineers and technicians were to be regarded as strata subordinate to the workers' rank-and-file structures. In *The ABC of Communism*, which he drafted in 1919 with Preobrazhensky as a popular commentary on the new programme, the problematic is formulated in even more trenchant language:

> All these circumstances make our work extremely difficult, and tend to a certain degree to promote the reintroduction of bureaucracy into the Soviet system. This is a grave danger for the proletariat. . . . Our party, therefore,

must do its utmost to avert this danger. It can only be averted by attracting the masses to take part in the work. The fundamental matter, of course, is to raise the general cultural level of the workers and peasants, to make an end of illiteracy, to diffuse enlightenment. In addition, however, a whole series of other measures is essential. Among these, our party advocates the following.

It is absolutely indispensable that every member of a soviet should play some definite part in the work of State administration. . . .

The next essential is that there should be a continuous rotation in these functions. The comrade must not stick for years to one and the same job, for if he does this he will become a routinist official of the old type. . . .

Finally, our party recommends, as far as concerns the general arrangement of the work, that by degrees the entire working population shall be induced to participate in the State administration. Here, in fact, is the true foundation of our political system.[100]

On 30 December 1920 Bukharin interrupted Lenin's speech to a meeting of Communist trade unionists and delegates to the Congress of Soviets, at the point where Lenin had called the Soviet State a 'workers' and peasants' state'. A few weeks later Lenin corrected himself: 'Comrade Bukharin is right. What I should have said is: "A workers' state is an abstraction. What we actually have is a workers' state, with this peculiarity, firstly, that it is not the working class but the peasant population that predominates in the country, and, secondly, that it is a workers' state with bureaucratic distortions."'[101]

In his book *Historical Materialism*, written in 1920, Bukharin once more summarized his analysis of bureaucracy in a polemic with the sociologists Pareto and Robert Michels:

But the question of the transition period from capitalism to socialism, i.e., the period of the proletarian dictatorship, is far more difficult. The working class achieves victory, although it is not and cannot be a unified mass. It attains victory while the productive forces are going down and the great masses are materially insecure. There will inevitably result a *tendency* to 'degeneration', i.e., the excretion of a leading stratum in the form of a class-germ. This tendency will be retarded by two opposing tendencies: first, by the growth of the productive forces; second, by the abolition of the educational monopoly.

And he concluded that under socialism, 'the power of the administrators . . . will be the power of specialists over machines, not over men.'[102]

The historical balance-sheet, however, shows that things evolved in the opposite direction in the USSR. The power of the specialists (rather, of all layers of the bureaucracy) became a power not only over machines but also over men, in the first place over the direct producers. The 'true foundation of our political system', the encouragement of all the working population to take part in the administration of the state, remained a dead letter. Today this is openly admitted in the USSR in countless revelations, some of them from the highest ranks of the Party.

Power was usurped by the bureaucracy. Not just for a short period but for the last sixty-seven years, the soviets have been without real power. How did things come to this pass? That is a question to which every historian, every practitioner of the social sciences, every communist who studies the history of the CPSU and the USSR, must find an answer.

In Bukharin's own intellectual biography we can locate, almost to the day, the turning point in his assessment of the danger of bureaucratic degeneration. In his speech on *The Proletarian Revolution and Culture*, given on 3 February 1923 in Petrograd, his earlier and later points of view can be seen cohabiting, as it were, alongside each other. On the one hand, he declares even more lucidly than before: 'Every proletarian revolution, in any country whatsoever, will inevitably be confronted, in the course of its development, with the terrible dangers represented by the internal degeneration of the revolution, of the proletarian state and of the party.'[103] The reason for this is the low level of cultural development of the proletariat in bourgeois society, and its extreme variations in material circumstances and class consciousness.

On the other hand, the only way Bukharin can see of avoiding this 'terrible danger' is the training of working-class technicians, engineers and managers, separate and apart from the mass of workers. The whole problematic of self-organization suddenly vanishes:

> This period of transition is the period during which the working class undergoes a transformation of its nature in the most diverse ways, *when it secretes from its reservoir of forces determined cohorts of men*, who pass through a cultural, ideological, technical, etc. transformation and emerge from this University in another existential form. . . . Thus you see that the significance of the period of transition, considered from this point of view, is that the working class, in conquering state power, while at the same time experiencing material hardship, trains by means of cultural work cadres who will enable it to govern the whole country with an energetic hand, to the extent that it places these qualified and trusted men in the most diverse posts.[104]

Bukharin is aware of the contradictions in his new position. The dangers of degeneration of the workers' state do not only derive from the weight and influence of specialists of bourgeois origin and with a bourgeois and petty-bourgeois mentality. They also stem from the fact that these specialists/officials/bureaucrats of bourgeois origin exert an influence, at least cultural and intellectual, upon the specialists/officials emanating from the working class. Nevertheless, Bukharin remains optimistic and apologetic in the face of the social and material differentiation taking place before his eyes:

> When we, when the Russian working class comes to train enough cadres, and
> . . . is able gradually to replace the cadres of the old intelligentsia and the old
> civil service, it will remove the first danger. . . . Our next task will be to
> stabilize these cadres by continually pumping in new blood, in an effort to
> prevent the cadres from becoming remote and turning into a monopolistic
> caste.[105]

This emphasis on the stability and authority of cadres, when combined
with Stalin's later maxim 'The cadres decide everything', would have
catastrophic effects on the mechanisms whereby power was exercised.
We have already seen some of these results: the negative selection of
cadres by appointment rather than election; the tendency to conformism
and monolithism, instead of critical debate and free expression; the
transfer of real power from the soviets to the Party *apparat*; the repressive labour legislation, including a de facto ban on strikes, and so on. The
'monopolistic caste' thus became a reality, in spite of the fact that it
expanded through incorporation of large numbers of technicians, intellectuals or bureaucrats originating in the working class.

In Bukharin's speeches between 1923 and 1928, the previous contradictions were 'resolved' in a blind faith in the cadres. By 1926 Bukharin
was almost hysterically reproaching Trotsky for his description of the
Central Committee majority as the 'bureaucratic faction'. 'One cannot
but agree,' he wrote, 'that bureaucratization of the governing party
would be extremely dangerous. But if the Central Committee represents
the bureaucracy . . . why should it not be set aside?'[106] In his most
extensive polemic against the Opposition, *Problems of Building Socialism*, he went so far as to say that 'the theory of [bureaucratic] degeneration is based entirely on social-democratic postulates'.[107]

Finally, in his theoretical work *The Road to Socialism*, which appeared
in 1925, the whole danger of bureaucratic degeneration is totally neglected. Social inequality in the towns, the higher earnings of 'senior
officials' and 'employees with responsibilities' are freely admitted, but
presented as an inevitable – and not even transitory – evil.[108] Lenin's
dialectical analysis of the demoralizing effects of such inequality on the
working class, and his practical conclusion that the income of Party
members should not exceed that of skilled workers, are completely
abandoned.

When Bukharin speaks in the same book of the gradual victory over
inequality, this relates exclusively to relations between the working class
and the peasantry. Nor does he have a word to say about *political
inequality* within the working class, between those members of the state
and party apparatus who exercise power in practice, and the broad

masses who are governed from above and upon whom no power devolves.

It is true that Bukharin, under the pressure of intense polemics with the Opposition, continued from time to time to make passing reference to the problem of bureaucratic tendencies. In a speech to officials of the Moscow Party organization on 5 January 1926, he accepted that relations within socialized enterprises were not 'totally socialist' because there was still a division of labour between 'administrators' and 'administered'. But such remarks should not be taken too seriously, especially as they were hedged around by systematic denunciations of the Opposition thesis that a process of bureaucratic degeneration was taking place in the USSR and the CPSU. Bukharin would answer such accusations by affirming that state power was in the hands of the working class, that the Party wielded power on behalf of the proletariat, that it had the bureaucracy in tow, and that to speak of a fundamental conflict of interests between the apparatus and the working masses was, implicitly, to head in the direction of overthrowing Soviet power.[109] Concrete analysis of a concrete situation – which Lenin had seen as the 'living soul of Marxism' – was replaced by warnings against 'subversive ideas' and undertones of repression. Already in 1927, Trotsky and the Opposition accused Stalin and the Party apparatus of openly using violent methods, in preparation not only for its expulsion but also for its physical destruction. Bukharin's reply was that to speak of a Soviet Thermidor was counter-revolutionary. Whom did history prove right in this instance?

It must, of course, be stressed that in 1928 Bukharin was to return to his earlier ideas. But by then he lacked any power to influence the course of events. He wrote: 'In the pores of our gigantic apparatus, elements of bureaucratic degeneration have come to nest which are absolutely indifferent to the interests of the masses, their standard of living, their material and cultural interests.'[110] Were these 'elements of bureaucratic degeneration' not already in control of all the levers of the state and of economic and social power?

Similarly, in his speech on the fifth anniversary of Lenin's death, Bukharin took up his old idea of the self-activity of the broad masses as a decisive means of combating degeneration. Lenin's organizational plan, he argued, 'develops directives geared to the masses which Vladimir Ilyich expresses in a concise but vivid formula: real participation by the popular masses'.[111] Curiously, however, this whole speech does not use the word 'bureaucracy' even once!

In the course of his intellectual evolution, Bukharin would several times return to these questions with considerable strength of feeling, albeit in rather 'Aesopian' references. For instance, the revival of his

concept 'new Leviathan' – harking back to his description of the imperialist state in 1916 as the 'modern Leviathan' – clearly implied that it was
relevant to the reality of the Soviet Union. On 30 January 1929, in a little-
known statement to the Politburo, he accused the Party leadership of
conducting a policy of 'militaristic–feudal exploitation', of 'undermining
the Comintern' and promoting 'bureaucratism in the Party'.[112]

The Aesopian language was particularly strong in his pamphlet
Finance Capital in a Pope's Gown (April 1930), in which the Pope and
'the Jesuits' are patent cover-names for Stalin and his Party apparatus.
Later there followed two remarkable documents: the 'Letter from an Old
Bolshevik', dating from the second half of 1936, which may be regarded
as Bukharin's political testament;[113] and the moving farewell letter *To a
Future Generation of Party Leaders*, which he read to his wife just before
his arrest and which was published in the West (and later in the USSR)
after the beginning of de-Stalinization under Khrushchev.[114] Finally, in
his carefully crafted closing speech of 12 March 1938 at the Third
Moscow Trial, before he was sentenced to death, Bukharin managed to
point the finger at Stalin with sentences like: 'Once again it has been
proved that to move away from the Bolshevik position is to move in the
direction of counter-revolutionary imposture.'

In his farewell letter to the Party, Bukharin writes: 'I feel my helpless-
ness before a hellish machine which . . . has acquired gigantic power,
fabricates organized slander, acts boldly and confidently . . . a degenerate organization of bureaucrats, without ideas, rotten, well paid, who use
the Cheka's bygone authority to cater to Stalin's morbid suspiciousness.
. . . Any member of the Central Committee, any member of the Party,
can be rubbed out, turned into a traitor, terrorist, deviationist, spy, by
these "wonder-working organs".'[115]

According to the report by the Menshevik Boris Nicolaevsky on his
interview with Bukharin in Paris in 1936, Bukharin is supposed to have
said: 'A second party is needed. When there is only one electoral list,
with no genuine alternative, then we have something that is tantamount
to Nazism. In order to distinguish ourselves clearly from the Nazis in the
eyes of the people of the West as well as those of Russia, we need to
introduce a system with two electoral lists instead of a single-party
system.'[116] It is interesting to note that just one month earlier Leon
Trotsky had also broken with the dogma of the single party. Unlike
Bukharin, however, he supported the idea of a *multi*-party system.

There remains one major enigma. How could a Communist, a Marxist
of Bukharin's calibre, reconcile this penetrating analysis of the degeneration of the Party and state bureaucracy – which had become, in his
estimation, semi-fascist – with the renunciation of any systematic politi-

cal struggle against those responsible for its degeneration? Stephen Cohen sums up the contradiction as follows:

> By 1929, Bukharin had come to share most of Trotsky's criticism of the party's internal regime. Unlike Trotsky, however, having sanctioned its development, he was its prisoner. His dissent and accompanying pleas for the toleration of critical opinion in 1928–29 were regularly rebuffed with quotations from his own, earlier sermons against the Left's 'factionalism', and his attacks on Stalin's 'secretarial regime' with derisive jeers: 'Where did you copy that from? . . . From Trotsky!' . . . His position was politically incongruous: driven by outraged contempt for Stalin and his policies, he remained throughout a restrained, reluctant oppositionist.
>
> Apart from public appeals too Aesopian to be effective, Bukharin, Rykov and Tomsky therefore colluded with Stalin in confining their fateful conflict to a small private arena, there to be 'strangled behind the back of the party'.[117]

The most common explanations for Bukharin's behaviour refer to his 'soft character' (Lenin's words), his 'organic centrism', his illusions until Kirov's death – not totally unrealistic, one might add – that Central Committee 'moderates' would put up a last fight (Ordzhonikidze, Kossior, Rudzutak, Kirov, et al.),[118] or his withdrawal from any action liable to split the Party. Each of these arguments contains an element of truth.

In our view, however, the deepest reason underlying Bukharin's vacillation, even after 1927 when he again recognized the possibility of a Soviet Thermidor, was his mistaken thesis that the seizure and exercise of power by the bureaucracy was attributable to internal party phenomena rather than to a socio-political regression in the country at large.[119] This explains why Bukharin addressed his farewell letter to 'a future party leadership' and not the mass of its members or the working class. It explains why Bukharin, till the very last moment before his torture and confession, continued to have a naive faith that Stalin would protect him. (Stalin was in fact playing a particularly cruel cat-and-mouse game with his unfortunate victim.[120]) And finally, it explains why, unlike Trotsky, he refused to call upon the mass of Soviet workers, youth and intellectuals to come out not only against Stalin and his faction but against the bureaucracy as a social stratum. All this becomes clear if we realize that Bukharin did not look beyond an internal reform of Stalinism (that is, of the bureaucracy), whereas Trotsky saw that it would have to be overturned by nothing short of a new revolution.

Any real balance-sheet of Bukharin's role must take account of the complicity of himself and his followers in the repression orchestrated by Stalin, first against the cadres of the Left Opposition in Moscow, then against the Zinovievist cadres in Leningrad. In a study of the 1920s and

1930s that appeared in *Pravda* on 3 October 1988, Academician Smirnov wrote:

> Even Rykov [Chairman of the Council of People's Commissars and Bukharin's closest political ally], at the Central Committee plenum in 1928, considered with reference to the Shakhty trial and the imprisonment of the German experts that the Party should make certain trials subordinate to political priorities. It should not allow itself to be guided by the abstract (!) principle of just punishment of the guilty. The question of imprisonment had to be approached less from the standpoint of the interests of Soviet legal practice, or 'the principle of justice in itself', than from that of the 'grand policy' of the Bolsheviks.

Thus was formulated a monstrous precept: that it matters little whether charges are true or false, the main thing is that they should be politically opportune. It was in accordance with this very principle that Bukharin and Rykov himself were to be found guilty and sentenced to death in 1938. One would be hard pressed to find an instance of Trotsky or his Left Opposition comrades making any concession to this principle, which is diametrically opposed to Marx's view that the Revolution is served only by the truth.

Was this stance a matter of pure tactics on the part of Bukharin and Rykov, or did it stem from genuine conviction? It is virtually impossible to give a definite answer. Communist, Marxist and socialist politics forms a knot combining firmly held principles with the capacity to conduct tactical manoeuvres. The balance between the two, which is itself unstable, involves extreme tensions when new phenomena suddenly appear in society. Quite clearly, Bukharin was not able to cope with such tensions. He sacrificed central principles (including the elementary rule: not to conceal the truth from one's own class) to tactical considerations. Trotsky has sometimes been accused of making the opposite mistake. Be that as it may, from 1928 on he cannot be indicted for the slightest tactical concession to Stalin and Stalinism.[121] But, as we have already said, behind Bukharin's tactical manoeuvres lay a political illusion, a wrong assessment of the social nature of the Party leadership and apparatus – one founded on a theoretical misconception.

It should be added that important groups belonging to the Left Opposition – to whom Trotsky made too many concessions until 1929–30 – committed the same mistake as Bukharin when it came to identifying the Thermidorean danger. Preobrazhensky, Pyatakov, Smilga and Radek, above all, underestimated the problem of the bureaucracy at that moment, in strong contrast with their lucid analysis of 1923–24. They saw the danger of Thermidor principally in an alliance between the kulaks, the new (middle bourgeois) NEP men and foreign capital – that is, they saw it almost entirely in economic terms. For this reason, they failed to appreciate the political dimension, the fact that the kulaks were manifestly incapable of joining together in common political action on a country-wide scale.

The key actors on the political front were the Stalinist faction, the bureaucracy.[122] This was the force which decided the destiny of the Soviet Union for half a century. The Soviet Thermidor came about through the dictatorship of the bureaucracy, and not as the result of a seizure of power by the kulaks or a restoration of capitalism.

8. Substitutionism and Policy Choices:
The Personal Fates of Mao Zedong and Deng Xiaoping

Bukharin was an honest and brilliant Communist theoretician, even if he became tragically entwined in a factional drama whose historical significance he did not grasp and in which he lost his political bearings. At a lower level of theoretical awareness, the trajectories of Mao Zedong and Deng Xiaoping dramatically illustrate the inability of power politics, pragmatism and realpolitik founded on substitutionism to shape the course of history. Both ended their careers by creating situations and promoting options that were the direct opposite of what they had initially planned.

When Mao unleashed the 'Cultural Revolution', he was concerned above all to win a power struggle inside the Chinese CP leadership. Having lost a majority on the Central Committee in the disastrous wake of the 'Great Leap Forward', he appealed to the youth against the Party apparatus and engineered a gigantic personality cult to underpin his claims to infallibility. This whole operation involved the suppression of any remaining elements of free inner-party discussion, and the spread of physical violence and other forms of repression against his real, potential or imagined opponents.

At the same time, the Cultural Revolution expressed, on the part of Mao as well as the broad masses, an elemental revulsion against the established Party and state bureaucracy. One cannot imagine Friedrich Ebert or Clement Attlee, nor Stalin or Brezhnev, mobilizing millions of people on the streets to clear out a horde of office-holders. Stalin's favoured weapon for his purges was the secret police.

The masses of youth (not just students) responded to Mao's appeal because they genuinely hated the bureaucrats and thought that the time had come to conquer greater equality and democracy. Indeed, it would distort the historical record to deny that a major component of mass spontaneity and political differentiation accompanied the first phase of

141

the Cultural Revolution.[123] But Mao's obsession with power politics, within the dogmatic framework of party as opposed to class rule, rapidly placed him in an insoluble dilemma. He dreamt of periodically shaking up the bureaucracy through mass mobilizations, to prevent its consolidation as a privileged caste like in the USSR.[124] But the real-world mobilizations began to escape his control, leading to political conflicts that endangered Party rule and to clashes between social layers of a kind that are inevitable where social differentiation is still a prevalent feature.[125]

Mao was thus caught in a vice. If he let the Cultural Revolution develop into a real political, anti-bureaucratic revolution, it would also overthrow his personal power and the pro-Mao faction in the CCP. He therefore chose, probably with an air of resignation, the other available option: to use the army to start repressing, or 'disciplining', the mass of Red Guards, as well as workers who were taking independent action.[126] Millions of urban youth were deported to the countryside. Bureaucratic 'law and order' was restored in the factories. Gradually the Party and state bureaucracy regained the upper hand.

As long as Mao was still alive and the 'Gang of Four' controlled the bureaucracy, it could appear that something basic had changed as a result of the Cultural Revolution. But Mao was under no illusion. He was convinced that the bureaucracy had won through, partly because of his own decisions. He died with a bitter sense of failure, telling his wife that he could not protect her and her faction for long, and that they would be brought down as soon as he disappeared. That is exactly what happened.

One should never forget that Mao shared Stalin's primary opposition to inner-party and workers' democracy, and his cardinal belief that only the CP leadership represented the working class. All other currents, even if 'nominally' representative of the workers and peasants, were really delegates of the bourgeoisie.[127] The inner contradiction of Mao Zedong Thought is thus quite evident: world history teaches us that rebellion is justified – except for rebellion against Mao Zedong Thought and 'the correct line of the Party'!

Throughout Mao's final period, the power struggle inside the CCP leadership and the bureaucracy was combined with a debate about conflicting economic policies, many details of which remain obscure. What transpired after Mao's death, however, has by and large clarified the issues at stake.

Mao's faction based its ideas for economic development upon central investment in the large-scale state sector, with a peculiar pattern of forced collectivization ('people's communes') that would allow excess labour to be retained in the villages through 'direct labour investment' at a low level of efficiency. The alternative proposed by Liu Shaochi and

Deng Xiaoping aimed to achieve higher efficiency and labour productivity through, on the one hand, partially decentralized investment to
modernize both urban and rural industry, and on the other, a re-
privatization of agriculture to unlock the productive forces of the peasantry. After a short transition, this was the pattern that was applied
when the Deng faction took power in the CCP in 1979.

But Deng was not just an 'economic liberalizer'. He had also been a
prominent victim of the inner-party terror during the Cultural Revolution. Indeed, in all probability he only saved his life by the narrowest of
margins – unlike his hapless ally Liu Shaochi, the former Party chairman,
who was murdered by the Maoists in especially cruel circumstances. Thus
Deng's return to power was understood not only by the Party bureaucracy but also by the broad masses as the prelude to a reduction in terror
and pressure, and at least the beginnings of intellectual and political
liberalization. The fact that Deng's economic policies implied an opening
to the capitalist world market inevitably contributed to that impression.

Nor was it mere fantasy. It corresponded to a real, though very partial
and contradictory, process. There is no doubt in our mind that Deng
genuinely opted for a partial and controlled political liberalization to
accompany the economic liberalization. Indeed, two consecutive
General Secretaries he had designated and groomed to succeed him, Hu
Yaobang and Zhao Zhiyang, became identified with a line akin to the
early stages of Gorbachev's glasnost. Deng tried to get rid of the real
Brezhnev-style gerontocrats around Peng Chen and Marshal Yang
Shangkin, moving them out of operational leadership into largely honor-
ary positions. The Marshal was formal president of the Republic.

Yet even more than Mao, Deng faced a dilemma that could not be
solved by someone who had never been willing to break with the so-
called 'four principles' – which included the Stalinist dogma of top-down
party rule, as opposed to class rule – and with the power and interests of
the bureaucracy.[128] From 1986 onwards, social discontent and ever more
open conflict broke out in the People's Republic of China. Sections of the
masses started to act in an autonomous way. There were peasant
demonstrations and strikes. There were workers' demonstrations and
strikes. Students and intellectuals operated as catalysts, slowly tying
together all these fragmentary movements into a general upsurge in
favour of democratic freedoms within the workers' state. The Beijing
student–workers' movement, which developed into the Commune of
May–June 1989, brought this process to a climax.

Like Mao during the Red Guards upheaval, Deng now had to choose.
And it soon became clear that he would opt for a violent and radical
repression of the mass ferment. This implied not only the massacre of 4
June 1989 and its aftermath, but also a factional realignment within the

CCP leadership. The two-cornered struggle between 'moderate liberals' around Deng and the 'conservatives' became a three-cornered fight in which the Deng faction increasingly had to support itself on the 'conservatives' against the more resolute 'liberals'. The CCP cadre and the Chinese people had seen in Deng a symbol of the shift away from that 'cultural revolutionary' political terror which they so much feared to see return. But now that same man successively eliminated his two chosen heirs, and unleashed a massive campaign of intimidation, persecution and terror, complete with appeals for public informing on opponents, torture of political prisoners, show trials, ruthless suppression of 'deviant' opinions, rigid censorship of the press, and systematic harassment of intellectuals. All the ills that Deng and his faction had denounced for ten years were reintroduced on his own initiative.[129]

Probably, Deng still believes that by defending the Chinese nomenklatura's monopoly of power and huge material privileges, he can save his economic policy of the 'four modernizations'. It remains to be seen to what extent this will prove true. But the essential lesson lies elsewhere. By sticking to power politics and the axiom 'dictatorship of the proletariat = rule by the Party leadership', Deng has become a prisoner of the very forces inside the bureaucracy that he initially tried, if not to suppress, then at least to curtail. What prevailed was not some 'intrinsic logic of liberalization' but the exercise of political power by the nomenklatura, in some of its most repressive terrorist forms.

A rejection of the substitutionist dogmas is an essential condition for consistent struggle against the bureaucratic degeneration of workers' organizations and workers' states. It in no way entails any spontaneist illusion about the class struggle, and is fully compatible with the much-needed efforts to build revolutionary vanguard parties. But it does require a correct view of the dialectical interrelation between the self-activity and self-organization of the class, on the one hand, and the vanguard party on the other. The classical formulation of that relationship was given by Trotsky:

> The dynamic of revolutionary events is directly determined by swift, intense and passionate changes in the psychology of classes which have already formed themselves before the revolution. . . .
>
> The masses go into a revolution not with a prepared plan of social reconstruction, but with a sharp feeling that they cannot endure the old regime. Only the guiding layers of a class have a political programme, and even this still requires the test of events, and the approval of the masses. The fundamental political process of the revolution thus consists in the gradual comprehension by a class of the problems arising from the social crisis – the active orientation of the masses by a method of successive approximations. . . .

Only on the basis of a study of political processes in the masses themselves, can we understand the role of parties and leaders, whom we least of all are inclined to ignore. They constitute not an independent, but nevertheless a very important, element in the process. Without a guiding organization the energy of the masses would dissipate like steam not enclosed in a piston-box. But nevertheless what moves things is not the piston or the box, but the steam.[130]

NOTES

1. It is true that for a time, Bebel, Kautsky and others maintained that the game would change if the ruling class directly threatened universal suffrage. But this reservation was progressively dropped. See, among others, M. Salvadori, *Karl Kautsky and the Socialist Revolution*, London 1979.

2. Recently, the leadership of the German trade-union federation has stated that the main reason why the SPD capitulated on 4 August 1914 and voted for the war budget was that it needed to defend the organization against the threat of repression and prohibition. *Referentenmaterial*, 1 May 1990.

3. It is sometimes added that the Party can make mistakes, but these can and must be corrected only through the normal channels of 'democratic centralism' (that is, in reality, bureaucratic hyper-centralism). For the thesis of the non-working-class character of all non-CP organizations, see the Stalinist Bible *History of the Communist Party of the Soviet Union (Bolsheviks): Short Course*, Moscow 1939, p. 359. The logical conclusion is the rejection of a genuine united-front policy, which can only be based upon the concept of the working-class movement as an organic whole. When the Stalinists do propose united fronts, it is only as a manoeuvre. This reached the heights of criminal folly in the 1929–33 period, when it was asserted that social democracy (or 'social fascism') had to be smashed before the Nazis could be defeated.

4. Whether differences could also be 'voiced' and fought out on the Central Committee was a more controversial question. But in practice this never happened after 1930, except under conditions of a de facto mass uprising.

5. The 1927 Congress of the RCP marked another major turning-point. The Opposition was called upon not only to apply discipline – that is, to defend majority positions in public – but actually to speak out against its own convictions and state that they had been wrong. In China the Maoist bureaucracy made a particular dogma out of the obligation of prisoners to recant and admit their 'guilt'.

6. Already in 1927, forged documents were circulated in the Party according to which the Opposition was delivering state secrets to foreign powers and trying to use the army for a *coup d'état*. See Michael Reiman, *The Birth of Stalinism*, London 1987, pp. 124–28.

7. In 1937 Stalin formally instructed the NKVD to employ torture in the interrogation of political opponents – a practice which had already probably been quite widespread on an unofficial basis. Many details on the use of torture to extract confessions are contained in the new edition of Roy Medvedev's *Let History Judge*, pp. 490f. At work here was a medieval concept of 'justice' according to which guilt had to be proved by confession or – what often amounted to the same – by incapacity to resist physical pain. The tortured person deserved to be tortured, because he was 'most probably guilty' in advance. A moving account of the psychological implications of this obsession is contained in the memoirs of one of China's leading journalists, Liu Binyan, *A Higher Kind of Loyalty*, New York 1990.

8. Dominique Desanti, *Les Staliniens*, Paris 1975, pp. 216f. After 1944 a large majority of intellectuals in France supported the Communist Party and servilely submitted to brain-washing about 'Hitlero-Trotskyism' by semi-illiterate Party bureaucrats.

9. H. Gortzak, *Hoop zonder Illusies*, Amsterdam 1985, pp. 126–27.

10. J.T. Murphy, *Stalin*, Zurich 1945 (published by Gutenberg, a social-democratic publishing house!), pp. 210–13. To his shame, Stafford Cripps wrote a glowing preface to Murphy's book. Walter Duranty, then Moscow correspondent of the *New York Times*, completely and persistently defended all the Stalinist frame-ups. See S.J. Taylor, *Stalin's Apologist*, Oxford 1990.

11. Rudolf Herrnstadt, *Das Herrnstadt Dokument*, Berlin 1990, pp. 182–83, 163, 173, 25. Herrnstadt's book on the origins of the concept of class (*Die Entdeckung der Klassen*, Berlin/GDR 1965) is an interesting and valuable work.

12. Merle Fainsod, *Smolensk under Soviet Rule*, Cambridge, Mass. 1958; Nicolas Werth, *Etre communiste en URSS sous Staline*, Paris 1981.

13. Quoted from Werth, p. 164.

14. The widow of Kuusinen, Stalin's main adviser on international policies, has stated that as early as 1937 her husband reformulated the idea of international revolution to coincide with territorial expansion of the USSR. Aino Kuusinen, *Der Gott stürzt seine Engel*, pp. 320, 106, 159–64.

15. The term 'Leninism', not to speak of 'Marxism–Leninism', was never used in Lenin's lifetime. It was coined by Zinoviev after Lenin's death, to justify the campaign against 'Trotskyism' and to weld together the Zinoviev–Kamenev–Stalin–Bukharin–Rykov–Tomsky grouping against the Opposition.

16. The classical formulations on the role of a vanguard are to be found in section II, 'Proletarians and Communists', of the *Communist Manifesto*. 'The Communists are distinguished from the other working-class parties by this only: (1) In the national struggles of the proletarians of the different countries, they point out and bring to the front the common interests of the entire proletariat, independently of all nationality. (2) In the various stages of development which the struggle of the working class against the bourgeoisie has to pass through, they always and everywhere represent the interests of the movement as a whole. The Communists, therefore, are on the one hand, practically, the most advanced and resolute section of the working-class parties of every country, that section which pushes forward all others; on the other hand, theoretically, they have over the great mass of the proletariat the advantage of clearly understanding the line of march, the conditions, and the ultimate general results of the proletarian movement.' In K. Marx, *The Revolutions of 1848*, Harmondsworth 1973, pp. 79–80.

17. 'The party needs socialist science, and that can develop only under conditions of freedom.' Engels to Bebel, 1–2 May 1891, in *Marx–Engels Werke*, vol. 38, p. 94.

18. The disastrous Soviet experience of agricultural collectivization, for example, would have been swiftly corrected if it had been possible to debate alternative economic programmes in the CPSU and democratically elected soviets.

19. Cf. Lenin: 'All members of the Party must make a calm and painstaking study of (1) the essence of the disagreements and (2) the development of the Party struggle. . . . A study must be made of both, and a demand made for the most exact, printed documents that can be thoroughly verified. Only a hopeless idiot will believe oral statements. If no documents are available, there must be an examination of witnesses on both or several sides and the grilling must take place in the presence of witnesses.' 'The Party Crisis' (19 January 1921), in *Collected Works*, vol. 32, pp. 43–44.

20. Cf. Rosa Luxemburg: 'Far from being a sum of ready-made prescriptions which have only to be applied, the practical realization of socialism as an economic, social and juridical system is something which lies completely hidden in the mists of the future. What we possess in our programme is nothing but a few main signposts. . . . But when it comes to the nature of the thousand concrete, practical measures, large and small, necessary to introduce socialist principles into economy, law and all social relationships, there is no key in any socialist party programme or textbook. . . . If such is the case, then it is clear that socialism by its very nature cannot be decreed or introduced by ukase. . . . Only experience is capable of correcting and opening new ways. Only unobstructed, effervescing life falls into a thousand new forms and improvisations, brings to light creative force, itself corrects all mistaken attempts.' 'The Russian Revolution', in *Rosa Luxemburg Speaks*, ed. Mary-Alice Waters, New York 1970, p. 390.

21. The late Hal Draper rightly insisted on the fact that this thesis embodied Marx's main contribution to the evolution of socialist ideas. See especially H. Draper, *Karl Marx's Theory of Revolution*, vol. 2, New York 1977.

22. Obviously an open civil war creates exceptional circumstances in which temporary restrictions may be introduced. In July 1936 in Spain, for example, after Franco's armies had drawn the battle-lines with their military offensive, neither the anarchists nor the social democrats were in favour of allowing the Falange to publish newspapers or to enjoy other democratic rights.

23. For a discussion of Trotsky's ideas on this question, see E. Mandel, 'La théorie de Trotsky sur le rapport entre l'auto-organisation de la classe et le parti d'avant-garde', *Quatrième Internationale*, April 1990.

24. 'The Russian Revolution', p. 391. Objectivity requires us to note that Rosa herself had her 'dark years'. In 1912–14, when faced with a dissident faction in the Warsaw party that included Hanecki and Radek, she did not hesitate to accuse them of being manipulated by the Tsarist secret police.

25. *Collected Works*, vol. 10, p. 310.

26. *Marx–Engels Werke*, vol. 32, p. 570.

27. F. Engels, Letter to Florence Kelley-Wischnewetzky, 28 December 1886, in *Marx–Engels Werke*, vol. 36, p. 589.

28. Letter to Sorge, 9 August 1890, in *Marx–Engels Werke*, vol. 37, p. 440.

29. See, among others, Wolfgang Ruge, 'Wer gab Stalin die Knute in die Hand?', *Neues Deutschland*, 20–21 January 1990; Mark Vandepitte, 'De Aufhebung van Lenin', in *Socialisme en Vrijheid*, Brussels 1990; and the various writings of Yuri Afanasiev.

30. In L. Trotsky, *Schriften zur revolutionäre Organisation*, Hamburg 1970, p. 73. Similar formulations can be found in the writings of Axelrod, Martov and Luxemburg. While Trotsky's assessment of Lenin was unjust, some of his warnings on the relationship between powerful and over-confident committees and working-class mass activity have been confirmed by history.

31. *Collected Works*, vol. 13, pp. 103–104.

32. *Collected Works*, vol. 10, pp. 19, 20, 21. Emphasis in the original.

33. Ibid., pp. 310–11.

34. Ibid., pp. 442–43.

35. A useful summary of Lenin's more 'libertarian' statements can be found in Marcel Liebman, *Leninism under Lenin*, London 1975.

36. Ralph Carter Elwood, *Resolutions and Decisions of the Communist Party of the Soviet Union*, p. 83. This and most other quotes here are taken from Paul Leblanc, *Lenin and the Revolutionary Party*, New York/London 1990.

37. Elwood, p. 87.

38. *Short Course*, p. 49. It should be noted that, under the Stalinist dictatorship, Party congresses and Central Committee meetings took place less and less frequently.

39. Ibid., p. 49. Cf. Ivan Pronine and Mikhail Stépichev, *Les normes léninistes de la vie du parti*, Moscow 1969, p. 74.

40. Pronine and Stépichev, p. 109. Underlying that 'rule' is the assumption that the leadership is always right. The former director of the Chinese Academy of Social Sciences, Su Shaozhi, stated in a critical comment on the tenth anniversary of the CCP Central Committee that initiated the reform course in December 1978: 'Nobody has the right to judge whether one is a Marxist or not.' *Shanghai World Economic Herald*, 26 December 1988, quoted in *Das Argument*, September/October 1989.

41. L. Onikov, *Probleme der Entwicklung der innerparteilichen Demokratie*. Onikov appears to represent the conservative wing of the Gorbachev apparatus. His insistence on a 'fluctuating' relationship between centralism and democracy leads to an explicit call for a stronger central authority today, while ignoring the need for permanent respect of certain minimum norms of democracy.

42. 'Le Tournant', *Nouvelles de Moscou*, 15 October 1989.

43. See 'Platform of the 46', in *The Challenge of the Left Opposition*, New York 1984.

44. A.P. Butenko, in *Voprosy Filosofii*, 1987, No. 2, p. 27.

45. See E.H. Carr, *The Bolshevik Revolution*, Harmondsworth 1966; and L.N. Kritzman, *Die heroische Periode der grossen russischen Revolution*, Frankfurt 1971, p. 252.

46. I.A.L. Rosenfeld, *Promyshlennaia politika SSSR*, Moscow 1926, quoted in Tony Cliff, *Lenin*, vol. 3, London 1978, p. 113.

47. Kritzman, p. 135.

48. Cliff, p. 89.

49. The divergence between industry and agriculture eventually led to the opening of a 'price scissors' that favoured the former over the latter and threatened the worker–peasant alliance. This was to become a growing concern of the Left Opposition and Trotsky from 1923 on.

50. For example, whenever the Mensheviks or SR factions came out against the White armies and counter-revolutionary governments, they were allowed to function legally on Soviet territory.

51. L. Trotsky, *The Revolution Betrayed*, London 1967, pp. 104–105.

52. V. Serge, *Year One of the Russian Revolution*, London 1972, p. 264.

53. The Bolsheviks' main proletarian leader, the Petrograd metalworker Shlyapnikov, half-jokingly and half-seriously apostrophized Lenin at the Tenth Party Congress: 'I congratulate you, Comrade Lenin, for exercising the dictatorship of the proletariat in the name of a non-existent proletariat.' Shlyapnikov headed the Workers' Opposition which, in spite of many errors, formulated most of the criticisms of the Party apparatus that would later be taken up in the 1923 Platform of the Left Opposition. See R. Daniels, *The Conscience of the Revolution*, Cambridge, Mass. 1960, chs. 5 & 6; and the selection in Kool and Oberländer, eds, *Arbeiterdemokratie oder Parteidiktatur*, Olten 1967, pp. 158–263.

54. *Collected Works*, vol. 32, p. 21.

55. L. Trotsky, *The First Five Years of the Communist International*, vol. 1, New York 1945, pp. 99–100.

56. This expression is actually taken from a speech by Plekhanov at the Second Congress of the RSDLP.

57. Quoted in Isaac Deutscher, *The Prophet Armed*, London 1954, pp. 508–509. In chapter 14 of that book, Deutscher gives several other examples of Trotsky's use of substitutionist formulations in 1920 and 1921.

58. Moshe Lewin's *Lenin's Last Struggle* (London 1969) offers a useful review of what happened in early 1923 within the CPSU leadership, although a full balance-sheet of Lenin's struggle with the bureaucracy has still to be written.

59. In Lenin, *Collected Works*, vol. 33, p. 314.

60. Ibid., pp. 428–29.

61. 'Better Fewer But Better', in ibid., p. 487.

62. Ibid., p. 288.

63. Lenin, *Selected Works*, Moscow 1977, p. 677.

64. Letter to A.D. Tsyurupa, 21 February 1922, in *Collected Works*, vol. 36, p. 566.

65. The attack had actually begun with Lenin's article 'How We Should Reorganize the Workers' and Peasants' Inspection', in *Collected Works*, vol. 33, pp. 481–86.

66. See his letter to the Politburo of 20 May 1922, in ibid., pp. 363–67.

67. In his posthumously published work *Stalin* (vol. 2, London 1969, p. 170), Trotsky asserts that Stalin presented the Party with a *fait accompli* by ordering the invasion of Georgia against the wishes of an overwhelming majority of the population.

68. For several years a new legend has been circulating that Trotsky shied away from Lenin's proposal of a bloc against Stalin. But documents recently published in the Soviet press (*Moscow News*, 22 April 1990) confirm that Trotsky alone on the Politburo voted in favour of communicating to all delegates the contents of Lenin's letter to the Twelfth Party Congress.

69. Trotsky, *Stalin*, vol. 2, pp. 177–78.

70. See the report of the conversations of the Soviet novelist Alexander Bek with Lenin's secretaries, in *Nouvelles de Moscou*, 23 April 1989.

71. *Stalin*, pp. 229–30.

72. V. Danilov, 'We Are Starting To Learn about Trotsky', translated in *History Workshop Journal*, Spring 1990, from the Siberian magazine *Eko*, Nos. 9–10, 1989.

73. Andrei Sorokin (member of the CPSU's Institute of Marxism–Leninism), in *Soviet Weekly*, 3 May 1990. Samuel Farber (*Before Stalinism*, Cambridge 1990) gives a much more critical account of Lenin's and Trotsky's attitude to soviet democracy from 1918 on. He asserts that Lenin opposed the legalization of other soviet parties that had been proposed by, among others, a leading Chekist. But the evidence recently come to light, as well as Farber's own account, are much more contradictory. He himself states that in 1921 Kamenev and Bukharin favoured such legalization.

Virtually from the time of its creation, the Cheka showed a marked tendency to become autonomous, and various figures – Latsis most clearly – sought to theorize this process. At the same time, serious phenomena of material corruption began to appear in its ranks. See V.A. Zhdanov's sharp denunciation of 11 July 1918, reproduced in *Nouvelles de Moscou*, 2 April 1989. Such criticisms were often supported by Lenin.

74. Dzerzhinsky is said to have stated in the mid-twenties that a Soviet Bonaparte was arising who would kill all the leading Bolsheviks. But it is unclear whether even then he believed, like so many in 1923–24, that Trotsky rather than Stalin would play that role.

75. 'So, in an amazingly brief space of time, an extremely strong central authority grew out of the anarchy that was the first, immediate consequence of the October Revolution – a power which, resting on an army and a huge bureaucratic apparatus, has transformed the local soviets into bodies merely governing themselves and secured for itself the decisive power throughout the realm. . . .

'There is a risk that the proletarian rank and file will become too meagre for the immense apparatus of domination erected on top of it. And insofar as this happens, the proletariat loses the power to direct and control the apparatus of domination it has built. The command structure of the Soviet bureaucracy and the Red Army begins to detach itself from the proletarian native soil, to make itself independent. It threatens to become an autonomous power standing above the class which only represents the idea of the proletariat, but whose despotic power, in reality, is exercised not only over the bourgeoisie and the peasantry but also over the mass of the proletariat itself.' Otto Bauer, 'Bolschewismus oder Sozialdemokratie' (1920), in *Werkausgabe*, vol. 2, Vienna 1976, pp. 279–80.

76. 'Die illegale Partei', in *Werkausgabe*, vol. 4.

77. Ibid., pp. 491–93.

78. 'Einführung in die Volkswirtschaftslehre', in ibid., pp. 866, 967–69.

79. Ibid., pp. 854, 859, 861.

80. Ibid., pp. 862, 863–64.

81. Ibid., p. 865.

82. 'Der Trotzkismus und die Trotzkistenprozesse', *Der Kampf*, 1937, No. 3, in *Werkausgabe*, vol. 9, pp. 711–12, 716–17.

83. Antonio Gramsci, *Selections from the Prison Notebooks*, eds Quintin Hoare and Geoffrey Nowell-Smith, London 1971, p. 155.

84. Ibid., pp. 238–39.

85. John Hoffman (*The Gramscian Challenge*, London 1984) manages to present Trotsky as the arch-advocate of coercion of the working class in the Soviet Union. A lifelong struggle against substitutionism, seventeen years of struggle against bureaucratic despotism, are wiped out with a quick stroke of the pen. As for Stalin, he is supposed to have had a more reasonable attitude of combining coercion with consent from below. A million communists killed – 'with consent from below'?

86. On the concept of latency in historical materialism, see Chapter 5 below.

87. When Stalin annexed Western Ukraine and Western Byelorussia under the terms of his pact with Hitler, he did not gain so much as twenty-four hours' respite against the Nazis' eventual military onslaught (except in the fortress of Brest-Litovsk). The direct military losses may even have been greater than the benefits as a result. On the other hand, the long-term political consequences were disastrous. The secret protocols of the pact with Hitler had strictly prohibited any propaganda in favour of a reconstituted Polish state, and the Polish Communist Party had been dissolved to assist in the imposition of these measures upon a resistant population. Thus, after the change in alliances in 1941, anti-Soviet hostility was so great, and Polish nationalism so resurgent, that the Polish Communists found

themselves unable to lead the national liberation struggle in the way that their comrades could do in Yugoslavia.

88. We shall discuss the concept of consensus politics, which is implied by vulgar realpolitik, in Chapter 5.

89. Letter to Kugelmann, 23 February 1865, in *Marx–Engels Selected Correspondence*, Moscow 1975, p. 159.

90. Quoted by Daniel Aaron in the *New York Review of Books*, 15 June 1989, from Dorothy Gallagher, *All the Right Enemies: The Life and Murder of Carlo Tresca*, Rutgers University Press, 1988.

91. 'The worst of it was that in a state where power was supposed to belong to the workers and peasants, most of the detainees were workers and peasants.' Sandor Kopacsi, p. 62.

92. 'The party leadership needs it [the apparat] to stay as it is, big, obsequious, obedient and unchanging.' Boris Yeltsin, p. 127. In his novel *Children of the Arbat*, Rybakov shows how this negative selection process could also be 'positive' for some children of the nomenklatura in the early stages of the Stalinist dictatorship.

Trotsky's most important remarks on the question are contained in three passages from *Stalin*: 'Stalin began to emerge with increasing prominence as the organizer, the assigner of tasks, the dispenser of jobs, the trainer and master of the bureaucracy. He chose his men by their hostility or indifference towards his various opponents and particularly toward him whom he regarded as his chief opponent. . . . Stalin generalized and classified his own administrative experience, chiefly the experience of systematically conniving behind the scenes, and made it available to those most closely associated with him. He taught them to organize their local machines on the pattern of his own machine; how to recruit collaborators, how to utilize their weaknesses, how to set comrades at odds with each other, how to run the machine. . . . he is deaf and blind to the formation of a whole privileged caste welded together by the bond of honour among thieves, by their common interest [as privileged exploiters of the whole body politic] and by their ever-growing remoteness from the people.' *Stalin*, vol. 2, p. 205.

'Not all the young revolutionists of the Tsarist era [were story-book heroes]. There were also among them some who did not bear themselves with sufficient courage during investigation. If they made up for that by their subsequent behaviour, the Party did not expel them irrevocably and took them back into its ranks. In 1923 Stalin, as General Secretary, began to concentrate all such evidence in his own hands and to use it to blackmail hundreds of old revolutionists who had more than redeemed this early weakness. By threatening to expose their past record, he browbeat these people into slavish obedience and reduced them step by step to a state of complete demoralization.' Ibid., p. 211.

'In the early period of the Soviet power the old revolutionary party was purging itself of careerists; in line with that, the committees were composed of revolutionary workers. Adventurers or careerists or simply scoundrels trying to attach themselves to the government in quite considerable numbers were cast overboard. But the purges of recent years were, on the contrary, fully and completely directed against the old revolutionary party. The organizers of the purges were the most bureaucratic and the most low-calibre elements of the Party. . . . Even these bands of the gilded youth are nowadays included in the Party and in the League of Communist Youth. These were the field detachments, recruited from the sons of the bourgeoisie, privileged young men resolutely ready to defend their own privileged position or the position of their parents. It is sufficient to point to the fact that at the head of the League of Communist Youth for a number of years stood Kossarev, generally known to be a moral degenerate who misused his high position to advance his personal objectives.' Ibid., pp. 237–38.

93. Freud discusses these phenomena in his work *Civilization and Its Discontents*.

94. Reich correctly insisted upon the importance of sexuality within the general need for individual freedom, but he later tended to give it excessive priority.

95. All references to Reich's ideas are based on Wilhelm Reich, *People in Trouble*, New York 1976; those to Bernfeld on his articles, especially 'Die Tantalussituation', reprinted in Helmut Dahmer, ed., *Analytische Sozialpsychologie*, 2 vols, Frankfurt 1980.

Among other interesting contributions to this work are pieces by Talcott Parsons, Horkheimer, Adorno, Habermas and Paul Parin.

96. Speech at the Thirteenth Party Conference, 16–18 January 1924, quoted in Trotsky, *Stalin*, vol. 2, p. 186.

97. Translated in N.I. Bukharin, *Selected Writings on the State and the Transition to Socialism*, ed. Richard B. Day, Nottingham 1982.

98. *Kommunist* No. 1, 20 April 1918.

99. Reprinted in N.I. Bukharin, *The Politics and Economics of the Transition Period*, London 1979.

100. Bukharin and Preobrazhensky, *The ABC of Communism*, Harmondsworth 1969, pp. 238–39.

101. *Collected Works*, vol. 32, p. 48.

102. *Historical Materialism: a System of Sociology*, University of Michigan, 1969, pp. 310, 311.

103. *Proletarskaia revoliutsiia i kul'tura*, Moscow 1923, p. 38.

104. Ibid., pp. 44–45. Emphasis added.

105. Ibid., pp. 48, 50. Emphasis added.

106. Bukharin, 'Die Partei und der Oppositionblock', speech of 28 July 1926, in Ulf Wolter, ed., *Die Linke Opposition in der Sowjet-Union, 1923–1928*, vol. 4, West Berlin 1976, pp. 156–57.

107. Bukharin, *Les problèmes de la construction du socialisme*, p. 266. Cf. in English *Building Up Socialism*, London 1926, p. 33.

108. *The Road to Socialism*, reprinted in *Selected Writings*. See especially pp. 274–81.

109. In *Die Linke Opposition*, vol. 5, pp. 464, 524–25; vol. 4, p. 469.

110. *Pravda*, 30 September 1928, quoted from A.G. Löwy, *Die Weltgeschichte ist das Weltgericht*, Vienna 1969, p. 363.

111. *Pravda*, 24 January 1929, quoted here from the German version 'Das politische Vermächtnis Lenins', in *Sozialismus*, September 1988, which is itself derived from the Italian translation of the Russian original.

112. Quoted from Löwy, p. 370.

113. Historians have argued about whether this 'letter' is based solely on Nicolaevsky's notes or was actually composed by Bukharin (or Bukharin and Rykov). See Stephen F. Cohen, *Bukharin and the Bolshevik Revolution*, London 1974, pp. 471–72. The letter's basic authenticity has not generally been contested, although Bukharin's widow does do this in Anna Larina-Bucharina, *Nun bin ich über zwanzig*, Göttingen 1989, pp. 316–23.

114. See Roy Medvedev, *Let History Judge*, New York 1971, pp. 182–84.

115. Ibid.

116. Löwy, p. 387. This report, which was published on the eve of Bukharin's execution, should not be confused with the above-mentioned *Letter from an Old Bolshevik*.

117. Cohen, p. 325.

118. See Pierre Broué, *Trotsky*, Paris 1988, pp. 353–59.

119. The Soviet author Mikhail Gefter clearly grasps this unity fetishism when he asks: 'And the Bukharin of 1928? What counted first and foremost for him? To defend the NEP against Stalin, or to preserve party unity even at the price of his own capitulation?' In Aganbegyan et al., *La seule voie*, op. cit., p. 91. See also Batkin's contribution to the same volume.

120. See Anna Larina-Bucharina, pp. 407–18.

121. This is how Trotsky put the matter: 'But, one of the Stalinists or their followers will say, don't you see that the Central Committee is making ready to purge the party of its rightists and that means precisely that Stalin is taking measures against Thermidor. No, we reply, the bureaucratic "purge" only facilitates the work of Thermidor. The new purge, like all those of the last ten years, will be directed against the Left Opposition and others, in general against the proletarian elements who think and criticize. . . . But even where the blows fall on the right wing they do not strengthen the party but weaken it. In the right wing, alongside of genuinely Thermidorean elements, there are others – hundreds of thousands, perhaps millions – who are deeply hostile to capitalist restoration but demand

the revision of the entire policy from the point of view of the town and country workers. The programme of these rightists is confused. They may become provisionally a prop for Thermidor; but they may also support the revival of the party along the revolutionary road. The Stalinist bureaucracy prevents them from understanding the situation. By its purge it tends primarily to stifle critical thought.' 'The Danger of Thermidor', in *Writings 1932–1933*, p. 79.

122. Stephen F. Cohen (p. 327) correctly points out that during the crucial formative years of the Stalinist dictatorship, Stalin tended to represent a consensus within the oligarchy, rather than being the protagonist of a specific policy line.

123. There are numerous books on the subject, one of the best being Maurice Meisner, *Mao's China*, London 1977. See also Livio Maitan, *Party, Army and Class*, London 1975.

124. Although Mao does not use the term 'bureaucracy', he explicitly denounces such typical practices as 'one-man management' at factory level, great income differentials, and the 'castification' of cadres' children. (See Helmut Martin, ed., *Mao Tse-tungs Notizen zum sowjetischen Lehrbuch Politische Oekonomie*, Hamburg 1975, pp. 82–84, 99, 114–15 and *passim*.) But after loftily proclaiming the people's 'basic right' to administer the state (and thus state industry), he lamely arrives at the conclusion that the factory manager's authority should be subordinated to that of the party committee. 'The people' = the Party committee. He cannot conceive of workers' management, least of all through freely elected workers' councils.

It is a subject of controversy whether Mao's 'anti-bureaucratic' inclination was a genuine reaction to negative developments in the USSR and China, or whether it was a result of his being put in a minority within the CCP leadership against the majority of the bureaucracy ranged behind the Li–Deng faction. The extreme bureaucratization of state and party in the 1949–64 period (vividly described in A. Doak Barnett, *Cadres, Bureaucracy and Political Power in Communist China*, New York 1967) tends to weigh in the direction of the first hypothesis.

125. On the conflicts within the Red Guards and Revolutionary Rebels, see Maitan.

126. Mao's alliance with Lin Piao, officially proclaimed his heir at the Ninth Party Congress, was based on the latter's control of the army. On the rise and fall of the Shanghai workers' commune, see Meisner.

127. See Mao Tse-tung, p. 60.

128. See *Selected Works of Deng Xiaoping 1975–1982*, Beijing 1984, p. 172. The four cardinal principles are: The socialist road equals the dictatorship of the proletariat, which can be exercised only under the leadership of the Communist Party, which must base itself upon Marxism–Leninism–Mao Zedong Thought.

129. On the terrorist nature of the repression of the Beijing Commune, and its exemplary function of warning the entire Chinese people against mass movements not controlled by the leadership, see among others *Massacre in Beijing*, a report by the International League for Human Rights and the Ad Hoc Study Group on Human Rights in China; Fathers/Higgins, *Tiananmen: The Rape of Peking*, New York 1989; and Simmie/Nixon, *Tiananmen Square*, Washington 1989. On the political paralysis resulting from Deng's repressive course, see among other sources the interview with Liu Binyan in *New York Review of Books*.

130. Trotsky, *History of the Russian Revolution*, vol. 1, London 1967, pp. 15–16.

4

Administration and Profit Realization: The Growth of Bourgeois Bureaucracies

1. The State Apparatus under Capitalism

In the course of its rise to historical dominance, the revolutionary bourgeoisie by and large appropriated the absolutist state apparatus and remoulded it to serve its own purposes.[1] It *could* do so because it was confident that its wealth and economic power would in the final analysis impose its will on any state. It *had to* do so because its class rule could not, and never can, rely exclusively upon its main weapon: economic compulsion.

The security of bourgeois political rule requires an acceptance of economic compulsion on the part of the great majority of the population who are not capitalists. This might be possible under normal circumstances. But from time to time sections of the masses rebel against the conditions of subordination, exploitation and oppression in which they are locked. Against such revolts, even if they are just potential, lay-offs, unemployment, the threat of starvation are not enough.[2] They can even have the effect of fuelling mass action.

In order to reduce the risks or to see it through explosive moments, the bourgeoisie needs both an apparatus of repression – '*la violence sans phrases*' – and an apparatus of ideological indoctrination of the exploited and oppressed, above all of the wage-earning proletariat. The bourgeois state thus plays a vital role for the reproduction of capitalist relations of production, without which capital accumulation cannot take place. Moreover, although surplus-value is the only source of capital and is essentially produced in the production process, the state also serves a key regulatory function in the capitalist economy.

The nature of capitalism is such that it can only exist under the form of many capitals – that is, of private ownership and competition. For the

153

same reason, no private capitalist or group of capitalists can express the general interests of the capitalist class in crucial fields of economic activity. In the political field this is even more obviously the case.

The 'ideal' or 'general' capitalist, then, can only be a non-capitalist, someone not directly engaged in the pursuit of profit maximization. The role of securing the general conditions of capitalist production and profit realization – for example, a well-functioning monetary system, an efficient fiscal and tariff structure – has to be transferred by the bourgeois class to special apparatuses, to the state. Otherwise, profit realization cannot occur under optimal, or even satisfactory, circumstances.

For specific historical reasons modern capitalism, already in its commercial and manufacturing phase but much more in the age of industrial and financial capital, has been structured by competing nation-states and their associated empires. The national market was the natural framework for the productive forces as they had developed up to the end of the nineteenth century. While international trade, unequal exchange and plunder of other countries (especially in Central and South America, Africa and Asia) counted for a great deal in the accumulation of Western, and later Japanese, capital, the production and realization of surplus-value were in the main geared to the national market.[3] For a whole period of transition, at least in the major countries, the level of development of the productive forces actually remained *below* the absorptive capacity of national markets. The revolutionary bourgeoisie had to fight to overcome pre-capitalist restrictions to free trade, while also protecting itself against an 'excessive' invasion of foreign goods.

Therefore, independently of any political considerations such as the socially integrative function of nationalist ideology, the capitalists' struggle to consolidate nation-states implied a transfer of competition to the international arena, to inter-state relations. Not only did bourgeois states need policemen, priests and teachers devoted to the defence of private property. They also needed armies and navies – more special apparatuses to which individual capitalists, and even the bourgeoisie as a class, could reliably surrender some of their sovereign rights and part of their income.

To be sure, acceptance of a powerful state machine is by no means the only tradition.[4] The young bourgeoisie had quite an experience of self-government,[5] which found ideological–political expression in a great distrust of the state. There was even a current of libertarian or semi-libertarian ideas which reached its peak in Jean-Jacques Rousseau and can in many respects be considered the direct forerunner of Marx's and Lenin's ideas about self-organization and self-rule of the toilers.[6]

However, as a 'fourth estate' of proto- or semi-proletarians began to

Table 3 Total Tax Receipts as % of GNP

	1955	1980
W. Germany	30.8	37.2
Britain	29.8	35.9
USA	23.6	30.7
Canada	21.7	32.8
Switzerland	19.2	30.7
Belgium	24.0	42.5
Netherlands	26.3	46.2
Sweden	25.5	49.9

Source: Figures from Eva Etzioui-Halevy, *Bureaucracy and Democracy*, London 1983, p. 119.

accompany the bourgeoisie in its historical rise, introducing its own practices of self-activity or even self-rule[7], the capitalists increasingly shied away from 'anti-statist' excesses. 'Law and order' now had to prevail at all costs, and that is impossible without a strong state. For a long period the real struggle within the ruling classes centred on the level of taxation that should be exacted from profits for the upkeep of the state. The very origins of parliament and the bourgeois revolutions lay there.

With the development of a mass labour movement and the entry of capitalism into its imperialist phase, the bourgeois state had a tendency to grow stronger and stronger – and to eat up ever larger sums of money. Thus, the US federal revenue collections moved from 1.3 per cent of GNP in 1880–81 to 3.3 per cent in 1930–31 and 18.1 per cent in 1960–61, while in Australia the totals climbed from 4.2 per cent of GNP in 1902–1903 to 8.6 per cent in 1932–33 and 17.1 per cent in 1960–61. As Table 3 shows, the tendency for taxation to rise faster than production and national income has continued.

Accordingly, the bourgeoisie remains divided between those who are and those who are not prepared to pay the price, or rather between proponents of various options and balances in commercial, monetary, social and international policy, each of which may require a quite different level or distribution of fiscal resources. But whatever the intensity of such disputes, government expenditure without transfer payments (that is, without revenue just transiting through state or para-state budgets) rose sharply between 1960 and 1974: for example, in Britain from 20.1 per cent to 38 per cent of GNP, and in Sweden from 25 per cent to 28.9 percent. In 1990, after more than a decade of ideological fanfares and demagogic mystification, government spending in the seven largest OECD countries stood at around 39 per cent of GDP.[8]

Late capitalism is indeed strong-state capitalism, in which all the functions of the state tend to increase. But, more particularly, the executive branch grows out of all proportion with the legislative and judicial branches. This is a reaction of the system to the changed relationship of forces between the classes which results from the advance of the mass labour movement and its penetration into parliaments, municipalities and other such bodies.[9] Ellul even asserts: 'In fact, the politician no longer has any real choice: decisions follow automatically from the preparatory technical labours.'[10]

The stronger the labour movement becomes within society, the greater is the danger that economic crises or big strike waves will lead to political explosions or pre-revolutionary situations, and the more the bourgeois state has to develop a new function of crisis-management.[11] This may take the preventive form of social legislation. It may take the operative form of state intervention in the economy to reduce the scale of economic fluctuations.[12] Or it may take repressive forms in an attempt to impose wage-freezes or to restrict trade-union freedoms and the right to strike. But each possibility implies a stronger executive branch of government. A growing number of civil servants is required to draft and apply various laws, decrees, budgets, monetary regulations, industrial and infrastructural policies, and so on.[13] These are submitted to governments and (less and less) to parliaments, which in nine cases out of ten rubber-stamp them without much ado. To paraphrase a classic saying: ministers and MPs come and go, but top civil servants and policemen remain.[14]

Etzioni-Halevy quotes a significant comment from the Fulton Committee report on the British Civil Service (1968):

> Because the solution to complex problems needs long preparation, the service must be far-sighted; from its accumulated knowledge and experience, it must show initiative in working out what are the needs of the future and how they might be met. A special responsibility now rests upon the Civil Service because one Parliament or even one Government often cannot see the process through.[15]

When one says 'the bourgeois state has a tendency to become a stronger and stronger state', one implies the growth of capitalist state bureaucracies. The first tendency is impossible without the second; indeed it is largely identical with it.

In the late twentieth century, we now have not tens but hundreds of thousands of state functionaries, and in some larger countries – depending on one's definition – several million. Central government employ-

Table 4   Growth of Public Employees in USA since World War Two

	Total number	Government/non-government ratio
1947	5,791,000	.10
1952	7,104,000	.11
1957	8,046,000	.12
1962	9,388,000	.14
1967	11,867,000	.15
1972	13,333,000	.16
1977	15,019,000	.16
1982	16,197,000	.16

Source: Marshall W. Meyer, William Stevenson, Stephen Webster, *Limits to Bureaucratic Growth*, New York 1985, p. 36.

ment per thousand of population rose in the USA from 0.7 per cent in 1821 and 3.1 per cent in 1901–1902 to 5.3 per cent in 1920–21, 11 per cent in 1941 and 14 per cent in 1970–71. In Britain it increased from 1.4 per cent in 1901–1902 to 2.6 per cent in 1920–21, 3.4 per cent in 1939–40 and 8.6 per cent in 1968.

The rise in the number of public employees is even more impressive, as we can see from Table 4.

These bureaucracies are structured in a way which reflects, without entirely duplicating, the hierarchy of bourgeois society itself. Lower, middle and top capitalist bureaucrats receive quite different incomes, enjoy quite different non-pecuniary benefits, and have quite different possibilities of accumulating capital and integrating themselves into the bourgeois class. They are also recruited from quite different social layers.[16] But the extreme poles of bourgeois society are not reproduced within the capitalist state apparatus. It has no permanently impoverished proletarian layers, nor does it secrete billionaires.[17]

To these various levels of integration into bourgeois society correspond distinctive mechanisms of assuring ideological conformity. Here also, as with the Soviet bureaucracy, what starts as functional ends up becoming social and ideological. A prison governor is a functionary who administers a prison. But no warder could become a governor, and no governor could become a top civil servant in the Ministry of Justice, if he had the unfortunate habit of letting prisoners escape or even setting them free. No fanatical pacifist could become head of staff of an army. The concrete mechanisms of this selection process are not the same as those which filter top politicians or top managers of capitalist firms.[18] But they are quite similar.

At lower levels of functional responsibility, this routine-based con-formism does not operate as smoothly as it did before the First World War. The general crisis of bourgeois social relations and values, which is tending to grow deeper, comes into play here. There can be no safe place for television administrators, teachers, university professors, church leaders, air traffic controllers, or even traffic policemen, who speak out against the iniquities of the capitalist system. Whether they remain steadfast under the threat of repression, whether they lose their job or keep it, will depend upon a number of circumstances. But as long as capital (that is, money) rules, they cannot become the majority in their profession. The function creates the organ. The organ remains bour-geois, with the task of facilitating the reproduction of capitalist relations of production and the general conditions of profit realization.

2. The Rise of the Para-state Bureaucracy

Since the late nineteenth century, the efforts of the mass labour move-ment to force through legislation alleviating the gravest hardships caused by capitalism, as well as a series of preventive social reforms initiated by the bourgeoisie, have led to the gradual, but in the long run phenomenal, growth of a new social stratum: the para-state bureaucracy. In many countries, this is as large as, if not larger than, the state apparatus proper.

The class nature of this stratum is much less precisely defined than that of the state bureaucracy. Part of it originates from the labour bureauc-racy – most obviously in the case of sickness insurance organizations, including hospitals, set up and controlled by the trade unions in Belgium, Argentina and elsewhere. Like the virtual union monopoly on unem-ployment hand-outs in some countries between the wars, such institu-tions significantly broaden the material–financial base of the labour bureaucracies, strengthening their power as well as their grip over the membership.

Both objectively and in terms of ideological implications, this is quite an ambivalent process, as may be seen most clearly in those social reforms in housing and transport which are summed up in the formula 'municipal socialism'. On the one hand, they are ways of asserting non-capitalist, tendentially socialist forms of social organization, values and mentalities. Not 'collectivism' versus 'individualism' but needs versus profits, solidarity and generosity versus egoism and greed, are the real oppositions in this trend towards the sharing of endowments among all: the strong care for the weak. We pity those whose myopic prejudices prevent them from registering this obvious fact. When public transport is made free in two European cities – Bologna and Athens – during the early morning hours when people are going to work, this is a break-through for a socialist mode of distribution, or need satisfaction, as opposed to a bourgeois one. It is even a step forward compared with the endeavours of craft unions, which generally care only for the strongest and best-paid wage-earners. Social reforms of the type we are discussing are designed to take care of all.

But if it is impossible to achieve the building of socialism in one country, it is even more unrealistic to build socialism in one municipality or one production cooperative. The administration of workers' hospitals, cooperative societies or socialist-led municipalities is intertwined by a thousand threads with the general mechanisms of bourgeois society, surplus-value production and profit realization. All need money to function. They even need more money to function better from a class point of view – that is, to assure services of higher quality to the toilers.

In many countries, huge sums of money pass through the hands of the para-state bureaucracy. In France, for example, the social security institutions administer funds practically equal in size to the entire state budget (nearly $250 billion in 1989). This creates a great potential for corruption. It was recently revealed that, in the United States, 10 per cent of health insurance expenditure is based on formally fraudulent claims.[19] Each case should be judged according to the real socialist–humanist criterion – whether it is to the benefit or harm of the patient's health.

Now, all this money must come from somewhere. Either the workers ultimately pay it themselves – which, other things being equal, means that satisfaction of the needs in question will be offset by lesser satisfaction of other needs. Or else it comes out of surplus-value, from taxes on the income or wealth of the capitalists – in which case there is permanent controversy and struggle between capital and labour, as well as between various sections of the bourgeoisie according to their willingness and capacity to pay and their habits of tax evasion.[20]

In this struggle the predominant class relations powerfully assert themselves. Even when the working class and the labour movement make significant gains, some sections of it become undermined, thwarted, deviated from their initial goals, by the way in which they have to interrelate with a functioning capitalist economy.

A free health service will be plundered by private pharmaceutical monopolies or semi-monopolies. The principle of meeting people's needs will be sapped by irresponsible, profit-inspired drugs advertising that stimulates over-consumption to the detriment of the patient's health. The quality of service will be impaired by shortages of funds from the state budget, by low pay for public employees, and by the deficiency of education and information available to the general public. In times of

economic depression – an inevitable periodic feature of capitalism –
major cuts in expenditure will occur. Real-estate speculators will tempt
hospital administrators to sell off land to private owners. And so on and
so forth.

All these considerations in no way diminish the progressive nature and
dynamic of social reforms. But they do indicate their limitations. If the
development of institutions along these lines sets up a trend to bureaucratization, this is not only for reasons of size or because of the need for a
large number of administrators. The para-state bureaucracies have to
fulfil a host of bargaining tasks, arbitrating between those who receive
benefits and those who hand them out, between those who hand them
out and those who fill the kitty, between central government and
municipal administration, between defenders and opponents of these
institutions, between those who criticize some of their unfair, undemoc-
ratic abuses and those who defend the top administrators
unconditionally.

What is true for social benefit institutions arising out of the labour
movement holds even more for those created by the bourgeois state
itself. Here the para-state bureaucracies are tightly integrated into the
bourgeois state apparatus, always keeping in mind its hierarchical structure. But it would be a mistake to draw a sharp counterposition between
'purely bourgeois' and 'purely labour' bureaucracies in this field. As a
strong labour movement has become a structural feature of many
imperialist and some dependent countries in the course of the twentieth
century – except in periods of reactionary dictatorship – so the labour
bureaucracies have deeply interpenetrated with the bourgeois para-state
bureaucracy.

Another development reinforcing this trend has been the growth of a
public sector in the economy owned by the state or the municipalities –
what Engels derisively called 'state socialism' but could more accurately
be described as state capitalism. Again this is not limited to the more
'mature' capitalist countries. In many dependent countries since the
Second World War, where imperialism exerts powerful pressure and the
native bourgeoisie was at least initially weak, it has been the only means
of economic 'take-off'.

To an ever greater degree, the bureaucracies of this public sector also
interlock with those of the state social services and of the social institutions created by the labour movement itself. A second general trend to
bureaucratization thereby affects the labour movement, especially the
political parties (first, the social-democratic and then the social-democra-
tized Communist formations).

Previously, mass parties and unions of the working class were dominated by bureaucracies emanating from the movement itself, including

elected representatives in state bodies. Now, a growing part of the bureaucrats dominating the reformist parties come from, or mingle with, the social-service and public-sector bureaucracies as well as top layers of the civil service. This shift in social origin and outlook increasingly loosens these parties from the unions and undermines any identification with the immediate material interests of their members. Hence the tendency for unions to assert a greater independence from the parties, or to enter into open conflict with them.[21]

A third phase in the bureaucratic degeneration of reformist mass parties started in the mid-seventies, with the growing penetration of capitalist businessmen proper, mainly from the 'information' sector, and the conversion of a number of reformist bureaucrats into managers, if not private owners, in the same sector. A typical example is the West German technocrat Detlev Rohwedder, who has successively been SPD deputy-minister for industry and energy (1966–72); managing director of the near-bankrupt steel firm Hoesch (from 1980 on), which he made profitable again through measures that included mass redundancies; and in 1990, chairman of the so-called *Treuhandanstalt* (Trust Institution) in the GDR, which has been administering the property of six thousand publicly owned companies and preparing their privatization.[22]

The emergence of municipal, state, para-state and public-sector administrators as the dominant layer of the reformist bureaucracy in capitalist countries has had a huge impact on the ideology and mentality of the Party leaderships. 'Municipal' socialism is identified with well-functioning – that is, well-administered – municipalities. The same is the case with 'social-service' or 'public-sector' socialism. So emerges the concept and the strategy of 'administrative socialism' ('*le socialisme gestionnaire*') as the cornerstone of electoral and long-term success. 'We can only win if we prove to be better administrators than the liberals and conservatives' (it isn't done any more to say 'than the bourgeois'). That is the new social-democratic credo. In fact, 'administrative socialism' turns out to involve the efficient administration of capitalism by 'socialists'.

Here the reactionary or even nakedly regressive aspects of the whole process overshadow what is progressive in it. The para-state bureaucracies often act in direct contradiction with the interests of the mass membership of the working-class movement, tending more and more to turn an indifferent face to the people they are supposed to serve. They thereby discredit the very idea of social services and public ownership of the means of production, which appears to at least part of the working class as a remote domain of wasteful bureaucratic machines, not fundamentally different from private corporations geared to profit.

The transfer of these services to regional or municipal control does not solve the problem. It does, of course, place them closer to the public, but it also tends to pile up administrative jobs and make the system more costly and top-heavy with officials. Many of these shortcomings could be remedied through part-time participation of citizens' committees in the running of services, or through forms of workers' control in the public sector. And it should not be forgotten that they do not wipe out the numerous advantages of cheap or free social services for the bulk of the working population. Nevertheless, in the framework of bourgeois society, this cannot by itself put an end to bureaucratization and its negative consequences for average working-class consciousness. Nor does socialist propaganda alone provide a solution.

The growing domination of the reformist parties by para-state bureaucracies has still worse effects in the general realm of ideology and politics, where it furnishes a social base and social explanation for 'consensus politics' and generates the tendency to *institutionalized class collaboration* which has emerged, especially since the war, in Western Europe.[23] Administrative socialism becomes a 'socialism' that administers the bourgeois state. Instead of Tarnow's famous formula about the economic crisis of 1929–32 ('We have to act as doctors at the sickbed of capitalism'[24]), there is now a wish to administer a 'healthy' capitalist economy on a permanent basis, albeit in exchange for some (fewer and fewer) reforms.

In reality, this administration ideology increasingly spawns economic policies that are virtually identical with those of the bourgeois parties – witness the austerity drives pursued in the eighties by social-democratic governments in France, Spain, Portugal and Italy, with the aim of increasing the mass and rate of profit.

At a higher historical level, two basic processes tend to coalesce in the ideological–political regression of reformist bureaucracies. *On the one hand, a growing 'socialization of wages'* means that a worker receives less of his or her pay directly in the form of money, and more in benefits disbursed when the wage-earner or dependant is sick, studying, unemployed, disabled or retired. This socialized or 'indirect' component is, of course, just as much part of the 'socially necessary' average price of the commodity labour power. However, the bureaucratization of benefit institutions, where 'independent' technocrats or even employers' representatives occupy a large number of positions, implies a loss of control by the mass of workers over at least part of the allocation and quantification of their own wages. The extreme complexity of benefit calculations, based on a host of laws, decrees and regulations in the face of which the individual wage-earner is hopelessly lost, serves to strengthen the self-justificatory ideology of these bureaucracies, much as the 'need for

162

secrecy' argument has bolstered the Soviet bureaucracy and its like. The demand for greater openness and a radical simplification of social security legislation is thus an essential component of the struggle against the bureaucracy here and now in the capitalist countries.[25]

The partial 'socialization' of the wage reflects one economic dynamic of mature and late capitalism. As the mass labour movement weighs more heavily in the class relationship of forces and social legislation plays a more prominent role in the affairs of state, a relatively greater share of the tax burden, both direct and indirect, falls on the shoulders of the working class rather than the capitalists. Social benefits, then, do not entail any basic redistribution of the national income from surplus-value to wages. The real redistribution takes place inside the wage-earning class at the expense of certain groups (smokers, heavy drinkers, motorists, households without children, and so on) and in favour of other groups. At the same time, the top layers of the state and para-state bureaucracies come to administer and thus to control huge sums of money – which is the source of continuous scandals, corruption and private appropriation, in close connivance with the shadier sections of the capitalist class.[26]

On the other hand, there is a long-term trend towards statification of the trade unions, and to the conversion of the labour movement into a fake completely subordinate to the bourgeois state and the interests of capital. This stems from the objective need for capital to tighten control over labour not only at the workplace but in society as a whole, as the historical crisis of profitability and of all bourgeois social relations becomes more acute. The tendency surfaces in the imperialist countries in periods of reactionary dictatorship, and is especially powerful in the Third World. But it is slowly asserting itself everywhere, even under conditions of bourgeois parliamentary democracy.[27] To be sure, it can to varying degrees be neutralized by counter-tendencies such as the periodic upsurges in union militancy. Even under dictatorships in their phase of decline – the Pinochet regime in Chile, for example – state-controlled 'yellow unions' can sometimes take on new life as genuine unions.

Nevertheless, both the 'socialization' of wages and the statification of trade unions are real historical trends, involving a gradual loss of the degree of autonomous control over living conditions which had previously been conquered by the labour movement. The bureaucratization of para-state institutions is thus a powerful motor for the transfer of such control to capital. And in the same sense, the labour bureaucracies present in these institutions tend to be gradually transformed into parts of the bourgeois state bureaucracy.

163

3. The Austro-Marxists' Tragic Misjudgement of the State Bureaucracy

The most lucid theoreticians of classical social democracy outside the revolutionary Left – that is, apart from Lenin, Rosa Luxemburg, Trotsky and Gramsci – had an intuition of these basic trends, at least in the radical period of their youth. This is especially true of Otto Bauer and of Rudolf Hilferding, whose work *Finance Capital* was one of the main inspirations for Lenin's *Imperialism*. In 1909 Hilferding concluded his *magnum opus* with this remarkable paragraph:

> Finance capital, in its maturity, is the highest stage of the concentration of economic and political power in the hands of the capitalist oligarchy. It is the climax of the dictatorship of the magnates of capital. At the same time it makes the dictatorship of the capitalist lords of one country increasingly incompatible with the capitalist interests of other countries, and the internal domination of capital increasingly irreconcilable with the interests of the mass of the people, exploited by finance capital but also summoned into battle against it. In the violent clash of these hostile interests, the dictatorship of the magnates of capital will finally be transformed into the dictatorship of the proletariat.[28]

During the 'mass strike' debate in German and international social-democracy, Hilferding came closer to Rosa Luxemburg's position than to Kautsky's. Already in 1903, before the experience of the 1905 revolution in Russia, he prophetically claimed: 'The general strike must be possible if socialism, the victory of the proletariat, is to be possible at all. For the general strike is the only instrument of power [*Machtmittel*] immediately at the disposal of the proletariat.'[29] His left-centrist consciousness reached its highest point in the German revolution of November 1918, when he wrote:

> We have the firm conviction that the hour of socialism has struck. What is at stake? In the first place the defence of the revolutionary conquests. . . . In that defence, all the workers are and will remain united. But it is possible to defend the revolutionary conquests only by pushing the revolution further. Our right is the right of all revolutions. . . . Our right is as unquestionable as all previous rights [legality], and the situation it has created means dictatorship of the proletariat.[30]

The next two months would see Noske's bloody repression of the Berlin Spartakus workers; the murder of Karl Liebknecht, Rosa Luxemburg, Leo Jogiches, Kurt Eisner and Hugo Haase; the results of the elections to the National Assembly leading to the formation of a coalition government between the SPD Right and the 'centre' bourgeois parties;

the radical curtailment of the shop stewards' (*Betriebsräte*) prerogatives conquered in 1918; and the de facto destruction of the workers' councils. All these developments revealed the illusions contained in the left-centrist position.

But even in 1920, when Hilferding, in his famous debate with Zinoviev, opposed the USPD's affiliation to the Communist International at its Halle Congress, he still argued that Germany was both economically and politically ripe for a socialist revolution, and that everything depended on the unity of action of the German working class. His opposition to Zinoviev's characterization of the reformist-led unions as 'yellow unions' was obviously correct.[31] He even defended the idea of limiting democracy for the class enemy in the struggle for the dictatorship of the proletariat. But hardly three years later, he would be a cabinet minister in a government coalition between the reunified right-wing and bourgeois parties. In his report to the 1927 Kiel Congress of the SPD, he would give a classical formulation of social-democratic consensus politics: a positive attitude to the parliamentary (that is, the bourgeois-democratic) state based upon the emergence of organized capitalism.

Again it would not take long for the illusions contained in the analysis to become apparent. Once more finance minister in a coalition government, Hilferding became the accomplice of an economic policy which led to sharp wage-cuts and mass unemployment. The great advocate of working-class unity of action stubbornly refused to countenance any unity of action with the mass KPD, thereby sharing the responsibility of that party's Stalinist leadership for the victory of fascism.

After the establishment of the Third Reich, Hilferding briefly reverted to a more radical position: namely, that the restoration of democracy required revolutionary socialism.[32] But soon he entered a period of despair in which he announced the triumph of a new totalitarian state economy that would enslave the population in both East and West.[33] Finally, the Pétain regime in France delivered him to the Nazis, who killed him in the Buchenwald concentration camp.

The theoretical source of Hilferding's tragic evolution was his excessive insistence upon the independent role of the state, and his associated lack of understanding of the class nature of the bourgeois state bureaucracy. In this he was inspired by the ideas of Kautsky, who in a comment on the 1921 Görlitz programme of German social democracy wrote: 'Between the epoch of states with a purely bourgeois–democratic form of rule and the epoch of purely proletarian states, lies the period of transformation of the one into the other. This corresponds to a political transition period, where government will generally take the form of a coalition.' Even where 'pure' bourgeois or social-democratic governments are 'democratically' constituted, they can function only by tolerating the other side – a clear a priori justification of 'consensus' politics if ever there was one![34]

After the experience of February 1934, it is hardly necessary to refute Kautsky's notion that his Austrian friends 'disposed of' (*'verfügt'*) the army, or to counter his obvious confusion of state form, government and the class nature of the state. The striking point is his systematic justification for the curbing of workers' self-activity and self-organization, including the suppression of strikes under 'socialism'.

In a way that broadly prefigured Stalinist and post-Stalinist ideologies, Kautsky openly defended the necessity for large bureaucracies. Indeed, he saw the independence of executive state power, and the concentration of its decision-making powers in a few hands, as one of the main conquests of civilization and historical progress, the great advantage to be gained from the division of labour.[35] Workers who opposed such an 'arbiter' role were supposedly representing their narrow, corporate interests against organs which embodied 'the collective interest of the whole of society'.[36] This fusion of bourgeois and bureaucratic ideology culminates – it would be surprising if it didn't – in a justification of social inequality.[37]

What is completely lacking from this argumentation is any grasp of the class nature of 'executive state organs'. The autonomy of the bureaucracy from real class interests is elevated to the level of an article of faith, in spite of the overwhelming mass of historical evidence to the contrary.

The young Hilferding did not share these views, either in *Finance Capital* or in his writings of 1918–21. But after he rejoined the SPD, he took them over lock, stock and barrel, and developed them in a much more sophisticated manner than Kautsky himself ever did. Unable to distinguish the electoral–parliamentary relationship of class forces from the existence of the state apparatus, he formulated the thesis that political parties (that is, parliamentary democracy) had become 'the essential element of every modern state. . . . Consequently, all parties are necessary components of the state, exactly like the government and the administration.'[38] We should not forget that when Hilferding wrote these lines, socialists already had the example of Mussolini's dictatorship before their eyes!

The political consequences of this theoretical mistake would be disastrous. German social democracy's main response to the rise of the Nazis would be to hope and appeal for the state apparatus to intervene against the fascists' violence and 'lawlessness'. The inevitable alignment of the top layers of the army, police and civil service with Big Business against Labour, in pre-civil-war conditions of extreme social tension, is not just the result of their class origins, interests and prejudices. It also corresponds to the functional nature of their thinking about the world. Police officers are there to protect 'law and order' which, in bourgeois society, is capitalist law and order geared to the protection of private property. Army officers are trained to defend 'the fatherland' (that is, the capitalist state) by means of arms. Under these conditions, Trotsky wrote:

> The mood of the majority of the army officers reflects the reactionary mood of the ruling classes of the country, but in a much more concentrated form. . . . Fascism impresses the officers very much, because its slogans are resolute and because it is prepared to settle difficult questions by means of pistols and machine-guns. . . . We have quite a few disjointed reports regarding the tie-up between the fascist leagues and the army through the medium of reserve as well as active officers.[39]

The fact that in Germany these layers preferred a bloc with the Nazis to any defence of the labour movement's democratic rights was systematically ignored in social-democratic conceptions. Successive blows, including the von Papen putsch, were met with retreats or capitulations without a fight. The road was thus opened for Hitler to take power without having to face organized resistance.[40]

The combination of theoretical error and political capitulation culminated in Hilferding's claim that social democracy's main merit was its successful prevention of a bond between the state apparatus and the Nazis. Unfortunately when his editorial article arguing this point appeared in the SPD journal *Die Gesellschaft*, in January 1933, Hindenburg had just invited Hitler to assume office.

Hilferding's theory of the state contained two further link-concepts: the political wage, and organized capitalism. Prices of consumer goods, as well as the level of real wages, were supposed to be *determined* by political relations of forces and thus, most centrally, by parliamentary election results.[41] (Hilferding did also mention extra-parliamentary class struggles, but as no more than an afterthought that played no role in the argument.) More generally, in the new 'organized capitalism' the law of value no longer ruled, even in the final analysis or in the long run. There was growing interpenetration between ever more centralized firms and an ever stronger state. 'Organized capitalism,' he went so far as to say, 'means in reality replacing the capitalist principle of free competition by the socialist principle of planned production.'[42]

The logical conclusion was that such a system of state-ruled economy, which suspended all the main laws of motion and inner contradictions of the capitalist mode of production, could no longer be described as capitalism. And when 'state rule' fused with despotism – that is, with the destruction of democratic freedoms – the wage-workers would be transformed into state slaves, utterly incapable of self-emancipation or the fight for socialism.[43] The personal tragedy is subsumed in an alleged historical tragedy of humankind.

Otto Bauer's thinking on the transition to socialism started from a similar position to Hilferding's in 1918–19, although he was then to the right of him politically. Bauer employed two 'objectivist' arguments to explain why the working class could not take power in Austria. First, although this might be possible in Vienna and some other towns, workers were in a minority in the rest of the country and a socialist government would be cut off from the countryside and its food supplies. Secondly, Austria like Germany was dependent upon the import of food and raw materials, so that Britain and the USA could use their control of the seas to impose a starvation blockade. The British and American proletariats were not ready to prevent that from happening. In other words: revolution was impossible because economic conditions inside Austria and political conditions in the West were not yet ripe for it.

This fatalistic approach to the question of state power did, however, receive a peculiar twist that would place Otto Bauer well to the left of Hilferding after 1920. Social democracy, he argued, should fight for and could secure an absolute majority in parliament, which could then be used in an attempt to conquer state power. But it should be understood that, precisely for this reason, the bourgeoisie would increasingly turn against bourgeois–democratic institutions.[44] The Linz Programme of 1926, drafted by Otto Bauer, explicitly stated that in the face of a reactionary coup social democracy should be prepared to go over to the dictatorship of the proletariat. Moreover, it should arm itself and the working class in readiness for such an eventuality, a kind of arms parity between the weak army and the workers' Schutzbund having already been imposed on the bourgeoisie in 1918.[45]

But when the chips were down, this perspective proved to be largely rhetorical. In 1927 the bourgeoisie set off on its protracted 'cold putsch', exactly as Bauer had foreseen. The workers responded with a spontaneous mass uprising in Vienna. The social-democratic city council repressed the workers and killed dozens upon dozens of them. The Schutzbund was marched out of the city, not into it to defend the unarmed insurgents.

The workers felt immensely cheated and disoriented as the bourgeoisie stepped up its repression, systematically dismantling all the positions that had been conquered in 1918–19 and after. All the socialist hopes were pinned on the outcome of elections. Otto Bauer glorified the retreat by saying that he had saved the country from civil war. But when civil war did break out in February 1934, under the worst possible conditions, the initiative had been left entirely in the hands of the enemy. And to cap it all, Bauer then tried to make the workers responsible for the defeat by arguing that mass unemployment had incapacitated them.[46] That they had been ready to fight in 1927, that the general strike which failed in 1934 would have been successful in 1927, that he himself bore the main responsibility for preventing it at that high-point of the real class struggle – all of this was blithely forgotten. Again, the illusion that somehow the state apparatus would not dare act against the power of the organized labour movement proved stronger than all the theoretical insights.

4. Third World Bureaucracies

After the Second World War, the pressures to modernize and industrialize as a reaction to the misery and inequities of colonialism became irresistible in a whole series of countries of the so-called Third World. For all non-proletarian political forces, it was a vital matter to prevent this pressure flowing into socialist revolution – as it was doing in China – and to divert it into channels compatible with bourgeois society. Yet neither imperialism nor the indigenous ruling classes (semi-feudal and/or capitalist) were able or willing to embark upon industrialization in a broad and consistent manner. Under these conditions, it was the state – directed either by capitalist forces (Argentina, India, Mexico, Brazil, South Korea) or by petty-bourgeois ones (Egypt, Iraq, Syria) – which started the process of large-scale primitive accumulation of industrial capital, in varying degrees of symbiosis or temporary antagonism with imperialism.

Such a course implied a huge expansion of state and para-state bureaucracies. And often it was the military bureaucracy which played the key role for a long period – the most notable example being Indonesia after the 1965 coup.

These bureaucracies by and large repeated the historical function of promoting industry which the absolute monarchy had once assumed in several European countries. Given the character of contemporary technology and the size of large-scale industry, the capitals controlled by the state were qualitatively greater than those of the eighteenth or early nineteenth century. By the same token, in comparison with anything ever seen in Europe, the number of bureaucrats was proportionately much larger and weighed much more decisively in 'civil society'.

Nevertheless, the broad similarities do need to be stressed. In all these societies money still ruled supreme – even in Nasser's Egypt, which was probably the most advanced form of 'statification' led by the petty bourgeoisie. When money rules, the accumulation of private money wealth is in the long run the basic motivation of all the powerful actors in the political–economic arena. Plunder of the state treasury and of private citizens becomes the source of tremendous fortunes, the best known being those of the Trujillo family in the Dominican Republic, the Marcos clan in the Philippines, the Somozas in Nicaragua, and the Mobutu family in Zaire. Richest of all has probably been the Pahlavi family in Iran. The wealth of the oil sheikhs of Saudi Arabia, Kuwait and the Arab Emirates – like that of the Sultan of Brunei, reputedly the second richest family on earth – is a special case where there is no real dividing line between ownership of the country's natural resources, the public exchequer, and the ruling families' private property.

The rise of Third World bureaucracies, however, is by no means just a problem of a handful of corrupt ruling circles, including the military.[47] The hypertrophy of the state, and its grip on key sectors of modern economic life, is a widespread phenomenon, as is the intrinsic drive of top bureaucrats to accumulate private capital. To replace the most corrupt cliques with other political forces would not alter the basic dynamic so long as bourgeois society and money wealth prevail. Iran after Ayatollah Khomeini is a good example in this respect.

What does inflect the general growth of Third World bureaucracies is the long-term logic of capital accumulation itself. When the private accumulation of capital – essentially through theft of public resources and corruption – passes a certain threshold, economic 'liberalization' and privatization are placed on the agenda and the weight of the state sector is gradually reduced. The pressure of the capitalist world market operates in the same direction. A new 'power bloc' takes shape, ever more closely combining 'national' private monopolies, state bureaucracies (including the military) and international capital. Brazil is the most clear-cut illustration of this tendency.

A restructuring, or restratification, of the Third World bureaucracies is an inevitable feature of this process. Parts of their top layers transform themselves into super-rich private capitalists. Others remain bureaucrats in the traditional sense of the word. The middle and lower ranks, whose standard of living tends to lose any relative edge or even to decline in absolute terms, gradually merge with 'white-collar labour', as they do in imperialist countries.

Since the heyday of the Peronist regime in Argentina in the early 1950s, all these phenomena have been the object of considerable debate and controversy, including among economists, sociologists and political scientists inspired in one degree or another by Marxism. In particular, the famous 'dependency debate' of the sixties and seventies centred on the question of whether the existence of international imperialism, and the dependence upon it of Third World countries, constituted an absolute barrier to modernization/industrialization. The most radical exponents of this theory were Raul Mario Marini and André Gunder Frank, who characterized all Third World ruling classes as 'lumpen-bourgeoisies'.

History has now largely settled this issue. There can be no doubt that a certain number of formerly semi-colonial countries have been able to transform themselves into semi-industrialized dependent countries.[48] To be sure, only a relatively small minority of Third World countries today fall into this category, and even for them technological and financial (credit) dependence is greater than ever. But it is evident that countries like Brazil, South Korea, Taiwan and even India are no longer 'semi-colonies' in the sense that the concept was used by Marxists from the beginning to the middle of the twentieth century. There, the process of national capital accumulation is not dominated by foreign capital. Nor is it subordinated to the interests of imperialism.

It is precisely in this context that we have to emphasize the role of state bureaucracies. They are involved in frequent conflicts with traditional private capitalists. But their own bourgeois character is clearly expressed in the function of the state sector as long-term promoter and subsidizer of a 'new' private capitalist sector.

5. The Bureaucracies of Large Capitalist Firms

Concentration and centralization of capital, one of the basic laws of motion of the capitalist mode of production, leads to the emergence of huge private firms as the main organizational form. These first took shape on a national basis under 'classical' monopoly capitalism. In the late-capitalist phase they have generally developed as multinational or transnational corporations.

Large-scale industrial, commercial and financial combines invariably beget large-scale internal apparatuses, for reasons of coordination, mediation, supervision and control.[49] A single entrepreneur, or a small board of directors, has to delegate power to manage such huge organizations. The managerial functions are divided among different branches and sub-services, each with its own hierarchy, and their coordination requires further instruments for the exchange of information. Paper constantly accumulates, and its handling again demands large staffs with their own hierarchy.

This trend is summed up in the constant growth of 'white-collar' and especially administrative personnel, as opposed to strictly defined 'production workers' in industry (see Table 5), although account should also be taken of other phenomena like the steep rise in the productivity of labour in direct production.

What characterizes these private corporate bureaucracies, exactly like

Table 5 Production and Administrative Workers in Manufacturing Industry in the USA

	Production workers	Administrative workers	A/P ratio*
1947	11,918,000	14,294,000	.20
1954	12,372,000	15,645,000	.26
1958	11,907,000	15,381,000	.29
1963	12,232,000	16,235,000	.33
1967	13,957,000	18,496,000	.32
1972	13,528,000	19,029,000	.41
1977	13,691,000	19,500,000	.42
1983	12,241,000	18,166,000	.48

*The A/P ratio is the ratio of purely administrative personnel (not all white-collar workers) to production workers.

Source: Meyer, Stevenson and Webster, p. 37.

the state bureaucracies, is their character as economic hybrids. Their ranks comprise neither capital-owners personally engaged in the maximization of profit, nor direct producers of goods or services for final consumers or other firms. They perform a mediating function between these two poles of economic activity. But the main concern of the personnel is to keep their jobs and secure promotion – quite a different motivation from that of competitive entrepreneurs or productive workers battling over the distribution of surplus-value. It is no accident that the term 'office politics' has been coined to describe the peculiar type of bureaucratic 'competition';[50] nor that the most ambitious bureaucrats in large corporations have come to be known as 'workaholics'.

Is the rise of corporate bureaucracies linked to the joint-stock company and its divorce between ownership and management?[51] This seems to us a dubious argument. Firms which maintain a legally private character are as deeply bureaucratized as so-called public companies. Much more decisive than juridical form is the need for a large firm to create a special apparatus to exercise functions which, initially, could be performed by the owners or a small group of top managers. The necessary multiplication of functions leads to a devolution of power.

One of the most striking shortcomings of Ludwig von Mises's theory of bureaucracy – which we shall discuss in greater detail in Chapter 5 – is his view that the growth of bureaucracies within large private corporations is due to the influence and pressure of economic regulation by the state. This is obviously not true of the old US monopolies like Standard Oil and US Steel, which emerged before there was any substantial economic legislation or intervention by the state. Similarly, although such intervention is much greater in Sweden than in Switzerland, there is no difference in the degree of internal bureaucratization within Swiss firms like Nestlé or Ciba-Geigy, on the one hand, and Swedish firms like Volvo, Asea or SKF on the other.

In reality, the growth of private corporate bureaucracies is closely linked to their expanding size. It is also correlated with the emergence of 'scientific management' and 'scientific labour organization' – that is, with the techniques and ideologies of Taylor and Gulick.

It is significant that when he was still a political scientist, the future US President Woodrow Wilson tried to apply the principles of business administration to public administration. Indeed, we might perhaps partially reverse the von Mises theorem. At least in the United States, the growth of public administration till the New Deal, and again from the 1950s on, was due to attempts to make it more 'business-like', more 'cost-effective', rather than to the spread of economic regulation by government agencies.

There is an important area of interaction in the development of public and private bureaucracies. The growth of the state under mature and late capitalism goes hand in hand with an increase in taxation, part of which weighs upon private firms. Fiscal laws become ever more complex, as well as more stringent, so that book-keeping and financial jiggling – in addition to their original function of keeping track of costs and profits – have increasingly to concern themselves with the avoidance or evasion of taxes. Sub-branches of private corporate bureaucracies, including legal advisers, develop with just that purpose in view.

Another dimension is more closely linked to the actual process of production. Parts of the private corporate bureaucracy are situated not in the office but on the shopfloor, or between the office and shopfloor. This 'industrial bureaucracy', as it has been called, encompasses all those supervisors who, unlike traditional foremen, are not directly connected with production but serve to exert stricter control over labour on the shopfloor.[52] Their number in a traditional factory (especially of the assembly-line type) is considerably larger than is generally assumed.

Moreover, the importance of this function within the tendential growth of corporate bureaucracies has been greatly underestimated by many neo-liberal and neo-conservative critics of bureaucracy. Such supervision is intimately bound up with the need for hierarchical control over the direct producer which, as we have repeatedly argued, lies at the heart of both the capitalist and the Stalinist organization of labour. Taylor, the 'inventor' of the formula of scientific management, did not fail to dot his i's and cross his t's when discussing the nature of the command hierarchy. Its whole purpose was to increase the likelihood of workers' compliance, by the imposition of strictly defined and measured tasks that would reduce their autonomy in the labour process.

Thirty years later, when it was a question of reducing the shopfloor autonomy of militant shop stewards on the pretext of not undermining the 'war effort' in the USA – a policy in which Stalinist trade unionists actively connived – the National War Labor Board representative Harry Shulman wrote no less unambiguously:

> Any enterprise in a capitalist or socialist economy requires persons with authority and responsibility to keep the enterprise running. . . . That authority is vested in Supervision [Shulman's capital letter]. It must be vested there because the responsibility for production is vested there, and responsibility must be accompanied by authority.[53]

And again two decades later, the move towards industrial semi-automation by means of numerically controlled machine-tools – the first phase of the third technological revolution – was essentially motivated by the managers' (the capitalists') attempt to break the power of the worker-machinist in the metalworking industry. As David F. Noble states in his remarkable book *Forces of Production*:

> Thus, the general purpose machine-tools remained the heart of metalworking, and here, despite the efforts of engineers and scientific management, *the machinist reigned supreme*.
>
> This, then, became the ultimate challenge of machine-tool automation: How to render a general-purpose machine-tool self-acting (that is, acting automatically according to prespecified management instructions, without labour intervention) . . . [54]

Noble goes on to formulate a more general thesis:

> In reality, the 'objective expert' comes to his work as prejudiced as the next person, constrained by the 'technical climate', cultural habits, career considerations, intellectual enthusiasms, institutional incentives, and the weight of prior and parallel developments – not to mention the performance specifications of the project managers and supporters. . . .
>
> In short, the concepts of 'economic viability' and 'technical viability' are not really economic or technical categories at all – as our ideological inheritance suggests – but political and cultural categories.[55]

This is miles away from Max Weber's axiom about 'technological constraints'. But it is a much more realistic description of the way in which bourgeois society actually functions.

174

6. 'Bureaucratization of the World'?

It is in this context that theories have emerged about a so-called 'managerial class', with its own hierarchy and a common mentality or even 'class consciousness' quite similar to those of the Soviet bureaucracy. From there to conclude that the whole world is undergoing bureaucratization is but a short step – and one that authors like Burnham, and to some extent Galbraith, have moved towards.[56] Empirical data, however, prove quite the contrary. Private corporate bureaucracies do not have sufficient cohesion to be able to act, even occasionally, as a collective social force comparable to the capitalist or the working class. Inner competition counts for much more than common interests. With regard to the US federal bureaucracy, H. Kaufman writes:

> The federal bureaucracy is such a collection of diverse, often competing and contradictory, antagonistic interests that many of its components check and neutralize each other. As a result of such divisions, rivalries, and opposing missions and interests, one of the principal barriers to an assumption of dominant power by bureaucrats is other bureaucrats.[57]

And if that is already true of the bourgeois state bureaucracy, how much more does it apply to the private corporate bureaucracy taken in its totality. That totality, in fact, exists only as a statistic. It has no concrete social being, hence no sociological relevance. This is largely due to its economic dependence on capital, but also reflects its interlocking with the general structure of bourgeois society.

Private corporate bureaucracies are hierarchically organized in such a way that each layer's social position and outlook are increasingly tied in to the different social classes. Top managers will try to integrate into the capitalist class, and not pursue 'class warfare' against the big bourgeoisie. Middle layers will tend to merge with the middle classes in general. And in spite of the formidable obstacles and the time-gaps between different capitalist countries, lower-level corporate bureaucrats – who, in reality, are just white-collar employees – will tend to unionize and move closer to the organized labour movement as such. Indeed, it is precisely the strong numerical growth of 'white-collar' labour within private firms which tends to overcome the main obstacle on that road – namely, personal competition and careerism. When salaries for white-collar workers become less dependent on individual situations and more closely tied to general conditions on the labour market, unionization has an obvious attractiveness in terms of immediate economic interest.

Meyer, Stevenson and Webster, in their trail-blazing *Limits to Bureaucratic Growth*, have convincingly argued that bureaucracies tend to generate fast-growing 'sub-bureaucracies' which are unable to adapt to a changing environment and over which the original bureaucratic structure tends to lose control.[58] They could have added that, in this respect, there is a substantive difference between the bureaucracies of private firms and those of bourgeois states and post-capitalist societies – one which stems from their functional character.

Private corporate bureaucracies have to be functional to profit realization and to the drive for profit maximization. Any cancerous growth of bureaucratic sub-bodies that undermines profit is eventually sanctioned: even high-flying managers get the sack if they do not deliver the goods.

The same is not true of state bureaucracies, whether in the East, the West or the South. Here too, of course, there is a similar limit to their growth. The mounting burden they impose on the economy as a whole might 'kill the goose that lays the golden egg' – that is, trigger a collapse of public finance or even (particularly in post-capitalist societies) jeopardize the production and distribution of goods. However, since their function is much less clearly defined and measurable than in the case of private businesses, it will be a much longer and more arduous task to hold back any dysfunctioning sub-systems, or to curtail the bureaucratic system as a whole.

7. The Contrary Logics of Direct Resource Allocation and Profit Maximization

There is a further, deeper reason why no 'managerial class' can emerge as a ruling class in capitalist society. The interests of state and private bureaucracies cannot override those of the capitalist class without calling into question its economic and social power. For under capitalism, the ways and means by which bureaucracies function economically are different from those which make businesses survive and prosper, or decline and perish. The two cannot coexist at the same level. The former have to be subordinated to the latter, lest capitalism itself disappear.[59]

Capitalist bureaucracies are funded by direct, a priori allocation of resources. Theirs is a procurement system. At the beginning of each year, or of a several-year period, the state, municipal or corporate budget sets aside a fixed sum for the wages and current expenditure of the relevant bureaucracy, which has an evident interest in keeping the total at the same level or in increasing it over the previous year. There is no cost-cutting incentive – quite the opposite. Towards the end of the budgeting period, bureaucracies actually have an interest in 'spending all they can' if, at that moment, expenditure is still below the allocation. The incentive is to reproduce or increase costs without regard for profit, not to reduce costs for the sake of profit.

This basically non-capitalist logic of expenditure naturally operates only in the higher echelons. Further down the hierarchy, employees have no more say over expenditure than do blue-collar workers. But those who can decide will tend to act in the way we have described, and their general attitude of indifference to cost-cutting will inevitably trickle down the ranks.

The behavioural patterns, motivations and mentalities which flow from the logic of a priori allocation are not necessarily irresponsible from the point of view of society in its totality. On the contrary, they can dovetail with the interests of the great majority of the population when they concern public expenditure already partly based on the principle of satisfaction of needs: health, education, public transport, culture, even some infrastructural expenditure. In all these areas, rigid or downward budgetary allocations are very often socially irresponsible, as well as being counter-productive in economic terms. If employees of the relevant apparatuses exert systematic pressure to raise the level of expenditure, this will generally have beneficial effects – although a distinction should be drawn between purely administrative costs or straightforward waste, on the one hand, and expenditure in the direct interest of consumers (the mass of the population) on the other hand. The actual direction of pressure will depend upon a multitude of factors whose detailed analysis is beyond the scope of this book.

The built-in tendency of capitalist bureaucracies to assure 'expanded reproduction' of their budgetary allowances also makes them liable to act in such a way as to promote their own growth. This too is contrary to the logic of profit maximization, which regards administrative costs as an imposition depressing the rate of profit, albeit one that is unavoidable and, under late capitalism, shows an inevitable tendency to rise.[60] An intelligent conservative observer, Cyril Northcote Parkinson, formulated this tendency to bureaucratic expansion in his well-known 'law'.[61] The dissident communist novelist from the GDR, Stefan Heym, has expressed it in Marxist terms of social (in the first place, material) interests.

Just think of one of these poor people at his desk, aware in his heart of hearts of his own superfluousness – how he sits day after day and has to justify his existence to the whole world, to prove that he has the right to draw his not even low salary. What colossal activities he has to carry out! He must issue one order after another, attend one meeting after another, read out one report after another, and above all else he must multiply. He must rise so as not to be knocked down from the position on which he climbs upward. If he is a section

177

leader, he must make sure that he becomes head of a department. But he can only do that if he begets at least two new sections out of his own, each with a new section leader who issues more orders, attends meetings, reads out reports and builds sub-sections, and so on *ad infinitum*.[62]

Particularly in periods of falling profit-rates and 'capital valorization crises' (that is, in long waves with a depressive tendency), strenuous efforts are made to block this self-expansion and to rationalize public and private administrative expenditure. Whether the present austerity drive will be successful in the long run remains to be seen. It has not happened in the past.

In the thirties and early forties, both under liberal 'New Deal' regimes and under fascist or fascist-like dictatorships, administrative costs rose considerably in spite of the grave crisis of profitability. Pressure from capital and governments to hold down costs can counteract but not essentially reverse the bureaucracies' natural inclination to act in the opposite direction. Conflicting social interests are at the bottom of this divergence in motives and attitudes. Paradoxically, the bourgeois state is eventually led to employ further controllers and controllers of controllers – that is, another layer of bureaucrats – to counteract the tendency of the bureaucracy to self-expansion.

An excellent synthesis of these contradictory trends can be seen in the way contemporary armies function and finance themselves. Armies are prototypes of a priori budgetary funding. But they are also inextricably bound up with profit-oriented capitalist industry, through their own system of procurement. Military bureaucracies order their hardware from private industry after much haggling over price and the 'cost-plus fixed profit margin'. Firms inevitably tend to quote inflated figures to push up their margin. The military bureaucracy tries equally hard to deflate them, not, of course, in order to decrease its overall expenditure but, on the contrary, to spend as much as possible on the best possible deals. The purpose of specific cost-cutting is to achieve and consolidate that overall expansion of expenditure, in a climate where the military budget has to be justified in parliament or before the public.

Given the irresistible power of wealth and money under capitalism, and the associated tendency toward personal corruption, there develops a refined form of interaction between the interests of private firms, military bureaucrats, state administrators (including legislators and municipal authorities) and even parts of the trade-union bureaucracy. The military brass will exert pressure on private firms to lower prices, while these firms will use various means, not stopping short of direct or indirect bribes, to weaken this pressure. At the same time, they will exert pressure of their own – through special lobbies, for example – to secure preferential treatment from politicians in connection with army contracts and even price levels. Such attempts to bypass the military bureaucracy may well be supported by local politicians who plead for the special interests of municipalities or regions where the armaments production is located.

Corporations earmark some of the profits from this procurement system to influence politicians' decisions, thereby creating a near-perfect feedback mechanism of self-expansion. The recruitment of top military brass, after retirement, to the board of directors will nicely close the circle. President Eisenhower, – ex-General Eisenhower – coined the term 'military–industrial complex' to describe this system. But the military input into it, unlike the industrial stake, does not follow a logic of profit maximization.

Similar tendencies of bureaucratic self-expansion are at work in the post-capitalist societies, but there is a decisive difference. The post-capitalist bureaucracies, at least in countries where they enjoy a monopoly of power, control the extraction of surplus labour at plant level and hence also the distribution of the social surplus product. There is no higher authority to which they have to bow in the economic field, although account should be taken of the partial pressure of the law of value (in the final analysis, world capitalism).

By contrast, capitalist bureaucrats, both public and private, do have a higher authority above them: that of the owners of capital. Irrespective of whether they behave rationally or irrationally from their own point of view, or from that of 'overall social interests' (insofar as such a yardstick can exist), they will be punished, demoted or even dismissed if they are deemed to have acted against the corporate or systemic interest in the production and realization of profit. Worse; they will suffer adverse effects if their number (and cost) has to be reduced in order to protect general profit levels.

Profit overrides the logic (the 'needs') of administration. And since the capitalists control the mechanical and human productive forces, as well as the products of labour including the social surplus, there is no way in which any administration can force them to take measures that are against their basic interests. Etzioni expresses this truth in other terms, but his conclusion is the same:

> in a factory, the elites which embody the production or profit goals must, functionally speaking, be more powerful than those which represent professional or artistic values. When those groups representing the secondary goals (or the means) are more powerful than those representing the prime goals, the organization is likely to be ineffective: for instance, a factory that

has such a dysfunctional elite hierarchy may make solid and well-designed products but no profits.

Hence the general rule: 'Effective elite hierarchy is one in which the structure of the elites and the hierarchy of goals (or goals and means) are congruent.'[63] As capitalism is a system of production for profit, it follows that efficient capitalist business bureaucracies are those which respect and submit to the goal of profit maximization.

8. Max Weber's Alternative Theory of Bureaucracy

Marx and Engels did not work out a systematic theory of bureaucracy but left only various analyses throughout their writings. Max Weber, however, did develop such a theory. It has acquired great prestige in the last few decades and is increasingly being taken over, *in toto* or in its main thrust, not only in academic circles East and West but also among political ideologues of nearly every shade. The contents of Weber's theory are well expressed in the following summary by Robert K. Merton:

> As Weber indicates, bureaucracy involves a clear-cut division of integrated activities which are regarded as duties inherent in the office. A system of differentiated controls and sanctions is stated in the regulations. The assignment of roles occurs on the basis of technical qualifications which are ascertained through formalized, impersonal procedures (e.g. examinations). Within the structure of hierarchically arranged authority, the activities of 'trained and salaried experts' are governed by general, abstract, clearly defined rules which preclude the necessity for the issuance of specific instructions in each case. The generality of the rules requires the constant use of categorization, whereby individual problems and cases are classified on the basis of designated criteria and are treated accordingly. The pure type of bureaucratic official is appointed, either by a superior or through the exercise of impersonal competition; he is not elected.[64]

Alvin W. Gouldner[65] adds to this summary the following quotes from Weber himself:

> The effectiveness of legal [in that context, 'bureaucratic' – AWG] authority rests on the acceptance of the following . . . That any given legal norm may be established by agreement or imposition on the grounds of expediency[66] or rational values, or both, with a claim to obedience at least on the part of the members of the corporate group.
> The choice is only between bureaucratism and dilettantism in the field of

administration. The primary source of bureaucratic administration lies in the role of technical knowledge. . . . The question is always who controls the existing machinery, and such control is possible only in a very limited degree to persons who are not technical specialists. . . . Bureaucratic administration means fundamentally the exercise of control on the basis of knowledge. This is the feature of it which makes it specifically rational. . . . Bureaucracy is superior in knowledge of the concrete facts within its own sphere of interest.

The content of discipline is nothing but the consistently rationalized, methodically trained and exact execution of the received order, in which all personal criticism is unconditionally suspended and the actor is unswervingly and exclusively set for carrying out the command.[67]

In other words, bureaucracies replace rule by amateurs with rule by experts; power exercised through whim, sentiment or prejudice with power exercised through impersonal formal rules; power exercised under semi-anarchic, unpredictable conditions with power imposed through rigid, foreseeable discipline; a largely irrational administration with a rational one.

For Weber, the essence of bureaucracy lies in the command hierarchy. The basis of power shifts away from personal towards administrative action. The power of *leaders*, whether hereditary or elected, is substantially weakened. The enhanced power of top bureaucrats is a function partly of their monopoly positions, partly of their ability to shroud their own workings in official secrecy. Bureaucracy therefore assumes considerably greater permanence than earlier administrative forms: 'More and more the material fate of the masses depends upon the steady and correct functioning of the increasingly bureaucratic organizations of private capitalism. The idea of eliminating these organizations becomes more and more utopian.'[68] This has sometimes been expressed in the formula of 'technological–organizational fatality' (*Sachzwang*).[69]

Weber's theory, despite all its critical aspects, is thus in large measure a defence and apology for bureaucracy.[70] Without doubt it provides an accurate account of how bureaucratic apparatuses actually function – many aspects of which had already been developed in Marx's early writings with which Weber could not have been familiar. But Talcott Parsons and other sociologists have indicated a number of weaknesses in the analysis.[71] Rule through expertise and rule through discipline do not necessarily coincide. Indeed they can (or, we should say, must) conflict with each other. Bureaucratic apparatuses do not operate in a social vacuum. What is 'rational' and 'efficient' for one social class or layer might be quite contrary to the interests and feelings of another.[72] Moreover, as Meyer, Stevenson and Webster have pointed out, for Weber efficient administration requires that the public should have little influence over state bureaucracies – a position inconsistent with any definition of democratic government save Weber's own.

All these criticisms are to the point. But they are overshadowed by a more essential failure. Max Weber assumes that bureaucratic rule is inherently rational. And that is not the case. Bureaucratic rule implies a combination of partial rationality and global irrationality, which exactly reflects the parallel combination in market economy and generalized commodity production – that is, capitalism itself – with whose historical rise the bureaucratic systems are closely bound up. It expresses the necessity of a more rationally functioning state to protect the interests of property-owners, one that will assure legal security, non-arbitrary use of monetary systems, safeguards against economic policies that hinder the free flow of commodities, and so on.

But these increments in rationality, for each person, firm or state taken separately, lead to a historically increasing irrationality of the system (the world) in its totality. And of that Weber is not aware.

Extreme rationality applied inside the organization of one firm explodes into the extreme irrationality of periodic crises of overproduction. Extreme rationality in the administration of nation-states and their armed forces leads to the extreme irrationality of ever more 'total' wars. Extreme rationality in juridical safeguards for individual property rights leads to the extreme, barbarous irrationality of dictatorial systems that completely disregard the integrity of a growing number of citizens. Extreme rationality in the inter-state 'policing' of minor conflicts leads to the potentially 'total' irrationality of humankind's physical destruction through a new world war, ecological disasters or an explosive crisis of food production.

These mounting contradictions are not due to some 'mistake' on the part of bureaucracies, experts or rulers. They are the inescapable result of the inner contradictions of bourgeois society (and the commodity production on which it rests), which we have referred to in many parts of this book as well as in previous writings.[73] Max Weber's inability to grasp this derivation reflects his uncritical acceptance of the ABC of bourgeois society: that is, surplus-labour production, profit realization and surplus-value appropriation in money form, accumulation of capital in money form for purposes of private enrichment under the pressure of fierce and permanent competition.

For Weber, this is all part and parcel of 'civilization', including the mass slaughter to which it has periodically led.[74] Under these circumstances, the global irrationality of the system is indeed an inexorable 'fact of life'.

These contradictions increasingly rebound onto the bureaucratic 'subsystems' of Big Business and state administration. If we leave aside the case of the post-capitalist bureaucracies – which are, however, supposed to fall under Weber's general theory as well – is it really true that big firms are run by top experts? Are they not rather run by financiers? Are they more and more efficient? What about the waste of material and human resources implied in the growth of bureaucracy? What about the state administrations which consciously 'plan' a reduction in public expenditure, with the result that, for example, half of the bridges in the United States threaten to collapse? What about the 'rationality' of blind obedience to orders that are not only inhuman or barbaric but even inefficient in simple technical terms? We could continue the list indefinitely.

Weber's theory of bureaucracy is, to a large extent, a rationalization of the growth and expansion of the Prussian state, with its specific – and contradictory – ties to an absolute monarchy, on the one hand, and a liberal, cultured bourgeoisie on the other. Franz Mehring sheds some useful contextual light on this aspect of things. In his non-apologetic study of the origins of the Prussian bureaucracy, he shows that it resulted from the distinctively military nature of the Prussian state, where a deep contradiction existed between the war-oriented monarchy and a nobility preoccupied with its immediate material interests.[75] The resulting hatred between the Junkers and the state bureaucracy would later be reproduced under Bismarck.

With the growth of capitalism, however, the Prussian bureaucracy also began to fulfil a second function: to clear the way for German unification with such initiatives as the customs union or *Zollverein* completed in 1852.

> The *Zollverein* developed as an economic necessity, . . . and out of it grew the *Zollverein* bureaucracy – not because it was recruited from the most select elements of the bureaucracy, but because activity in the *Zollverein* broadened their view and steered them beyond the narrow economic interests of Junkerdom east of the Elbe towards the cultural interests of the modern world. It is this bureaucracy which prepared the Prussian state for its 'German vocation', and there was some truth in it when it prided itself, with truly bureaucratic complacency, on being the genuine elite of Prussia.[76]

In Weber's theory we find a clear reflection of these illusions concerning the legitimacy of the Prussian bureaucracy. On the other hand, as Engels stressed, its delusions of absolute power under rising capitalism were rooted in its petty-bourgeois origins:

> The bureaucracy was set up to govern petty bourgeoisie and peasants. These classes, dispersed in small towns or villages . . . cannot govern a large state. . . . And it was exactly at that stage of civilization when the petty bourgeoisie

was most flourishing that the different interests were most completely intertwined. . . . The petty bourgeoisie and the peasants cannot, therefore, do
without a powerful and numerous bureaucracy. They must let themselves be
kept in leading strings . . .

But the bureaucracy, which is a necessity for the petty bourgeoisie, very
soon becomes an unbearable fetter for the bourgeoisie. Already at the stage of
manufacture official supervision and interference become very burdensome;
factory industry is scarcely possible under such control.[77]

The Prussian bourgeoisie was congenitally tied to the state bureaucracy. But these ties were contradictory, and the growing political impo-
tence of the bourgeoisie finally exploded in the unsuccessful revolution of
1848. If Bismarck and the Prussian Junkers fulfilled that revolution's
testament, they did so by leaning heavily on a pre-bourgeois state
bureaucracy whose conservative and conformist elements were deeply
marked by irrational ideologies and motives. All this would gush to the
surface in the war drive of the Second Reich, and still more in the
submission of the German elites to the Third Reich and their endorse-
ment of its imperialist goals. Weber was unable to foresee, let alone
counter, these tendencies. Marxists at least foresaw them. The most lucid
among them made realistic proposals about how they could be checked.

Weber also erred in underestimating the weight of irrational arrogance
and prejudice among bureaucrats, closely linked to their pre-capitalist or
proto-capitalist character. To a large degree, the modern bourgeois
bureaucracy developed in a straight – if 'self-reforming' – line from the
bureaucracy of the absolutist state. Ludwig von Mises grasped this more
clearly than Weber. Thus, in the preface to his book *Bureaucracy*, he
quotes from a text by a Prussian minister of January 1838:

It is not seemly for a subject to apply the yardstick of his wretched intellect to
the acts of the Chief of State and to arrogate to himself, in haughty insolence,
a public judgement about their fairness.

Half a century later, the rector of Strasburg University could make a
similar statement:

Our officials . . . will never tolerate anybody's wresting the power from their
hands, certainly not parliamentary majorities whom we know how to deal
with in a masterly way. No kind of rule is endured so easily or accepted so
gratefully as that of highminded and highly educated civil servants. The
German State is a State of the supremacy of officialdom – let us hope that it
will remain so.[78]

In point of fact, the prototype of the modern state bureaucracy comes
from Austria rather than Prussia. Whereas Prussian absolutism involved

an essentially military state, in which the bureaucracy was subservient to the martial aim, the Austrian bureaucracy, especially after its strengthening by the reforms of Joseph II, embodied much broader social and economic purposes than those of the army establishment. It acquired greater power than in Prussia, largely because of the numerous social and national conflicts which divided the ruling classes in the Empire. And it internalized an 'enlightenment' ideology that made little headway in the Prussian bureaucracy. This did not make it less inclined to despotism, although it remained more vulnerable both objectively and subjectively.

Weber's theory of bureaucracy reached its greatest popularity at a time when 'organized capitalism' seemed to be all-powerful – that is, during the long wave of expansion following the Second World War. This postwar Weberianism in politics and sociology corresponded to triumphant neo-Keynesianism in the field of economic policy. State intervention through expert bureaucrats was supposed to guarantee forever full employment, economic growth, rising standards of living, social peace, a real brave new world.

Then the big crises erupted one after the other: explosions in Third World countries; a general crisis of bourgeois social relations culminating in May 1968; a turn from the long expansionary wave to the long depressionary wave in the early seventies. Illusions in the rationality of state intervention now started to wane. But the apparent recourse to 'the free market' did not solve any of the fundamental problems; it even heightened them. 'Organized capitalism' turned into 'disorganized capitalism'.[79] Weber's theory cannot explain that. Marxism can.

The Japanese experience, which is often held up as the most efficient model of late capitalism, has largely been 'overdetermined' by the directive role of the MITI ministry. As a number of objective commentators have pointed out, including in Japan itself, this model was born out of wartime needs and the post-war recovery from devastation, and although it has been imitated with some success in Taiwan and South Korea, it is difficult to see how it could be transplanted today to Europe or North America. Whether it will weather the storm of the next recession, or itself turn into 'disorganized capitalism', remains to be seen.

9. Schumpeter's Views on the Trend to Bureaucratization

Joseph Schumpeter was by far the most important representative of the Austrian school of economists, to which he tried to give a new and more dynamic direction. He proved able to grasp most clearly, after Marx, the nature of capitalism as a system of uncontrolled growth, coining the formula 'creative destruction' to define its basic characteristic.

It is thus no accident that towards the end of his life, Schumpeter devoted his last book to the problem of bureaucracy. Its very title, *Capitalism, Socialism and Democracy*, indicates to what extent he was concerned with the contradictory and universal aspects of the bureaucratic phenomenon. His approach is certainly superior to Weber's, because it comes more tellingly to grips with the basic dynamic of the economic system in question.

Schumpeter posits a trend towards bureaucratization as a form of self-destruction stemming from the inner contradictions of capitalism. Monopoly capitalism saps the entrepreneurial spirit, both by increasing the delegation and formalization of power within the firm and by exercising a negative influence on economic efficiency. Technological innovation becomes routinely organized. Thereby, bureaucratized capitalism moves in the direction of bureaucratized socialism.

In these analyses, Schumpeter may be seen as the real father of the theory of 'convergence between the two systems' that gained considerable popularity in the sixties. He further argued that since monopoly capitalism begets large-scale unemployment and underemployment of resources, bureaucratized socialism will appear as a lesser evil and people will democratically opt in favour of it.

Thus, unlike the neo-liberals Hayek and von Mises, the other main representatives of the Austrian school, Schumpeter did not believe that bureaucracy was necessarily incompatible with civil liberties, or that it equalled the 'road to serfdom'. He inclined more to Weber's view that a certain 'rational' form of bureaucratic rule could be made acceptable (and sufficiently flexible) through a consolidation of political democracy. But as he shared the bourgeois liberals' distrust of the potential competence of the working class, he could not visualize anything other than a hyper-centralized form of socialism, considering democratic socialism to be utopian at least in the field of economic management. Not surprisingly, then, he could take only the Stalinist Communists seriously in his analysis.[80] *De gustibus non est disputandum.*

10. Power and Wealth

In the final analysis, the problem of the weight and limits of capitalist bureaucracies boils down to the problem of the relative autonomy of the state apparatus vis-à-vis the ruling class as such and the rule of money wealth in bourgeois society. No serious Marxist ever denied a degree of such autonomy, as may be seen most plainly in Marx's theory of

Bonapartism and its later development by Trotsky, Thalheimer, Gramsci and others. The question is: what are its limits?

We have already dealt with the manifold ties of the top bureaucratic layers to the bourgeois class, bourgeois interests, values, mentalities, ideologies and prejudices. More important, however, is their insertion into bourgeois society as it actually functions, under the rule of money wealth and money power. No capitalist bureaucracy, whether private, semi-public or public, can free itself from that dominion. All top bureaucrats, even if they rebel in spirit, sooner or later go the way of all flesh, attempting to translate their power into private capital accumulation.[81] That is the key dissimilarity between bourgeois and pre-capitalist or post-capitalist societies. In the latter, power overrides money; owners of money wealth can be expropriated by those who hold power.[82] In the former, no state – including the Nazi one – has been able to overcome the sway of money wealth. Whoever does not grasp this difference, does not understand the little nuance between having and not-having.[83]

The saga of Italy's Mediobanca perfectly illustrates the peculiar relationship between state power (including state ownership) and private Big Business under late capitalism. For a period, the state-owned Milan merchant bank Mediobanca, run by Italy's *éminence grise* Enrico Cuccia, operated as a holding company through which the most powerful billionaire families – Agnelli, Pirelli, Garolini, De Benedetti, et al. – controlled their respective corporations. 'A classic example of the Cuccia method is the way he preserved the Pirelli family control of its tyre and cable business, although it has only 6 per cent of the equity. This has been achieved through a "syndicate" that includes the great and the good of Italian finance which supports the family at all costs. The Pirellis return the favour if their allies need assistance.'[84]

Nowadays, as Mediobanca moves to add Italy's largest insurance company, Assicurazione Generale, as the jewel in its crown, the political establishment headed by Christian Democrat Andreotti and Social Democrat Craxi have brought considerable pressure to bear to weaken this club of industrialists and bankers. The intrigue involved the appointment of the chairmen of two other Milan-based state banks, Banca Commerciale Italiana and Credito Italiano.

Pirelli once said: 'What Cuccia wants, God wants too.' And Andreotti is supposed to have replied: 'We have to bear in mind that it is not possible that a private establishment above good and evil should do as it pleases.'[85] We shall have to wait and see whether Cuccia's power will really be weakened through the appointment of more malleable directors of the two state-owned banks. One banker at least is convinced that politicians would not go far in compromising Mediobanca's operations: 'It would be an act of sado-masochism', he is alleged to have said. But the reality of money power is such that even before these nominations occur, 'a number of the big families like the Agnellis and the Pirellis have . . . started to strengthen their positions within their own companies' – let's bet with the help of credits, including from the state-owned banks.[86] Power such as this – and similar stories could be told from other capitalist countries – can never be broken up without the expropriation of the big capitalists' wealth.

For a long time, observers of things social have been fascinated by Lord Acton's dictum: power corrupts, absolute power corrupts absolutely. The Marxist Stefan Heym has recently repeated it, drawing the logical and correct conclusion that there is an absolute need for social control from below.[87]

But if we consider the actual functioning of bourgeois society through five centuries, especially in mature and late capitalism with its growing bureaucratization of socio-economic life, then the formula which best fits reality has to be substantially different. It should read: Power corrupts. A lot of power begets a lot of corruption. But in the epoch of capitalism, no power can be absolute, because in the last analysis money and wealth rule. Big wealth corrupts as much as, if not more than, big power. Huge sums of money beget huge power and therefore corrupt absolutely. You can eliminate near-absolute power only if you do away both with the strong state and with huge money wealth.

NOTES

1. See Perry Anderson's classic study *Lineages of the Absolutist State*, London 1974.

2. The Prussian minister von Puttkammer is supposed to have said that in every strike appears the hydra of revolution. This is a slight overstatement – but it contains a kernel of truth.

3. Immanuel Wallerstein, Samir Amin and, to a lesser extent, André Gunder Frank have at various times argued that metropolitan capital accumulation originates mainly from exploitation of the 'periphery' through trade and prices. This thesis gravely underestimates the centrality of surplus-value production in the metropolis, and of the industrial revolution and industry in general. Needless to say, it is strongly at variance with Marx's *Capital* and cannot be verified by empirical data. Samir Amin has recently moved away from that extreme position.

4. This tradition was especially marked in France, where the early stages of the Revolution traumatized the bourgeoisie and led to its embracing the strong, centralized Napoleonic state.

5. See Marx on the self-organization of the bourgeoisie in Saint-Quentin and other medieval towns. Marx to Engels, 27 July 1854, in *Marx–Engels, Selected Correspondence*, Moscow 1975, p. 81.

6. Lucio Colletti (*From Rousseau to Lenin*, London 1972) accurately traces this affiliation between Rousseau's radical concept of direct democracy and Lenin's defence of soviet power in *State and Revolution*. In his subsequent break with Marxism, Colletti goes back on his insights.

7. The Paris Commune of 1792–93, for example, took seriously the ideals of liberty, equality and fraternity, transforming them from bourgeois into potentially anti-capitalist values. See Engels to Kautsky, 20 February 1889.

8. Eva Etzioni-Halevy, *Bureaucracy and Democracy*, London 1983, p. 115; and *The Economist*, 19 May 1990.

9. Etzioni-Halevy, pp. 57–58. See also E. Kamenka, *Bureaucracy*, Oxford 1989, pp. 125–29. Ralph Miliband's *The State in Capitalist Society* (chs 4 and 8), London 1969, is the best work on the shifting centre of gravity of the bourgeois state. Jean Meynaud, who is not a Marxist, notes the same tendency in *La Technocratie*, Paris 1964.

10. Jacques Ellul, *The Technological Society*, London 1965, p. 259.

11. In a certain sense, the French Regulation School believes the system to be capable of secreting mechanisms that more or less automatically guarantee the reproduction of capitalist relations of production and the bourgeois order, independently of state intervention. This underestimates the explosive character of successive crises of capitalism in the twentieth century.

12. The Keynesian and neo-Keynesian variant is the most obvious but by no means the only one.

13. Hitler's Autobahn system, for example, had already been designed by ministerial technocrats of the Weimar Republic in the twenties.

14. Especially in the USA, parliament has developed a sub-bureaucracy of congressmen's secretaries and assistants to cope with the mounting, and ever less controllable, mass of proposed legislation and related controversies.

15. Etzioni-Halevy, p. 93.

16. See Miliband.

17. Except in some Third World countries.

18. See E. Mandel, 'The Role of the Individual in History: the Case of World War Two', *New Left Review* 157, May–June 1986.

19. *International Herald Tribune*, 8 July 1990.

20. The fiscal realm puts to the test the attitude of Big Business to bourgeois legality. Evasion of the law begins to appear as legitimate and to foster a new branch of business in its own right. Hence the growing criminalization of whole layers of the big bourgeoisie under late capitalism, and its coexistence with *mafiosi* eager to 'go legit'.

21. The most striking recent examples have been the general strikes in Spain and Greece against socialist-led governments; the confrontation that erupted in 1989 between the Swedish social-democratic government and the trade unions; the open break of the Kinnock Labour leadership with the mass-based anti-poll-tax federation; the major dispute between the Belgian teachers' union and the Catholic–Social Democrat government coalition in 1990; and the massive opposition of the French trade unions to the Rocard government's attempt to whittle away some of the social security conquests.

22. *Süddeutsche Zeitung*, 2 July 1990. This process seems to have gone furthest in Spain. The Belgian daily *Le Soir* writes as follows of the 1990 congress of the Spanish PSOE: 'Nearly seventy per cent of the 871 Socialist delegates currently occupy political posts. . . . Most of the delegates could have been chauffeur-driven to the congress in their official cars. . . . As the Spanish press has noted, although the 871 delegates represent a 'socialist workers' party', they do not include a single worker among them! They are above all teachers, with also a lot of lawyers, functionaries, economists, engineers and doctors.' *Le Soir*, 10–11 November 1990.

23. The prototype was the 1937 no-strike agreement in the Swiss metal industry, which has now operated for more than half a century.

24. Tarnow was one of the main theoreticians of the German trade-union federation, ADGB.

25. The authoritative Marxist study of 'the social wage' is Anwar M. Shaikh and E. Ahmet Touak, *National Accounts and Marxian Categories*, draft copy, December 1989.

26. See, among others, Hans-Jürgen Schulz's book on the *Neue Heimat* scandal in West Germany: *Die Ausplünderung der Neuen Heimat*, Frankfurt/Main 1987.

27. Some proponents of the 'corporatist' thesis assume that there is a growing equalization of power between trade unions and big corporations or employers' associa-

tions in the West. For a refutation of such ideas, see Leo Panitch, *Working Class Politics in Crisis*, London 1986.

28. R. Hilferding, *Finance Capital*, London 1981, p. 370.

29. Hilferding, 'Zur Frage des Generalstreiks', *Die Neue Zeit*, 1903–1904. The real initiator of the mass-strike theory was Parvus. See his article 'Staatsstreich und politischer Massenstreik', *Die Neue Zeit*, 1895–96.

30. Hilferding, 'Worum handelt es sich?', *Die Freiheit* (daily of the USPD), 23 November 1918.

31. See Hilferding's counter-report of 15 October 1920, in *Protokoll über die Verhandlungen des ausserordentlichen Parteitags der USPD in Halle vom 12. bis zum 17. Oktober 1920*. The experience of the general strike against the Kapp–von Lüttwitz putsch in the same year, in which the reformist unions called for a general strike and even for the formation of a workers' government, certainly vindicated Hilferding's criticism of Zinoviev's ultra-left definition. On the other hand, his analysis seriously underestimated the role of the reformist bureaucracy and its ideology as barriers to mass struggle, especially in pre-revolutionary and revolutionary conditions when it could openly resort to counter-revolutionary initiatives.

32. Hilferding, 'Revolutionärer Sozialismus', *Zeitschrift für Sozialismus* No. 5, February 1934.

33. Hilferding, 'Staatkapitalismus oder totalitäre Staatswirtschaft?', in Armin Hetzer, ed., *Dokumente der Arbeiterbewegung*, Bremen 1977. This article, which first appeared in the Menshevik organ *Sotsialisticheskii Viestnik* No. 8, 25 April 1940, polemicized with Trotsky's view that the bureaucracy was the ruling social layer in the USSR. But Hilferding's argument that it was 'the state' which ruled begs the question. For how can one divorce the state from those who compose and lead the state apparatus?

34. Karl Kautsky, *Die proletarische Revolution und ihr Programm*, Berlin 1922, pp. 106, 101.

35. Ibid., p. 130.

36. Ibid., p. 158.

38. Naturally it is administrative, managerial and scientific labour which is better paid under Kautsky's 'socialism', as it is under capitalism, on the specious grounds that no one would otherwise wish to do such demanding work. But is it not incomparably *less* nerve-racking and injurious to health and life than the labour of a miner, and *more* agreeable and stimulating than that of a refuse collector or construction worker? Why then should these latter categories be paid four times less than top managers, technologists and scientists?

38. Hilferding, 'Die Aufgaben der Sozialdemokratie in der Republik', in *Protokolle über die Verhandlungen des Sozialdemokratischen Parteitags in Kiel vom 22. bis 27. Mai 1927*, p. 220.

39. Trotsky, *On France*, New York 1979, p. 112.

40. If the Reichswehr hesitated for a time about the prospect of a Nazi dictatorship, this was not because of any principled opposition but because it was not sure of how the working class would react. As soon as the cowardly policy of the SPD and KPD leaderships became clear, it gave Hindenburg the green light to call on Hitler to form a government.

41. Hilferding, 1927 report, p. 219.

42. Ibid., p. 218. In many ways we can consider Hilferding – together with Bukharin and his concept of 'state monopolist trusts' – as the real forerunner of the Stalinist concept of 'state monopoly capitalism' which achieved wide currency after the Second World War.

43. Hilferding actually made the masses responsible for the victory of fascism (and also, implicitly, of Stalinism). In 1935 he wrote in a letter: 'The truth is that the masses fastened on to Hitler (and not only 'Germany'). Pitiably squeezed, the workers, certainly most of them, have played a disappointing role.' Letter to Paul Hertz, 17 January 1935, quoted in Cora Stephan, ed., *Zwischen den Stühlen: Oder über die Unvereinbarkeit von Theorie und Praxis: Schriften Rudolf Hilferdings 1904 bis 1940*, West Berlin 1982, p. 279. All evidence available today shows that judgement to have been quite false. The German workers desperately wanted to act against the Nazis in the decisive months of 1932 and 1933. It was the leaders who refused to fight, for reasons of organizational fetishism,

parliamentary cretinism, illusionary opportunism, or outright fear of mass struggles.

44. Otto Bauer, 'Rätediktatur oder Demokratie' (March 1919) and 'Weltrevolution' (May 1919), both in *Werkausgabe*, vol. 2, Vienna 1976; 'Kapitalherrschaft in der Demokratie' (1928), in *Werkausgabe*, vol. 9, pp. 202f; and 'Die illegale Partei'.

45. This shows how favourable the relationship of forces had been for the proletariat in November 1918 – and how easy it would have been for it to take power.

46. O. Bauer, 'Der blutige 15. Juli' and 'Die politische und wirtschaftliche Lage Oesterreichs', in *Werkausgabe*, vol. 3; 'Die illegale Partei', pp. 381–82.

47. One of the most striking instances of private military enrichment was the Indonesian general in charge of the Pertamina oil company, who is said to have accumulated (that is, essentially embezzled) half a billion dollars.

48. See E. Mandel, 'Pays semi-coloniaux et pays dominés semi-industrialisés', *Quatrième Internationale* 13/3, April 1984. In our discussion here we leave aside the political–social motivations of the 'modernizing' sectors of the ruling power bloc in the semi-industrialized countries – factors which should not however be underestimated.

49. There is an extensive bibliography on the subject. See, among others, Marshall Dimock and John Hyde, *Bureaucracy and Trusteeship in Large Corporations*, TNEC study No. 11, Washington 1940; William F. Whyte, ed., *Industry and Society*, New York 1946; William E. Moore, *Industrial Relations and the Social Order*, London 1946.

50. See, for example, William H. Whyte, *The Organization Man*, New York 1956.

51. This has been alleged by, among others, Robert A. Brady, in *Business as a System of Power*, New York 1943.

52. Alvin A. Gouldner, *Patterns of Industrial Bureaucracy*, Glencoe, Ill. 1954.

54. Quoted in Nelson Lichtenstein, *Labor's War at Home: The CIO in World War II*, Cambridge 1982, p. 179.

54. David F. Noble, *Forces of Production*, New York 1984, p. 81. Emphasis added.

55. Ibid., p. 145.

56. The term itself is the title of a well-known book by Bruno Rizzi, first published privately in French in 1939. B. Rizzi, *The Bureaucratization of the World*, London 1985. For Galbraith, see his concept of the 'technostructure' in *The New Industrial State*, Harmondsworth 1969.

57. H. Kaufman, 'Fear of Bureaucracy: A Raging Pandemic', in *Public Administration Review*, 1981, No. 41, pp. 5–6.

58. *Limits to Bureaucratic Growth*.

59. The outgoing chairman of British Rail – which is still supposed to be a public service – declared in early January 1990 in a speech to the Chartered Institute of Transport: 'Our duty is not to run a service that is desirable – it is to run a service that is profitable.' (*The Observer*, 14 January 1990.) This policy has already cost many human lives. It will cost many more – and in the long run, from a macro-economic (and even more a macro-social) point of view, it will lead to losses far greater than any short-term profits.

60. Gillman even developed a theory that higher costs of surplus-value realization have become a permanent feature of contemporary capitalism. See G.M. Gillman, *The Falling Rate of Profit*, London 1957.

61. See C.N. Parkinson, *Parkinson's Law*, London 1958.

62. Stefan Heym, *Einmischung*, Munich 1990, p. 226.

63. Amitai Etzioni, *Complex Organizations*, New York 1975, p. 157.

64. R.K. Merton, *Social Structures and Social Theory*, Glencoe, Ill., pp. 151–52. Weber's *Wirtschaft und Gesellschaft* has been edited in English by A.M. Henderson and Talcott Parsons, as *Max Weber's Theory of Organization*, New York 1947.

65. *Patterns of Industrial Bureaucracy*.

66. Weber's dual formula harks back to the contradictory theories of state legitimacy in Greek Antiquity: Plato's normativism and Aristotle's realism. Their contradictions, especially those of Aristotle, have been exploded by the experiences of Stalinism and fascism, where, after all, 'really existing laws' were also applied, and innocent people were sentenced, imprisoned and murdered on a 'legal' basis.

67. Max Weber, pp. 329, 339, 254.

68. Quoted from the chapter on bureaucracy (*Wirtschaft und Gesellschaft*, pt 3, ch. 6), in *From Max Weber: Essays in Sociology*, eds H.H. Gerth and C. Wright Mills, London 1970, p. 229.

69. See the summary in Meyer, Stevenson and Webster.

70. See Michel Crozier, *Actors and Systems: The Politics of Collective Action*, Chicago 1980.

71. See Parsons's comments in Henderson and Parsons, p. 59.

72. Cf. Gouldner, pp. 20–21. Gouldner correctly suggests (pp. 26–27) that, had Weber studied industrial (intra-factory) bureaucracies, this contradiction would have leapt to his eyes.

73. See the final chapter of E. Mandel, *Late Capitalism*, London 1975.

74. In his inaugural speech at Munich University, Max Weber in 1895 justified Germany's turn towards 'world power politics' (*Weltmachtpolitik*) as he would justify colonial wars of conquest by Germany and the First World War. In his lecture of 1919 to students at Munich University ('Politics as a Vocation', in Gerth and Mills, eds, *From Max Weber*, pp. 77–128) Weber drew a distinction between an 'absolute ethic' or 'ethic of ultimate ends' and an 'ethic of responsibility'. The latter, which always implies a judgement on the balance-sheet of positive and negative results, obliges the politician to take responsibility for the practical consequences of his action (or inaction). Weber thus takes his stand with a variant of moral relativism. But he does not add, as Marxists would do, that the withering away of such a relative standard is desirable; that moral relativism rests in the last analysis upon social conflicts reflecting the opposition of material class interests; and that the withering away of 'dual morality' is conditional upon the emergence of a classless and stateless society.

It is thus inconsistent and rather hypocritical of Weber, and especially latter-day Weberians, to reproach the Bolsheviks and revolutionary socialists in general for the application of moral double standards. Indeed, within the framework of an 'ethic of responsibility', a judgement on which forms of injustice a politician should prefer will clearly be determined by class interests and class prejudices. Weber himself enthusiastically endorsed colonial conquests and imperialist wars which cost millions and millions of human lives. Were those really the 'lesser evil'?

75. See F. Mehring, *Die Lessingslegende*, Stuttgart 1920, pp. 103–104.

76. F. Mehring, 'Ein altpreussischer Bürokrat', in *Zur Deutschen Geschichte*, vol. 3, Berlin 1947, p. 325.

77. F. Engels, 'The Status Quo and the Bourgeoisie', in *Marx–Engels Collected Works*, vol. 6, pp. 87–88.

78. Ludwig von Mises, *Bureaucracy*, Yale University Press 1944, pp. iv–v.

79. See Claus Offe, *Disorganized Capitalism*, Oxford 1985.

80. J. Schumpeter, *Capitalism, Socialism and Democracy*, London 1943, p. 363.

81. Typical in this respect is what happened under the Nazi dictatorship. Even the relatively austere Hitler became a very rich man, and Goering a billionaire. All top and middle layers of the Nazi administration were utterly corrupt. And contrary to a certain legend, the SS leaders were literally obsessed with the accumulation of gold and money and tried to integrate their spreading slave-labour empire with 'normal' capitalism.

82. Until the fifteenth century, relatively weak kings could still confiscate big bankers' fortunes, as the ungrateful Louis XI did to Jacques Coeur who had financed all his wars to promote the unity of France. But in the sixteenth century Emperor Charles V, though ten times richer and more powerful, could no longer cancel his debts to the Antwerp and German bankers. Economic power had shifted decisively in favour of the capitalist class.

83. The Polish Marxist Stanislaw Kozyr-Kowalski has developed an interesting critique of Weber's theory of social classes. While showing that its emphasis on property is close to Marx, he also brings out the crucial differences, among which is Weber's inclusion in the capitalist ruling class of those whose privileges derive exclusively from education. 'Ownership and Classes in Max Weber's Sociology', *Polish Sociological Bulletin* 1/4, 1982.

84. *Sunday Times*, 20 May 1990.

85. *International Herald Tribune*, 15 May 1990. Paradoxically this problem was raised only after it had been privatized!

86. *Sunday Times*, 20 May 1990. At the same time, it was reported that Mediobanca – which wields its power through a web of interlocking ownership – wanted to extend its (that is, the Big Families') control over Italian industry through privatization of the *Banca Commerciale Italiana*. (*International Herald Tribune*, 15 May 1990.) By November it appeared that a compromise had been reached through the creation of a 'superbank' around the Banca di Roma, in which public and private shareholders were both associated. Cuccia gave his blessing to this superbank because it will continue to collect money for Mediobanca, which will remain under the control of the 'syndicate'. *Panorama*, 4 November 1990.

87. Stefan Heym, p. 258.

5

Self-administration, Abundance and the Withering Away of Bureaucracy

1. The Actuality of Political Revolution

When Trotsky first raised the prospect of a political anti-bureaucratic revolution in the USSR, this caused a great scandal among communists and left social democrats in the mould of Otto Bauer. Even his most gifted, though quite critical, follower, Isaac Deutscher, expressed doubts about its realism as late as 1963.[1]

History has now given its verdict, and it weighs heavily in Trotsky's favour. A real process of political revolution did indeed begin in Hungary in October–November 1956, in Czechoslovakia in 1968–69, in Poland in 1980–81, and in the GDR, Czechoslovakia and Romania in 1989. An embryo of one has emerged in the People's Republic of China.

Curiously enough, while some left critics of Stalinism remain sceptical about the 'feasibility' of the political revolution, the head of the Soviet state himself repeatedly used the word 'revolution' to describe what was needed to put the USSR back on the tracks toward socialism.[2] Indeed, like Trotsky and Deutscher before him, he used the historical analogy with the French revolutions of 1830, 1848 and 1870 to identify the quality of a *political* revolution. This extends or consolidates the social system born of a prior social revolution (1789–94 in the case of France), enabling it to realize its full potential. It is thus the very antithesis of a social counter-revolution.[3]

The likelihood of a political anti-bureaucratic revolution hinges on several questions: the depth and explosiveness of the systemic crisis; the extent of the antagonism between the toiling masses, essentially the working class, and the bureaucracy or its top stratum, the nomenklatura; the relationship of forces between the major classes and class fractions; and the capacity of the nomenklatura for self-reform, pointing in the direction of its own suppression. The four historical alternatives are: victorious social counter-revolution (restoration of capitalism); continued self-reproduction of the bureaucracy, with the possibility of protracted crisis and further decomposition;[4] radical self-reform of the bureaucracy; and a victorious political anti-bureaucratic revolution.

Again the verdict of history is clear on at least two of these possible outcomes. The depth of the systemic crisis cannot be denied by anyone who looks reality in the face,[5] while the degree of hostility between the working class and the nomenklatura is even greater than revolutionary Marxists assumed. Trotsky's suggestion in 1936 that the workers were unwilling to rise for fear that 'in throwing out the bureaucracy, they would open the way for a capitalist restoration' does not in any case apply today.[6] And the narrow limits of bureaucratic self-reform have been strikingly demonstrated by the evolution of Tito, Khrushchev, Mao and Deng. They are in the course of being confirmed by the Gorbachev experiment too.

If one central conclusion can be drawn from the perestroika–glasnost process, it is that unless a 'revolution from below' overtakes the 'reforms from above' (and they are just that, not a 'revolution from above'), it is impossible to eliminate the obstacles that huge bureaucratic machines place in the way of radical reforms.

What characterizes a *victorious* political anti-bureaucratic revolution is not only the sweep of mass actions but also the high level of consciousness and revolutionary leadership. It is not so much a question of mechanically repeating formulas from 1917, 1927 or 1936 ('dictatorship of the proletariat', 'real soviet power', 'collective ownership of the means of production and exchange', 'dominance of central planning', and so on). The point, rather, is to secure their real content, in terms which relate to mass consciousness as it has been shaped through the traumatic experiences of Stalinist and post-Stalinist dictatorship.

This real content is clear enough. The producers, collectively and in their concrete forms of articulation, have to be the real masters of the major means of production and exchange. They democratically decide on the broad priorities and proportions in which existing resources are to be allocated. The remaining or reappearing nuclei of the former ruling classes are prevented from hiring wage-labour beyond a strictly limited threshold. The accumulation of capital remains severely restricted.[7] Equality prevails in the assured distribution of basic goods and services for all. These guarantees should be written into the constitution and changed only by 75 or 80 per cent of the popular vote. The political conditions for their erosion would thus become impossible or nearly so, especially if political power was firmly in the hands of the working people.

If the political revolution achieves all these safeguards, it will undoubtedly have secured a new social order against the restoration of capitalism. The vast majority of producers/consumers will be integrated into the running of society and will therefore consciously identify with it. The economy will become more efficient through the elimination of bureaucratic mismanagement, the main source today of the massive waste and disproportions. With regard to these effects, we can confidently base ourselves on extensive empirical evidence and reasonable working hypotheses. But to create the political prerequisites for such a successful revolution is quite another matter. It will probably take some considerable time.

No final answer can yet be given to the decisive historical question. Could a victorious political revolution in the post-capitalist societies qualitatively reduce the dimensions and weight of the bureaucracy? Could the withering away of the state (nobody seriously proposes its immediate abolition) really gain and keep momentum? Or would a somewhat slimmer and chastened bureaucracy take over and maintain its basic grip on society? If political revolution failed then the prospects for capitalist restoration would greatly increase.

This question stretches beyond the political revolution per se. It also concerns the destiny of victorious revolutions in the capitalist part of the world. Will they be able to avoid bureaucratic degeneration, or grave bureaucratic deformations, even in the 'ideal' case of an international socialist society embracing all the main industrialized and semi-industrialized countries? In other words: can the functions that the bureaucratic apparatuses have usurped from society, taken as a whole, gradually be devolved to the mass of citizens? Is that vision of Engels and of Lenin's *State and Revolution* as utopian as nearly everyone claims it to be?[8] If not, what are the prerequisites for a radical extension of self-administration in the world as it is, with the working masses as they are today?

2. The Political Preconditions of the Withering Away of the State

The gradual withering away of the bureaucracy, and in any case a radical contraction of its scale and weight in society, implies first of all a politically weaker state. The larger the political centralization of power, the stronger the state, and the stronger the bureaucracy.

In the minds of many contemporary sociologists and political scientists, a weakening of the state has become identified with a reduction in the power of the secret police or the repressive apparatus. This chimes in with the 'reductionist', vulgar-Marxist view of the state and the bureaucracy. In reality, however, even in the Soviet Union and the United

States, not to speak of Western Europe and Japan, the broadly defined repressive apparatuses account for only quite a small percentage of the upper and middle layers of the bureaucracy, of the people who exercise state functions in a position of command over other people. The major parts of the state administration are to be found elsewhere, and that is where we have to look if we want to know what a withering away of the state would really mean.

The first prerequisite for a weaker state is a qualitative growth of *political* democracy, for the state is above all a machine for exercising political power. Concretely, a whole series of administrative centres – starting with ministries and their regional equivalents – have to be abolished and replaced by self-administrative bodies. Today many of these ministries are redundant: they duplicate functions that are already largely performed by parallel institutions. A ministry of transport, education or health duplicates respectively the railway, airline and other such administrations, the school and university administrations, and the hospital and public-health administrations where some socialized system is in operation.

The suppression of these ministries, and the devolution of their powers to self-administrative bodies, would not entail a rise of new bureaucracies if it was tied to a sharp cut in the number of full-time functionaries and a sweeping process of decentralization.[9] The key tasks could then be assumed by local or community bodies such as schools, hospitals, railway centres, power stations, telecommunications centres, and so on.

Of course, this could not be done rapidly with all ministries. There would still be conflicts of sectoral interests and problems of coordination, to which we shall return in a moment. But the upper and middle layers of officialdom could certainly be thinned out – naturally we do not call a teacher, doctor, nurse, radar technician or electrician a 'bureaucrat'. We would be so bold as to propose such a cut in every advanced industrialized country to the tune of 50 per cent.

As important as this numerical reduction, if not more so, is the *qualitative* extension of political democracy. This has to be pluralistic and all-pervading. A multi-party system with free, democratic elections and the greatest possible broadening of all human rights and political freedoms (freedom of association, assembly and demonstration; freedom of the press, religion, cultural and scientific creation, thought, research, etc.) – all these are absolute preconditions for the enlargement of political democracy.[10] The power of the state to limit these freedoms, especially for reasons of 'state security', has to be drastically curtailed.[11]

Here the classical Marxist critique of bourgeois democracy comes into its own. To be sure, it is essential to guarantee these formal rights and freedoms. But it is likewise essential to give the mass of the people the means to enjoy them. There is no contradiction between these two principles – contrary to what Stalinists (or neo-Stalinists) and dogmatic liberals (or neo-liberals) traditionally argue.

The example of press and media freedom confirms this general rule. The formal guarantees are: no censorship, either by the state, by proprietors or by professional associations; freedom for any significant group of people to found and operate a newspaper independently of any public or private 'authority'; freedom from criminal prosecution for words written in the press or spoken on radio and television, except in circumstances precisely defined by the law and subject to the verdict of an elected jury in open court. Which liberal, not to say libertarian, defender of the freedom of the press could quarrel with that clear formal definition?

But in order to guarantee that all citizens can *equally and practically* enjoy that freedom, *additional* material conditions have to be created. Access to print-shops and radio or TV stations should be free of charge, on terms that would have to be quite flexible to prevent excessive waste – say, all groups presenting 10,000 signatures would have access to a daily, 5,000 to their own weekly, 1,000 to their own fortnightly, 500 to their own monthly, 100 to a column and individuals to the letters page in a general pluralist weekly or monthly. Periodic review of these conditions in the light of sales, or an increase in signatures, would make them even more democratic.

Even the freedom of advertising could be guaranteed. People would be free to choose the paper in which they preferred to place their advertisement. But the revenue would be put in a common pool to finance the press as a whole.

Overall administration of the press system, and of its necessary financial resources, would be in the hands neither of state or municipal institutions nor of journalists' associations but of bodies freely elected by the journalists, workers and technicians in the sector and, pro rata, by the mass of citizens at large. The total costs would be decided by freely elected central bodies responsible for the priority allocation of national resources: parliament, a central workers' council, an economic senate.

Such a real, materially guaranteed freedom of the press for all would not limit the formal freedom of the press for any individual. At least, we have never heard any convincing argument to the contrary. It would restrict the freedom of individuals to launch and own *large* daily newspapers or television stations without sufficient popular support in the form of signed endorsements. It would thus prevent any individual from cornering the market, from establishing a monopoly of the national or even local press. But what is wrong with that? Such 'freedom' for a few individuals suppresses freedom for a great number of individuals, whereas in the extended political democracy we propose, *all* individuals would enjoy the freedom of the press.

It can hardly be denied that under capitalist conditions, a small number of magnates – Murdoch, Maxwell, Hersant, Goldsmith, de Benedetti, Berlusconi, Springer, Bertelsman, et al. in Europe – have gained control over a large part of the daily press. The financial costs of launching a new paper have risen so much that they are beyond the means even of large mass parties like the West German SPD or the British Labour Party. Claude Julien recently summed up the situation as follows: 'Fifty-four million "equal" citizens had the right to buy TF1 [the now privatized French TV channel]. Only two of them, Messrs Lagardère and Bouygues, became potential buyers.'[12]

Nobody could seriously argue that this is superior or equal to the real freedom of the media that is part of an old socialist programme. In fact, there is an old bourgeois–liberal/conservative tradition which openly stands for the limitation of democratic freedoms out of fear of 'majority' or 'mob' excesses or repression. Logically, they defend the curbing of freedoms themselves – above all the freedom of the majority – on the pretext of defending their own (minority) freedoms. The rights of capitalist private property take precedence over freedom. Against those who advocate restriction and repression, whether through capitalist strong states or post-capitalist state bureaucracies, socialists unreservedly support democratic rights and freedoms for all.

The extension of political democracy implies that representative, indirect forms should be complemented by a wide range of direct democracy. Here too a classical Marxist critique of bourgeois parliamentary democracy comes into its own.

Under capitalism parliamentary democracy is a regime in which the unequal distribution and use of wealth implies inequality of political power. Liberal theory assumes that once universal suffrage has been achieved, the ballot box ensures equal political weight for each individual. But this is an obvious fiction, as rich people can influence the electorate in ways that are not open to ordinary citizens. During the last presidential elections in the United States, for example, both the Republican and the Democratic Party spent tens of millions of dollars, essentially on TV slots. In the Japanese general elections of 1990, the ruling conservative party spent more than half-a-million dollars on *each* of its 380 candidates. Which group of ordinary citizens could possibly match that kind of financial effort?

Furthermore, parliamentary democracy is, by definition, indirect democracy. The mass of citizens do not continuously exercise their sovereign power but alienate it to representative institutions. If one takes large countries such as Brazil, Japan, Germany, France or Britain, and *a fortiori* the USA, USSR, India or China, then tens or hundreds of millions of people 'delegate' their sovereignty to no more than a thousand people in central parliaments. Even if elected regional bodies are added, the figure is still only a few tens of thousands.

This alienation of sovereignty (democracy, after all, does mean rule by the people) inevitably produces huge administrative apparatuses which have to mediate between the elected representatives and those who have to apply, and especially live with, their decisions. A general rule can be formulated: the larger the country, the greater the shift in decision-making power from the citizens to representative bodies, and the larger the bureaucratic state (and para-state) administration.

Important areas of direct democracy should therefore be carved out in political life, in order radically to reduce the scope and weight of the bureaucracy. Citizens' bodies in neighbourhoods (for large cities), towns and villages could assume many of the duties of municipal and regional councils, and not a few of the state administration. Local federations of enterprises, run not by functionaries but by people rotated from these bodies without additional pay, could play a major role in the same sense. That is, after all, what a 'commune system' is all about.[13]

Another form of direct democracy would be large-scale use of the referendum. This poses least problems on questions of a local or regional character. But on national issues, too, despite the many misgivings in the socialist movement, it could serve an educative function and help to stimulate democracy.[14] This is the balance-sheet of the only experience of referenda being widely used over a long period of time, in Switzerland.

All these forms of direct democracy – and several others could be suggested[15] – are not substitutes but complements to universal-suffrage institutions. After the traumatic shocks of fascist, military and Stalinist dictatorships, the working masses throughout the world are deeply committed to free democratic elections to parliament-type bodies. It would be suicidal for socialists to set themselves against that commitment in the name of some spurious dogma echoing the arguments of the Bolsheviks and the Comintern between 1917 and 1921.

The special conditions that led the Bolsheviks to restrict universal suffrage in the first Soviet constitution – the fact that the proletariat was only a small minority of society – do not obtain today in any major country of the world, with the possible exceptions of Indonesia and Pakistan. (Rural wage-earners and landless peasants should obviously be reckoned as part of the proletariat.) The justified wish for a qualitative increase in the scope of direct democracy can perfectly well be realized in a system where the rights of a parliament-type body are limited by the rights of other chambers representing sectors of society (nationalities, producers, women, and so on). Greater frequency of elections, plus the right to recall representatives, would dramatically reduce the 'distance' of parliamentarians from their electors, as well as their tendency to make demagogic electoral promises which they have no intention of keeping.[16]

3. The Social Conditions for a Radical Increase in Self-administration

For all these anti-bureaucratic processes to be implemented in real life, a series of social conditions must exist. Large masses of people must be able and willing to assume tasks necessary for the administration of the 'general affairs of society'.[17] This in turn requires as its main premiss – to which too little attention has been paid until now – a sharp reduction in the working day (or week). There are many reasons why this is a central problem today both in the West and the East, but what concerns us here is that no real qualitative progress can be made toward self-government unless people *have the time to administer the affairs of their workplace or neighbourhood.*

As long as the average man or woman spends ten hours a day at work or between home and work – not counting women's 'second workday' at home – they have neither the time nor the psychological inclination to spend another four hours attending meetings or performing administrative labour. Self-administration and self-management will then to a large extent remain formal and fictitious, irrespective of any 'bad intentions' of political parties, politicians or entrenched bureaucrats. The commune system will automatically give rise to an additional bureaucracy, as the Yugoslav example so sadly proved. Logically, we have to assume that the half-workday of four hours, or the half workweek of twenty hours, would provide the ideal conditions for self-administration on a mass scale.

Another key prerequisite is the suppression of secrecy which, like the strong central state, secretes a plethora of bureaucrats to guard it, as well as agencies to discover and punish its real, potential or imaginary violators. *Without the broadest possible access to information, no serious self-administration is possible, whether in economic life or in other fields of social endeavour.* This is particularly relevant to conditions in large enterprises, where the fragmentation of labour – one of the key elements in alienation – cannot otherwise be overcome. People must know exactly what they are producing, for what reason and with what purpose, before they can even think of themselves taking decisions about the nature and allocation of the products of their labour. The computer and the range of time-sharing systems make such universal access to information incomparably easier to achieve than it was in the past.[18]

But this is not enough. People must be able to use the available information. A minimum of general culture and professional skill, deriving from a high level of education, are obviously indispensable for a qualitative enlargement of self-administration.[19] It might be objected that this is presuming too much, on a planet where there are still four hundred million illiterates in the Third World alone, and standards of literacy are declining in countries like Britain and the United States.[20] No doubt this would be an insuperable obstacle to an overnight deployment of self-administration. But no serious socialist advances such a proposal: we are talking of a *gradual process* that will extend over several generations.

There is absolutely no reason to assume that illiteracy could not be wiped out everywhere in the world in a time-span of fifty years. After all, even a relatively underdeveloped country like Cuba has virtually achieved this in less than thirty years. It is absurd to think that certain people or 'races' are inherently incapable of reaching high levels of cultural and technical education. All that needs to be done is to fix universal literacy as a top priority, and to allocate the necessary resources. As Hegel and the young Marx realized, however, you can't teach people to become free, and to enjoy particular freedoms, without their actually experiencing those freedoms. People also have to educate themselves, to learn the art and science of self-administration by starting the practice immediately, on a broad scale.

Will society thereby incur mistakes and losses? It undoubtedly will. But of which system of administration is that not true? If one draws a balance-sheet of the colossal waste that humanity has endured through capitalist mismanagement and bureaucratic mismanagement – not only of economic resources but of human lives lost in wars and internal repression (literally hundreds of millions in this century) – then the likely costs of a transition to self-administration appear slight indeed.[21]

A further objection raised by well-meaning critics like Michael Harrington, or less well-meaning social democrats, is that most people are simply not prepared to spend a lot of their time in endless meetings.[22] To some extent a simple confusion is involved here. It would certainly be preposterous to imagine that everyone would discuss and decide about everything – indeed, the very idea of a progressive devolution of bureaucratic functions to the mass of citizens implies a basic thrust towards *decentralized* decision-making and administration. Only then could the participation of everybody in public administration ('every cook', in Lenin's famous phrase) be realistically conceived. Evidently the same people will not participate in the running of farms, textile plants, power stations, machine-building factories, banks, hospitals, schools and theatres. Still less will they have to run day after day from a self-management meeting at their workplace to a bus-users' self-administration meeting to a meeting to decide on regional or national energy policy to one discussing measures to combat pollution of the Rhine, Ganges or Amazon. Self-administration does not entail the disappearance of delegation. It combines decision-making by the citizens with stricter control of delegates by their respective electorate.

But is it not the case that the majority of citizens are too indifferent to social problems, too much inclined 'to spend their evenings in front of the TV', for them to assume these new tasks? Again there is an element of misunderstanding in this question. We have already suggested the formula: four hours of non-administrative work plus four hours of administration a day (or, if you prefer, twenty hours of each a week). If self-administration stays within those time-limits, it does not increase the total workload. It does not reduce leisure or sleep. Inasmuch as there is a valid kernel in the objection, it simply confirms that a radical reduction in the working week is a prerequisite for expanded self-administration.

The real weakness of such counter-arguments, however, lies in their contradictory concept of human nature, which harks back to the old debates of Locke and Adam Smith, or even Hobbes and Aristotle. On the one hand, they maintain that private self-interest is what motivates people. But on the other hand, they assume that people remain blind to private self-interest as soon as it is not mediated by 'market mechanisms' and eternal 'economic laws'. Everybody is supposed to be inclined to 'enrich themselves', and to have the right to do so. But the workers are accused of being 'selfish' and 'envious' when they defend their material interests against those of privileged classes or social layers.

In reality, the *homo oeconomicus* of liberal theory is not an eternal human type but a historical phenomenon specific to certain social conditions under which people live and think about the world. Inasmuch as we are dealing with human beings who have been conditioned by centuries if not millennia of commodity production, of institutionalized scarcity, real or induced, of the universal struggle for existence with its competition and its drive to accumulate individual wealth, private self-interest does loom large in the consciousness of most citizens, including workers. But for that very reason, because it *is* in their 'private' interest, the majority of people will probably be prepared to take part in some forms of self-administrative activities.

If a quarterly residents' meeting decides on the provision of adequate heating for the block or neighbourhood, will the relevant households really not be motivated to attend? Is it not also their concern at what frequency buses run in a given area, or where the stops are located? Do they not have a vital interest in the workloads and rhythms at their workplace? Are they indifferent to the choice of canteen food at their office or factory, or their children's school? Are they passive on such 'general' questions as pollution in their town and the relationship between their money income and the prices of accommodation, food, holidays or public transport (insofar as these are not yet distributed free of charge)? And will they not feel moved to act to defend the guarantee of full employment?

'Human nature' is largely a representation of human needs, which include the need for self-fulfilment or, as Amitai Etzioni puts it, 'self-actualization without submission, in a peer situation, without any hierarchical relations'.[23] Contrary to the assumptions of so many critics of 'Marxian utopianism', it is precisely the Marxian project of the withering away of the state which corresponds to this fundamental aspect of human nature. For the largest part of its presence on this planet, humankind has lived without states and without bureaucracies.

When we suggest that most citizens will grasp the opportunity to involve themselves directly in decision-making processes, we are not assuming that they will be motivated by the commandment 'to love one's neighbour'. We simply believe that the pursuit of self-interest is not the sole prerogative of stock-exchange sharks, take-over experts, yuppies, industrialists, bankers, small shopkeepers or professional politicians.

We will even go further. People will be indifferent to meetings of the kind we have just described if they have the impression that they are mostly a fake, that the real decisions have already been taken elsewhere. As people are generally more intelligent than the average liberal–conservative (or, alas, social democrat) gives them credit for, they rapidly spot the difference between rubber-stamp gatherings and meetings with real teeth. The first type breed cynicism and apathy, as does the non-fulfilment or reversal of election promises. But the second type set up a virtuous circle of participatory democracy based on self-interest, in which a general social commitment can gradually increase in parallel with the successes of self-administration.[24]

4. The Economic Conditions for Self-administration

If the ultimate source of bureaucracy and state power lies in scarcity, then the withering away of the state depends on its gradual elimination in a climate of abundance. Definitions are needed here in order to avoid semantic disputes which divert attention from the real issues.

It is of course possible to define 'abundance' as a regime of unlimited access to a boundless supply of all goods and services. We have many times pointed out the absurdity of such a notion, which was also expressed in Stalin's talk of 'ever-increasing needs'.[25] It really would be a nightmare if men and women were to 'consume' goods and services every minute of their lives.

The continual accumulation of more and more goods (with declining 'marginal utility') is by no means a universal or even predominant feature of human behaviour. The development of talents and inclinations for their own sake; the protection of health and life; care for children; the development of rich social relations as a prerequisite of mental stability and happiness – all these become major motivations once basic material needs have been satisfied. One has only to look at how the upper reaches of the bourgeoisie conduct themselves with regard to food, clothing, housing, furniture or 'cultural goods' to note that for those who already 'live under communism', rational consumption takes the place of a restless pursuit of more. In fact, it often implies a reduction rather than a growth in the quantity of goods consumed, although huge, irrational waste certainly continues to prevail in other fields.[26]

We can conclude from this that the correct theoretical definition of abundance is *saturation of demand*. A product may be said to be plentiful when the marginal elasticity of demand for it is around or below zero – a level, we should note, at which its distribution free of charge is economically more efficient than further sales at declining 'real' prices, since distribution costs are then sharply reduced. Long-range statistical series, above all in Western Europe, furnish overwhelming evidence that a large number of goods already fall into this category in the richer countries – not only for millionaires but for the mass of the population.

It might be thought that the growing diversity and industrial transformation of basic goods (thirty varieties of bread in German bakeries, for example) contradicts this trend. But the same law asserts itself. If one's average daily consumption of bread stabilizes or gradually declines, for reasons of health or even taste, one cannot just go on consuming an 'ever greater variety' of differently packaged and processed bread. Limited quantity imposes limits on variety and quality too.

This argument might appear more open to doubt in the case of services. But if one defines consumption of services as essentially passive (similar to the consumption of goods), then the same law is applicable. People cannot just consume an unlimited quantity of air trips, telephone conversations or television programmes within the space of one lifetime, where there is increasing concern for such questions as health, happiness and mental/psychological stability. An overdose of anything just kills.

Of course, the picture tends to change if we substitute creative praxis for passive consumption of services. To describe as 'consumption' such activities as playing the piano, painting pictures, modelling vases, practising sports, climbing mountains, making love, walking in parks and woods, watching birds, rearing animals, talking with friends, educating children, caring for the old and the sick, writing books – that would be, to say the least, rather inappropriate. Far from putting plenty out of reach, the flowering of such 'really human' practices requires precisely a reduction of time devoted to the acquisition and consumption of material goods and services. It presupposes increasing plenty and increasing leisure.

Today we have become aware, with much delay, that dangers to the earth's non-renewable resources, and to the natural environment of human civilization and human life, also entail that the consumption of material goods and services cannot grow in an unlimited way.[27] Saturation of demand, of consumption, is not only possible; it is absolutely necessary for the survival of humanity. That is one of the reasons why it has become a life-and-death question to eliminate a system which institutionalizes scarcity by stimulating demand for ever-changing goods, with all the attendant frustrations and psychological or even macroeconomic irrationalities.

Does our definition of abundance or plenty as saturation of current consumption imply an expert's (or philosopher's) arrogance of the Platonic type or, worse, a white man's arrogance with regard to the needs of people in the Third World and to 'cultural pluralism' in general?[28] Not at all. We have never proposed for one moment to limit economic growth or *world* consumption, as soon as the basic needs of people in the Northern hemisphere have been satisfied. Nor have we ever dreamt of maintaining the present international division of labour, which inevitably breeds phenomena of unequal exchange.[29] It would appear obvious that all basic needs of all the world's inhabitants will have to be fulfilled before there can be any talk of general abundance. That is one of the most powerful arguments against the myth of 'socialism in one country' or in a small number of countries.

The goal of abundance, then, imperiously demands a radical international redistribution of current production and existing productive resources, including human resources, so that people in the Third World can become masters and producers of advanced technology adapted for their own and the world's needs.[30] In a socialist world, the number of teachers, doctors, scientists, mathematicians, technologists, computer programmers or machine producers in the Southern hemisphere will be proportional to the share of the world's population that lives there, and not to the present structure of trade.[31]

The concept of saturation for the passive consumption of goods and services hinges on a theory of needs which is indeed hierarchical. It divides them into basic needs, secondary needs that become indispensable with the growth of civilization, and luxury, inessential or even harmful needs. Agnes Heller's remarkable book on this subject dovetails nicely with the Maslow–Etzioni hierarchy according to which the needs for physical gratification and security are the most urgent, followed by the need for affection and respect, and then by the need for self-realization or 'self-actualization'.[32]

Some authors have alleged that such a hierarchy is 'tyrannical' by definition. There is an element of truth in this, since our definition of abundance implies a *priority* in the allocation of resources to the satisfaction of basic needs for all, and then to the reduction in the workload for all. But it is sufficient to identify this 'kernel' to see that a much stronger charge of tyranny can be laid at the door of those who argue against that priority. Instead of a 'tyranny' of the majority vis-à-vis the luxury needs of a small minority, they favour continuous or at least spontaneous growth of consumption for that small minority. We can see neither the logic nor the justice in such a substitution.

Furthermore, a priori resource allocation, resting upon democratic majority decisions, does not impose absolute restrictions on consumption choices supported by large minorities. A division of resources is possible along proportional lines. Even less does it involve curbs on the right of every citizen himself, or herself, to produce whatever they wish even with a heavily increased personal workload. The only proviso is that this should not directly or indirectly force others to engage in production for that individual's own gratification.

Precisely because aggregate resources are finite, a systematic priority for luxury needs implies systematic non-satisfaction of some basic needs for the less fortunate majority. Tremendous social resources are today used (and wasted) to that end, including through the use and abuse of credit. 'Cultivating the new rich', as journalist Claire Martin calls it, involves in her estimate no less than $7 trillion of credits that are mainly used for speculative purposes such as take-over bids.[33]

To determine priorities by 'market laws' – that is, through the unevenness of income and wealth – also imposes excessive workloads on the big majority, together with increasing stress and health hazards.[34] Why then should that same majority, above all those who devote much of their life to material production, not have the right to make these decisions?[35] Anyone who wants to work eighteen hours a day to have a third TV at home, when society refuses to produce more than a given number of sets, could receive all the requisite tools with which to produce it in a private shed. That is his or her perfect right. But they have no right to dictate, by 'market laws' and a labour market, that the mass of producers should work 50, 40 or 36 hours a week instead of 30, or worse, that tens of millions of Indians or Chinese should go without a bicycle just because 20 per cent of the inhabitants of the richest countries (less than 5 per cent of the world population) have different priorities from everyone else.

The charge of 'intellectual arrogance' would be justified if some outside body were to *impose* such priorities upon the majority of citizens.

208

But that is the exact opposite of our notion of a real increase in self-administration. Governments, parties, planning boards, scientists, technocrats or whoever can make suggestions, put forward proposals, try to influence people. To prevent them from doing so would be to restrict political freedom. But under a multi-party system, such proposals will never be unanimous: people will have the choice between coherent alternatives. And the right and power to *decide* should be in the hands of the majority of producers/consumers/citizens, not of anybody else. What is paternalist or despotic about that?

A further objection has been raised by Philippe Van Parijs, who defends the concept of 'general abundance' against the 'good-by-good' approach first proposed by Oskar Lange and then developed by myself. For Van Parijs, the latter would involve economic inefficiency from a 'neo-classical' point of view.[36] While adding that this would not, in and of itself, be a mortal sin, he proposes an alternative solution of 'weak abundance', whereby all human beings would be assured a minimum income to distribute as they saw fit among various goods and services.

The problem, however, is precisely that such a universal money grant could be spent on any good or service. There is no reason to suppose that all or even most people would necessarily spend it on basic necessities, especially if they have additional incomes. So you could still have children deprived of food while their parents spend part of their allowance on alcohol or a colour television – as any study of welfare handouts in 'rich' countries will easily demonstrate. The psychological revolution resulting from guaranteed satisfaction of basic needs cannot be achieved through a universal money grant.[37]

If it is argued that the world's resources are insufficient to satisfy basic needs for all humans beings on this planet, without fatally endangering the environment, we would reply that today as much as 50 per cent of the world's total productive capacity is unused or employed on arms production and other wasteful or destructive purposes. That huge reserve, if converted to useful ends, would be more than enough for everyone on earth to have the means to eat, to clothe themselves, to get an education, to be cured of illness within the present limits of medical science, and to receive a minimum of decent housing. To be sure, economic growth would have to continue for some time to assure abundance of all goods and services that have become cultural–historical necessities. But not for ever.[38] And already today there is a material basis for significant moves toward abundance, self-administration and the withering away of the social division of labour between bosses and the bossed-over.

It might finally be objected that the whole industrial system as it exists today presents a deadly threat to the environment, and that this would become intolerable if it were to be deployed still further. The argument is, to say the least, dubious. For although the ecological danger is steadily increasing, it has not yet crossed the point of no return. And the kind of redeployment of resources that we have in mind would have protection of the environment as one of its main priorities. Abundance, as we have defined it, is therefore still within the reach of humanity.[39]

5. The Institutional Conditions for Abundance

Different economic systems, sets of relations of production and economic policies all ultimately imply different forms of resource allocation. Marxists do not reify relations of production. No more than Mr Capital or Mrs Land can you meet Mr Plan or Mrs Market on the street. Relations of production are always *social relations* of production, between given groups of human beings. The real problem for social science – which, from a Marxist point of view, is never 'pure' economic or political science – is to discover which social group imposes a given form of resource allocation, for what reason, in whose interest, and with what consequences for those who suffer the specific priorities and dynamics.

As long as the 'general affairs of society' are taken care of by a special group of people, the bureaucratic apparatuses, state ownership of the means of production and decision-making power over surplus-product allocation almost automatically entails a large degree of bureaucratic control over the economy as a whole. Of course, the degree and harmfulness of that control can vary widely, as can the forms of its hybrid combination with petty-commodity production and incipient capitalism. In the same way, under capitalism the despotism of the market may be exacerbated by the rule of large monopolies, or it may be tempered by social legislation and various conquests of the labour movement.

But whatever the intermediary forms, despotism of the state and despotism of capital (of money wealth) represent two different forms of allocation of material and human resources, or two different forms of deciding priorities.

We would insist that the state and capital are the two primary sources of despotism – that is, of radical restrictions on freedom of choice for the mass of producers/consumers/citizens. The alternative is not either plan or market. As we argued in Chapter 1, it is simply not true that central planning automatically implies the growth of large-scale bureaucracies.[40] Those who seek to show this by pointing to the Soviet Union fly in the face of the evidence that it was the *prior* establishment of bureaucratic dictatorship which was followed by peculiarly bureaucratized forms of planning and a general hypertrophy of the state.

Similarly, we can say that huge factories or transport systems, trade and telecommunications centres, not to mention big schools and hospitals, do not 'automatically' result in the emergence of large-scale bureaucracies. Nor do relatively important areas of market economy in post-capitalist societies automatically result in the growth of capitalism. For all these developments to generate new qualities (bureaucratization, restoration of capitalism, etc.), material factors such as the size of institutions, the nature of technology or even the existence of money are insufficient. The social framework, the relationship of forces, the outcome of struggle between key social groups, classes and class fractions are decisive.

Max Weber himself points out that before the emergence of bourgeois bureaucracies, patrimonial bureaucracies prevailed under the regime of what we might call semi-feudal, absolutist state power. Patrimonial bureaucracy was characterized by the sale of key state functions, including tax collection, to the highest bidder. It was one of the main sources of widespread corruption and permanent fiscal crisis, reflecting a certain relationship of forces between the landowners, the court nobility, the super-rich financiers/speculators, and the rest of the rising bourgeois class. Before modern bureaucracies could take over, this relationship of forces had to be modified, as it was in Britain after the 'Glorious Revolution' and in France as a result of the revolution of 1789.

We have seen that there are certain institutional frameworks which guarantee and consolidate the rule of a privileged bureaucracy in post-capitalist societies. The question that has to be asked is: what are the institutional preconditions for a gradual emergence of abundance, and thus for the withering away of bureaucracy and the state? Our answer is: processes of resource allocation that involve free, conscious and a priori choices on the part of the producers/consumers/citizens. The mass of the people must have the *power* to take these decisions, and a set of articulated institutions must be established to enable them to do so.

These institutions cannot cover every single allocation decision, at least not during a long transition period. Some will have to be left to the market. Some, though only a residual number, will probably remain fairly 'technocratic'. But before the market sets the exact purchasing and selling price of, say, potatoes, both wholesale and retail, the mass of the people must have the power to determine which foodstuffs will be distributed free of charge, and whether potatoes should be included among them. Similarly, before scientists and technocrats resolve how nuclear power stations might be built or maintained at a maximum safety level, the people must have the power to decide democratically whether they should be built or maintained at all.

Let us start from what already exists in all states under various forms of bourgeois parliamentary democracy. The government, or rather the top layers of the bourgeois state bureaucracy, present annual proposals for the apportionment of, let us say, 5 per cent of national income to institutions of national defence and security, 8 per cent for purposes of education, R&D and 'culture', and 7 per cent for health. These three priorities, then, already account for 20 per cent of available resources. Their allocation is decided a priori, a year (or, in fact, several years) in advance. The proposals are open to discussion and revision in parliament and through the pressure of public opinion. Large parliamentary minorities like the British Labour Party under Thatcher, or extra-parliamentary forces such as the Spanish trade unions under Felipe González's 'austerity socialism', can put forward alternatives and even force the government to amend its proposals. But a persual of what actually happens in the main capitalist countries of the world will show that the projected outlays are not basically altered as a result.

A system of democratically centralized planning (articulated self-management) could extend this 20 per cent to 50, 60 or 75 per cent of available resources, as soon as the level of material wealth permits it. In addition to a priori decisions on 'national defence' (if these still exist), education and health, there could be a priori allocations with regard to food, basic clothing, public transport, housing and home comfort (heating, gas, electricity, water, basic appliances, perhaps radio and television). The reason for setting these priorities would be formally the same as the reason why, in a bourgeois state, the army, police and judiciary are given such scrupulous attention. They are fundamental safeguards of the social order.

Once the majority of the people are freely committed to build a *socialist* social order – and as long as they do not choose this, the project remains just a political goal, not an ongoing historical process – the satisfaction of basic social needs ('abundance') will be gradually guaranteed for all. Society has the sovereign power to decide that the economy should function in a way that makes this possible. And it thereby creates a yardstick by which progress towards it can be measured.

When we advance from bourgeois to socialist democracy, the a priori allocation of economic resources advances from 20 per cent to 50–60–75 per cent. But this is achieved by democratic means – means, in fact, which make society, and especially the economy, qualitatively more democratic than it can ever be under capitalism. A choice of internally consistent models of large-scale a priori allocation ('central plans') would be submitted not to parliament but to the voters. The decisions would be made transparent – that is to say, general figures and statistics would be translated into what they mean for the mass of individuals in concrete, practical terms. After broad pluralistic debates, the mass of the people would then determine the priorities on the basis of universal franchise.

The qualitative rise in democratic decision-making would, as we have already suggested, entail a major process of decentralization. Only the general framework (basic proportions of the division of national resources) would be nationally, one day internationally, determined. All other decisions would be delegated to regional, district, branch-wide or neighbourhood bodies, each one democratically elected after free debate. Two rules of thumb might be applied in this respect. Decisions should be taken at the level at which they can most easily be implemented. And they should be taken at the level where the greatest percentage of people actually affected by them can be involved in the decision-making process. Obviously it cannot effectively be decided at village level how to prevent and reverse the pollution of the world's great rivers, but nor can a region with fifteen million inhabitants mark out every pedestrian crossing within its compass. Nevertheless, all the elected decision-making bodies would operate within the guidelines fixed by a universal vote on general priorities.

Such an institutional framework involves a much lesser degree of delegation of power than that which supports either bureaucratic state despotism or the despotism of capital – in the latter, the mass of producers 'delegate' decision-making power to a handful of big capitalists and top managers, without being asked whether they wish to do so or not. It also involves a qualitatively higher integration of ecological, feminist and national concerns, which is by no means the least of its merits.[41]

When all is said and done, however, the social product is created at the workplace. It is then centralized by being transferred to other places. Institutional safeguards for a gradual decline in bureaucracy therefore concern the degree of power that the producers have directly to control a fraction of their products. Again this has to include an element of delegation, as parts of current production have to be centralized under any social system – at least at present, or presently foreseeable, levels of technology.[42] But when blue-collar and white-collar workers have a large amount of decision-making power at the workplace – probably including the right to dispose of part of current output for their own consumption or for direct exchange[43] – their real control over the social product increases substantially in comparison with what exists under the despotism of capital or bureaucratic despotism.

The idea that 'Marxian socialism' implies a complete socialization and therefore planning of the whole of current production, or at least an ever-growing part of it, is essentially of Stalinist origin and in total contradiction with the writings of Marx and Engels. What socialism meant for them was a socialization (social appropriation) of a large part of the social *surplus product*, for reasons both of social justice and of economic efficiency, as explained in the *Critique of the Gotha Programme*. It did not at all involve alienation of the producers' right to dispose of the rest of the social product as they saw fit – indeed, that would contradict the very definition of socialism as a regime of *freely associated* producers.

Moreover, intermediary bodies controlling the social product/surplus product would also be democratically elected on a pluralist basis, with delegates subject to recall by their electorate. The proceedings of such institutions would be given wide-scale publicity.

A system of the kind we have outlined would mark a major advance in the economic preconditions for the withering away of bureaucracy. For so many people to be involved in general assemblies, in councils of workers, women, consumers, residents and citizens, as well as in local, regional, national and branch-wide conferences of such councils, a radical reduction of the working week is an absolute prerequisite. It is also essential that people should be free from constant worry about their own and their children's material needs.

The objection has been raised that we are projecting a withering away of bureaucracy by making everyone into a bureaucrat.[44] But bureaucracy is synonymous not with organization, centralization and the exercise of authority per se, but with their *usurpation by special (and specialized) bodies of people, divorced from the mass of society and professionally paid to carry out their functions*. When ordinary people progressively assume these functions, they do not become 'bureaucrats'. They organize and administer for themselves and by themselves – and that is what we mean by saying that bureaucracy withers away.

6. Is 'Free Enterprise' an Effective Antidote to Bureaucratic Despotism?

In his book *Bureaucracy*, published in 1944, Ludwig von Mises, doyen of the Austrian neo-classical or marginalist school of economists, set forth the classical, and classically simplified, case in favour of capitalist free enterprise. There are two methods for the conduct of affairs within the frame of human society, he argues; one is 'bureaucratic management', the other is 'profit management'. Bureaucratic management is inherently despotic and totalitarian. Even under conditions of political democracy, state interference with free enterprise – that is, the welfare state – saps the profit motive and thereby opens the road to despotism.[45] Only free enterprise, a generalized market economy, guarantees freedom.

Since the systemic crisis broke out in the USSR and the Stalinist regimes collapsed in Eastern Europe, this theme has been taken up by a chorus of ideologues in the West, and by the great majority of their colleagues in the East. As Alec Nove expressed it in a nutshell: either bureaucratic (state) despotism or the free market, *tertium non datur*.[46]

Nevertheless, there are many weaknesses in the reasoning of von Mises and his followers, some of the most basic of which we shall try to identify here. Von Mises correctly relates the nature of economic systems to the form of ownership of the means of production.[47] Essentially, in his scheme of things, only two such forms are possible: either private ownership or state ownership. But this is neither a logically nor a historically tenable position. In reality, there are at least four basically different forms:

1. private ownership by the direct producers (what Marxists call petty-commodity production);

2. private ownership by capitalists who, in exchange for a wage, hire others to use the means of production and appropriate all the goods so produced;

3. state ownership of the means of production, with no free access to them by the mass of producers (what is today known in the USSR as 'command economy');

4. social (collective) ownership in which the direct producers have broad access to the means of production and to consumer goods and services (what we have called democratically articulated self-management, a regime of freely associated producers).

A moment's thought, together with some elementary knowledge of the economic history of Europe between the fifteenth and twentieth centuries, are enough to see that the differences between the first and second of these forms are much greater than between the first and the fourth. And a study of political history will indicate that the second system, which is praised to the skies by von Mises, is perfectly compatible over long periods with a lack of political freedom and civil liberties for the mass of the people, or even with bloody tyranny. Such extreme forms of repression are rarely found under the first system. It is impossible to conceive them under the fourth.

A summary passage in von Mises's book helps us put our finger on the crucial flaw in his argument:

> The very fact that labour is, under capitalism, a commodity and is bought and sold as a commodity makes the wage-earner free from any personal dependence. Like the capitalists, the entrepreneurs, and the farmers, the wage-earner depends on the arbitrariness of the consumers. But the consumers'

choices do not concern the persons engaged in production; they concern things and not men. The employer is not in a position to indulge in favouritism or in prejudice with regard to personnel. . . .

It is this fact, and not constitutions and bills of right, that makes the receivers of salaries and wages within an unhampered capitalist system free men. They are sovereign in their capacity as consumers, and as producers they are, like all other citizens, unconditionally subject to the law of the market. In selling a factor of production, namely their toil and trouble, on the market at the market price to everybody who is ready to buy it, they do not jeopardize their own standing. They do not owe their employer thanks or subservience, they owe him a definite quantity of labour of a definite quality.'[48]

Virtually every sentence is wrong here – that is to say, it does not correspond to the real situation of the wage-earners in capitalist society, or to the real dynamics (laws of motion) of the capitalist economic system.

Are the wage-earners 'sovereign in their capacity as consumers'? Only if 'sovereignty' is reduced to a capacity to divide their wages as they see fit among an existing range of consumer goods and services. But after all, is that not the case in the despotic state economy of the USSR? Surely the term 'sovereignty' also implies a capacity to satisfy needs, especially those which are considered to be vital. The last two centuries show with crystal clarity that in a generalized market economy, 'consumer sovereignty' may be limited in two basic ways: on the supply side, by insufficient availability of goods and services; on the side of 'effective demand', by a lack of the purchasing power to gain access to available goods and services.

Let us further note in passing that there is a third limitation of consumer sovereignty under actually existing capitalism: namely, the capacity of big monopolies – especially in the retail sector dominated by supermarket chains – to manipulate consumers' choices. As a number of American sociologists, by no means Marxists, have shown, the average shopper already displays growing anxiety and saturation problems when confronted with the endless mushrooming of product varieties. Often she or he is not aware of what is happening:

You enter a supermarket at your peril. The store manager knows better than you do how you will behave – which way you will walk, where you will look. And he exploits his knowledge with a ruthlessness guaranteed to shoot holes in your bank account. Even the giant food manufacturers, who have to pay for the privilege of having their products advantageously displayed, are impotent pawns, themselves manipulated by the grocery superpowers as mercilessly as their customers.[49]

Rather imprudently, von Mises summarized the classical case for market economy in the formula: 'The capitalist system of production is an economic democracy in which every penny gives a right to vote.'[50] Every penny! The trouble is that whereas every voter has a single vote in democratic elections, not every individual counts for just one on the market. Von Mises's strange concept of 'economic democracy' gives most people one or two votes, and a tiny minority a thousand votes. If you have 500,000 households with 1,000 votes each, and 100 million households with an average of 1.5 votes, then it is easy to see that the small band of big capitalists will have a permanent absolute majority: 500 million votes against 150 million. They will have become all but irremovable – except through a revolution.

The main defender of the faith today, Milton Friedman, illustrates in an equally simple and clearcut formula how the liberals misrepresent the functioning of the capitalist system:

If [a person's] income does depend on what he does, on the difference between the prices he receives for selling his services and the prices he has to pay for the item he buys – if it depends on the difference between receipts and costs from the point of view of a business enterprise or wages and costs for a worker, and so on – then he has a very strong incentive to try to insure that he sells his services in the best market for the highest price.[51]

This might be an accurate description of the economics of generalized petty-commodity production, such as has never in fact existed. But it certainly does not correspond to the workings of capitalism.

The average wage-earner owns no 'money-bearing' capital, or only the most insignificant amount. His annual income does indeed depend on what he does – or, to be more precise, on what he is allowed to do and whether he is allowed to do it during that particular year.[52] Let us estimate that income at $30,000. The income of a capitalist, on the other hand, depends far more on what he owns than on what he does. If he owns $50 million, if the average monopoly rate of profit is 20 per cent and if he can achieve capital increments of $20 million, then the additional money that will fall into his hands in the course of one year will be $30 million – a thousand times the wage-earner's income.

A capitalist household owning $50 million would not even qualify for the club of the 'super-rich'. The wealthiest man on earth, at some $400 billion, is said to be the Japanese tycoon Yoshiaki Tsutsumi.[53] At an average rate of interest of 7 per cent, this would 'produce' $28 billion a year, without Mr Tsutsumi having to lift his little finger or to take the slightest risk. Those $28 billion a year, if reinvested, would in turn yield nearly $2 billion a year, which would yield a further $150 million a year

. . . But let us stop there. We are already talking of capital accumulation to the tune of $30 billion a year, $80 million a day, $55,000 a minute. It is hardly surprising that when Paul Getty, another super-rich tycoon, was asked how much he owned, he answered: 'If I knew how much I owned, I wouldn't be one of the richest people in the world.'

Now, there is a structural connection between the availability of supply and the tremendously uneven stratification of effective demand under capitalism – a connection which again largely escapes our neo-liberal dogmatists. The distribution of 'effective demand' – that is, of actual purchasing power – not only makes businesses spontaneously orient towards the markets 'where they can get the highest price'. Often it also means that they simply do not produce goods for which profits are below the average. Sometimes, smaller firms try to occupy these 'niches'. But where costs are generally high, and alternative investment opportunities abound, consumers' needs, not to speak of 'consumer sovereignty', will just go by the board.

The case of cheap housing in West Germany (and Japan) is a perfect illustration of this point. For a long period, the building of cheap apartments has been in sharp decline, falling from a peak of 447,000 in 1956 to a low of 41,000 in 1988.[54] The result is that there is now an acute shortage. At the same time, however, hundreds of thousands of 'secondary residences' have been built for wealthier people, many of them occupied for only a couple of months a year. We shall not go here into such matters as social justice, which mean next to nothing in the language of neo-liberalism. But we are entitled to ask what has become of 'economic democracy' and 'consumer sovereignty' in all this.

The distribution of income under capitalism encompasses a *structural inequality of status* which von Mises conjures away with his ambiguous formula that the wage-earner is 'free from any personal dependence'. Insofar as this suggests a contrast between the status of a wage-earner and that of slave or a medieval serf, it would appear to be making a valid, and uncontroversial, point. But insofar as it suggests that the *only possible* forms of personal dependence are those of liege bonds, 'owing thanks and subservience' in the feudal sense of the term, it succeeds only in confusing the issue. *Economic dependence is a definite form of dependence.* And the specific form of income distribution under capitalism constantly reproduces such economic dependence of the wage-earners upon the capitalists.

Wages and salaries, whether they are high or low, only allow the mass of the wage-earning class to enjoy a certain level of consumption.[55] Given the constantly rising start-up costs of a large enterprise, they do not enable workers to escape the proletarian condition that compels them to sell their labour-power to the owners of the means of production at the prevailing market price – that is, at a price which oscillates precisely around the total costs of the goods and services that enter into the reproduction of their labour power.

Only the capitalists derive an income from ownership of capital (their accumulated wealth). This income provides them with the means not only to acquire basic goods and services and items of luxury consumption, but also to purchase new means of production and to hire additional workers. To put it in other terms: the 'savings ratio' of lifetime income is insignificant or nil for the overwhelming majority of wage and salary earners.[56] But it is very high for the average capitalist and astronomical for the top bracket.[57]

This structural inequality in revenues, and therefore in status, not only implies that the wage-earner depends for employment and consumption level entirely on the capitalist class.[58] It also entails a brutally direct dependence on the employer, and a lack of personal freedom, in the field of production.

Even if the wage-earner is not expected to show thanks to his employer, he does owe him blind obedience in the workplace. Von Mises and other apologists of capitalism talk a great deal about the blessings of competition. But they forget to mention one obvious fact of life: namely, that competition sets up a compulsion to cut production costs, including labour costs, and that therefore the strictest possible control over workers at the point of production, for the purposes of a maximum extraction of surplus labour, is inherent in the operation of capitalism.

It is simply not true, then, that by selling their labour-power to the employer, wage-earners 'do not jeopardize their own standing'. Not only do they 'jeopardize' it daily, they surrender virtually all freedom and autonomy at the workplace, where they have to submit to the boss's commands.

Similarly, when von Mises writes that 'consumer choices concern things and not men', he is engaging in an arbitrary fragmentation of the economic totality. Yes, when you choose between two pairs of shoes, with different prices and different qualities, you are dealing with 'things' and not with 'men'. But the shoes happen to be produced by men with the aid of other things (means of production). In order to manufacture cheaper shoes, the capitalists have to turn the screws on living men and women, not only on things. And those screws hamper, mutilate and alienate all their human aspirations and capacities, in a way not dissimilar to a 'command economy'. In a system of 'unhampered' capitalism, the prison-like factory regime is one of unhampered despotism, where even the time a worker spends at the toilet is dictated and supervised by the bosses, and the individual may be penalized or even dismissed for such 'ungainful' and 'economically inefficient' activities.

'Free enterprise' is no antidote to state despotism; it is no guarantee of broader human freedom. And yet there is an alternative, a *tertium datur* – an economic system in which the mass of producers/consumers freely decide what to produce, how to produce it, and how much of it to allocate to certain priorities in the realm of individual and collective consumption. No one has ever put forward a serious argument to show why such a producers' democracy, combined with political democracy and the broadest pluralism and openness in public life, would be inherently totalitarian or despotic. It seems evident that it would be qualitatively less despotic than either the bureaucratic 'command economy' or the capitalist market economy, because it would qualitatively expand the sphere of autonomy and self-determination for the mass of the population.

7. Capitalism, Planning and Economic Calculation

Unable to answer these arguments, certain diehards of 'unhampered capitalism' fall back on a second line of defence. They are ready to concede that 'economic democracy' in the real sense of the term would follow from alternative models of economic organization, and that abolition of private ownership of the major means of production would be a necessary, if certainly not sufficient, precondition. They continue to insist, however, that such models would be inherently much less efficient, and more wasteful, than capitalist free enterprise.

This line of reasoning too harks back to debates which began in the early years of this century. The Austrian school tried to prove that without a market, precise economic calculation would be impossible, and that a planned economy would therefore always imply arbitrariness and waste in the allocation of scarce resources.[59] What the producers/consumers gained in freedom and autonomy in a system of democratic self-management, they would lose in access to consumer goods. The supply of these (or their quality or diversity) would be seriously restricted, if not in absolute terms then in relation to what 'free capitalist enterprise' would provide. Thus, dogmatic liberals attempt to turn the socialist argument against capitalism against itself: what is the point of 'freedom' if it is freedom to starve? Hayek gives us a good example in his latest book:

> So many people already exist; and only a market economy can keep the bulk of them alive. . . . Since we can preserve and secure even our present numbers only by adhering to the same general kinds of principles, it is our duty – unless we truly wish to condemn millions to starvation – to resist the claims of creeds that tend to destroy the basic principles . . . [60]

Here again the argument teems with half-truths and sheer sophisms. The fact is that *all* economic calculation under capitalism and in societies transitional between capitalism and socialism has to be imprecise. As long as the economic actors behave in a fragmented way, because labour is not yet completely socialized, a unified aggregate practice is impossible. Each independent actor constantly changes the overall situation, thereby modifying what can be known and what needs to be known. A 'universal brain', of the kind that we saw Trotsky mocking in Chapter 1, can never exist.

If private businesses or monopolist tycoons were capable of exactly predicting production costs and sales revenue, it is hard to see what purpose the market would serve. The function of the market is precisely to give signals or information on the basis of which businesses modify their calculations and projections. But this implies that the initial calculations were incorrect. Otherwise, there would be no need for correction.

This intrinsic fallibility of all economic calculation and projection is essentially rooted in: (a) the impossibility of exactly predicting the behaviour of millions or hundreds of millions of consumers; (b) the impossibility of determining the precise duration in which the costs of long-term, fixed investments will be recuperated, owing to the uncertainty of technological obsolescence, fluctuations in the rate of profit, changes in the economic conjuncture, etc.; (c) the unpredictable effects of the class struggle on wage costs; and (d) variations in the availability and the cost of credit. We could add a number of other factors, but these are sufficient to state our case.

The surprising conclusion, therefore, is that private businesses do not find themselves in an essentially better position than that of 'central planners' with regard to their capacity for precise economic calculation and prediction. Indeed, the similarities are much greater than the differences.

Does this mean that private businesses and central planning boards are both in the dark when it comes to cost calculation and the anticipation of future earnings? Of course not. If that were so, neither a planned economy nor a capitalist economy could function for one year. While both systems start from the impossibility of making precise calculations and predictions, they apply in practice the method of *successive approximation*. They adjust their operational cost-prices by recomputing what they will have to pay for the replacement of inputs. They continually attempt to improve their forecasting of consumers' behaviour, by developing more accurate market research. They try to predict the twists and turns of innovation in products and production techniques.[61]

All these correctives are unable to overcome completely the imprecise character of calculations or predictions. And a high price is paid for their imperfection. Under capitalism, the price is periodic general crises of overproduction for all, and bankruptcy for some. Under the 'command economy', the price is structural underproduction of low-priority goods and services, with the consequent growth of disproportions between sectors.

There is a striking, and by no means fortuitous, parallel between the pseudo-prices used within big capitalist combines and those which would operate in a system of planned, articulated self-management. Hayek, more realistic and less dogmatic than von Mises, already saw what every capitalist manager knows: planning is an unavoidable component of economic management in any society based upon large-scale production.[62] Thus practice tends to vindicate those economists who, in answer to the liberal dogma of the impossibility of economic calculation under socialism, referred to the potential of the step-by-step approach and the use of pseudo-prices or quasi-prices.[63]

The notion that the capitalist economy, as it has functioned for a century or more, is essentially based on market mechanisms and market-price calculation is unrealistic. It is simply not true – as innumerable advocates of generalized market relations, including most recently Alec Nove, have argued – that there are millions of goods in industrialized countries whose prices are established through the law of supply and demand.[64]

The law of supply and demand does often, not always, influence price fluctuations of such goods as potatoes, socks or television sets. It certainly does not determine the prices of the great majority of goods in Nove's multi-million basket, which must largely be made up of tools, machines and spare parts. What prevails here is a hybrid between a priori allocation and the profit motive. Most large machinery is built to order, not bought ready-made after some hunting around in shops. 'Competition' does not originate production. The only goods produced are those which are actually ordered. Prices do not fluctuate under the influence of competition. Most parts are not commodities at all, but are produced as a function of technical coefficients, like the parts of a motor-car that come together on an assembly-line. They have no real prices, hence there are no price fluctuations.

The production costs of the great majority of such goods are calculated not in market prices but in 'quasi-prices'. When the chassis-building department of a large automobile combine calculates the costs of its chassis, it does not do this on the basis of the law of supply and demand since it will not be selling its product to the assembly-line.[65] It just projects into the future what was measured in the past, after the sale of a previous number of finished cars. No interest on capital invested in chassis production is added to that cost-price calculation.

This raises a more general question. If there is no intrinsic difference between the imperfections of economic calculation under capitalism and under a 'command economy', how are we to explain the latter's ever greater dysfunctioning in the last two decades? What is the *differentia specifica* of the 'command economy' in respect of economic growth?

Our answer ties in closely with the analysis of the bureaucracy that we have developed throughout this book. Because of its economic nature, the sources and forms of its income, the bureaucracy – and hence the 'command economy' which it controls – is more conservative, less flexible, less capable of adaptation to new challenges, and less responsive to a changed environment – except in periods of acute crisis and in certain priority sectors – than is an advanced capitalist economy. It is not, as Milton Friedman contends, that the lack of a free market deprives it of signals about what is amiss. Rather, it reacts more slowly to the available signals, since there is a built-in incentive to falsify, or not to transmit, information.

Having said this, we do however need to make an important comparative qualification. The more the capitalist economy becomes monopolized, the more the monopolies (not just private business bureaucracies but the financial tycoons themselves) act like brakes upon economic growth in quite a similar way to that which prevails in a 'command economy'. David F. Noble notes:

> It is only in the reductionist fantasies of economists that decisions about new technologies are made strictly on the basis of hard-boiled no-nonsense evaluations and refined analytical procedures for estimating their cost-effectiveness. This is not to say that profit-making is not a motive; it is. . . . In reality, which is considerably less tidy than any economic model, such decisions are more often than not grounded upon hunches, faith, ego, delight and deals. Whatever economic information there is to go by, however abundant, remains vague and suspect.
>
> Not only does this handicap the purchaser of new equipment, it also plagues the independent investigator who is trying objectively to assess the economic viability of a new technology. Reliable data is simply unavailable or inaccessible. . . . Moreover, companies have a proprietary interest in the information, for fear of revealing (and thus jeopardizing) their position vis-à-vis labor unions (wages), competitors (prices) and government (regulations and taxes). And the data is not all neatly tabulated and in a drawer somewhere. It is distributed among departments, with separate budgets, and the costs to one are the hidden costs to the others. In addition, there is every reason to believe that the data that does exist is self-serving information provided by each operating unit to insulate it from criticism and enhance its position within the firm.[66]

Again both the 'command economy' and actually existing capitalism display an incapacity to optimize growth which is more similar than dissimilar. Again the *tertium datur* suggests itself. For in a democratically planned and self-managed economy, the producers would have a powerful incentive to try out opportunities for rational technical progress. Their labour time, and so their leisure or 'real life' time, would be indexed to economies in production time. They could 'call it a day' as soon as a given quantity of goods and services had been produced, under strict quality control exercised by freely elected consumers' representatives. What group of workers would refuse to test a new technique if it meant they could go home after four instead of seven or eight hours of work?

8. Economic Rationality and Social Rationality

The term 'rational technical progress', which we introduced in the previous section, opens a whole new area of debate between liberals and socialists.

Liberals assume – sometimes tacitly, sometimes on the basis of sophisticated mathematical models – that micro-economic and macro-economic rationality coincide. The latter, insofar as it is thought to be capable of calculation, is reduced to an aggregation of the former. The evidence, however, does not bear out this assumption – and not only because of the 'externalities' which neo-liberals try somehow to compute in money terms.

Maximum efficiency at the level of the firm is not automatically identical with maximum efficiency at the level of the economy as a whole.[67] For example, a cut in the workforce to increase profitability might benefit a thousand enterprises to the extent of $2 billion, but it might at the same time cost the community $4 billion in lost output and dole payments to people deliberately prevented from working.[68]

A similar profit-and-loss balance can be seen in the case of public spending on infrastructure, health or education. For individual enterprises (and individual capitalists), a cut in such expenditure might save $10bn a year in taxes. Let us even grant to the naive 'supply-side economists' what the US economy under Reagan and Bush has proved to be a false assumption: namely, that this whole sum would be automatically invested and, through a multiplier effect, increase current production by some $20 bn a year, or $100 bn over a five-year period.

Nevertheless, if we compute the higher transport costs from inadequate maintenance of bridges and roads, the loss in output and exports from poor standards of training, the increase in sick-leave and accidents, all due to the lower level of public expenditure, and if we arrive at a total loss of $150 bn over five years, then it is once more evident that 'optimization' is not the same in micro-economic and macro-economic terms. Higher profits for individual firms are more than offset by greater losses for the economy as a whole.

Economic criteria, of course, are not by themselves sufficient for a full evaluation of the comparative rationality of different social systems. We also have to introduce the concept of macro-social rationality (optimization) into the analysis.

Economic efficiency is not the be all and end all of human endeavour. It is an *instrument* for the achievement of human welfare, the satisfaction of human needs and aspirations, nothing more. If the pursuit of ever greater economic efficiency enters into conflict with these goals, if it entails mass killings or even a nuclear war, if it undermines the physical and mental health of millions, if it threatens the environment in which men and women live, then it has to be limited for these very reasons. Micro-economic rationality should be fully subordinate to macro-social optimization.[69]

Some have argued that it is precisely the market, with the pressure of market prices and the profit motive, which alone allows such a computation to be made. Let the polluting firms, it is said, pay high taxes or fines for polluting the environment, and they will search for alternative technologies.

But this kind of argument rebounds on the apologists for capitalism. Taxes and fines do not generally have a prohibitive effect. Polluters will continue to pollute (even if, perhaps, less than before) so long as existing technologies allow them to amortize previous investments, and so long as their legal departments find them thousands of ways in which to limit the burden of fines and taxes. Besides, it is not possible to measure precisely the effects of pollution and threats to the environment, especially over a long period of time. Nor can human suffering and loss of health be expressed simply in terms of reductions in anticipated income.

In all these areas, value judgements and scales of priorities come into play. Just as bourgeois ideology takes it for granted that 'national defence' or police protection of private property is an 'absolute value',[70] so society has the perfect right to judge that high standards of education for all its children, or high levels of health for all its members, is an absolute value independent of the cost of schools and hospitals, or the salaries of teachers and medical personnel.

Only if taxes and fines were capable of resulting in confiscation could they be considered effective tools for the prevention of further damage to the environment. But in that case, the outcry from the defenders of 'free enterprise' would be as clamorous as if they were faced with outright bans on the use of certain technologies.

Once we reduce the problem of economic efficiency to its proper dimensions, the need to combine micro-economic rationality with macro-economic optimization speaks rather against generalized market economy and in favour of democratic planning. We have outlined the case for this in Chapter 3.

Let us just stress once more that we are not proposing a rapid end to market mechanisms, which will persist throughout the period of transition from capitalism to socialism. Our solution includes precise measurement of production costs through a stable currency and a system of consumer-goods prices – except for those distributed free of charge – corrected by the operation of the law of supply and demand. The difference between this and generalized market economy (with or without private ownership of the means of production) resides in the long-term dynamic of the economy and society as a whole. Key allocations of scarce resources – say, 50 to 75 per cent of the total – would be decided democratically and a priori by the mass of the people themselves, and not left to the vagaries of market fluctuations which, in reality, are governed by the big bank accounts.

The neo-liberal arguments about despotism, as opposed to the consolidation and extension of human rights, cannot in fact be squared with their dogmatic assertions about micro-economic efficiency. An undeniable and growing element of *social injustice* is involved in the quest for micro-economic maximization of private profit. Thus, when the multinational Philips decides to sack 40,000 wage-earners, as it recently did, it is not penalizing workers for having 'priced themselves out of the labour market'. Even if we assume that Philips' wage-costs were 10 or 20 per cent 'too high', these were such a small component of the total costs of computer production that their reduction to a 'more acceptable' level would still have cut the cost of Philips computers by no more than 2.5–5 per cent. The losses sustained in computer production were far greater than this modest difference.

The truth of the matter is that the sackings resulted from faulty investment decisions, misconceived production models, and mistaken predictions of market behaviour. All these shortcomings were the responsibility of management and management alone. But 40,000 individuals are paying the price for decisions over which they had no say whatsoever.

Such episodes are among the general phenomena of economic and social crises stemming from the operations of capitalist production geared to profit. They provoke growing questioning of the system as such, and periodically lead to mass reactions and wide-scale revolts.

Whereas Max Weber assumed that technological constraints would make such revolts impossible, the history of the twentieth century proves otherwise.

For their part, neo-classical conservatives face a clear contradiction between defence of the profit motive and private property, at all costs and as the number one priority, and the extension or even maintenance of civil liberties and human rights. When the chips are down, the weight of the argument unfailingly shifts in favour of 'economic efficiency' and the curtailment of human rights.

In the case of von Hayek, this reactionary turn is truly pathetic. Not only does he plead for restrictions on universal suffrage; he even hopes for a return to Religion, the Family and Traditional Authority.[71] The wheel has turned full circle. The conservative neo-liberals become legitimate heirs of the *ancien régime* or its Vichy-type parody, open enemies of the historical causes defended by classical liberalism. They become de facto defenders of bourgeois state bureaucracies, without which Traditional Authorities and their values cannot be imposed upon society.

Like social–historical crises produce like ideological reflexes among the pillars of a reactionary social order. But after the nightmare of Stalinism, socialists can again act as they traditionally did (and many never ceased to do): as the staunchest, most resolute defenders of human rights, which they refuse to sacrifice to some fetish of micro-economic efficiency.

Advocates of full-scale marketization in the former Soviet Union, cheered on by not a few Western pseudo-liberals and even social democrats, proclaim: Beware of too much glasnost, lest it get in the way of perestroika.[72] There lies the real choice for the years to come, and not between 'command economy' and the market.

9. Obstacles on the Road to Self-administration and Self-management

The withering away of the state and bureaucracy, and of scarcity and commodity production, is not an easy process. Indeed, the building of socialism is not an easy process – otherwise, it would already have existed for a long time. What we are talking about is the gradual disappearance of a given set of institutions, forms of social life and thinking which support them, particular motivations of individual, group and collective behaviour. These have been with us for centuries if not millennia, but they have by no means always existed. So although their withering away is difficult, it is not incompatible with 'human nature' as it has empirically presented itself in the history of the species.

227

The most important obstacle corresponds to a real problem, not just to myth or prejudice. At the present level of technological and organizational development, specialist knowledge is the knowledge of specialists, and these 'special groups of people' will remain for a long time to come. To eliminate them would lead to a catastrophic regression in the wealth and well-being of the great mass of the population. Some 'trade-off' between current consumption or welfare and the relative power of specialists will therefore have to persist well into the future. The problem cannot be reduced to that of raising the general level of culture and skill. Once all people active in the health sector have studied until the age of eighteen or twenty, they will still not all be able to perform surgical operations. In other words, the social division of labour cannot be simply 'abolished'; it can only gradually wither away.

Social security has often been cited since the time of Schumpeter as an example in this connection. The development of the welfare state, both East and West, has increased the complexity of legislation on such matters as pensions, maternity leave or disablement allowances, with the result that most cases involve the application of dozens of different rules and regulations. No individual wage-earner could hope to cut through this intricate web that has been set up, so it is said, not to crush but to protect him or her. We will therefore tend to rely on experts – that is, bureaucrats – either in state or para-state bodies or in civil organizations.[73]

This obstacle is real. But it is partly countered by three trends in contemporary society. First, we must make a careful distinction between power relations and the devolution of power on the one hand, and the *articulation of power* involving specialized knowledge on the other hand. Decisions about the allocation of social labour (available resources) to health and social security should and can become the prerogative of the mass of citizens. There is bureaucratic alienation if and only if they are left in the hands of governments and state bureaucracies, Big Business or 'the market'. But one cannot seriously argue that the capacity to perform operations has been taken away from the mass of the population and concentrated in the hands of 'a minority of surgeons'. That would be a philistine prejudice against science in general – although one does, of course, have to take into account the patient's right to full medical information.

Second, the great diversification of scientific and other specialist knowledge, far from enhancing the power of experts, decisively limits it. Power is always social power, power of some human beings over others. A surgeon has power over his patient. But an energy expert has power over him, and in turn an architect or town planner has power over the energy expert. Controllers of food standards have power over all of them. Each of these powers shrinks, however, to the extent that specialized knowledge increases and is spread over greater numbers of people, and society as a whole decides in a sovereign manner how many resources will be put at the disposal of surgeons, energy experts, town planner, food controllers, and so on. As more and more of these decisions are fully socialized, bureaucratic power is diminished rather than increased.

Third, the trend towards specialized access to information on social security matters can be substantially reduced if protection is based essentially on non-monetary, non-market mechanisms. When the consumption levels of pensioners, pregnant women, invalids or university students are socially guaranteed through free access to certain goods and services, the need for complex regulation of each individual case will be sharply reduced.

More serious problems on the road to self-administration are posed by the complexity of social life. The trends of objective socialization of labour and growing cooperation at basic levels of social life are contradictory. They involve parallel tendencies of centralization and decentralization which make mechanisms of mediation unavoidable.

There are 500,000 parts in a supersonic jet airliner, which require 500,000 separate designs. It is quite possible to have tens of thousands of workers cooperating, in the broadest sense of the word, in the production of the finished article, on the basis of the maximum information available. It is likewise possible that, at the level of the shopfloor, office or integrated group, conscious cooperation might take over completely from hierarchical systems, whose logic is bound up more with surplus-labour extraction than with technical constraints.

Nevertheless, it remains a fact that the bringing together of all these designs and parts requires bodies that are engaged in permanent mediation. It is hard to imagine that this will not remain a full-time job, representing a form of social division of labour not likely to wither away before a completely new technology is born. And it is at least possible, if not likely, that such professional mediators will retain some power over people.

What is true in the field of production also applies to distribution, transport, telecommunications, culture, health, and so on. Will there ever be hospitals so small and so adapted to neighbourhood conditions that no intermediary needs to act between patients and medical personnel? The minimum size of an efficient hospital, equipped with the latest appliances, is such that an administrative staff remains a necessity, at least for the foreseeable future. No one can just walk into a hospital and choose the bed they like. And so, intermediaries will have some power over people, which will continue to be the source of some abuses.

More disturbing are the conflicts that will persist during the process of the withering away of the state: conflicts between social, individual and group interests; between local, regional, national and international interests; between different gender interests; between age-group interests; between majority and minority ethnic interests, and so on. Marxists – beginning with Marx, Engels and Lenin – have never proposed the chiliastic thesis that a classless, socialist society will display perfect harmony among all human beings. They have simply contended, on the basis of much evidence from the distant past as well as clearly discernible trends for the future, that even serious conflicts will not require any 'special apparatus', any state or bureaucracy, for their resolution. Social groups in no way specialized in repression – schools, 'extended family' communities, neighbourhoods, workplace assemblies, meetings of producers/consumers, etc. – will take care of them without need for outside 'assistance'.[74]

It might be thought that such procedures would give rise, if not to new bureaucracies and repressive apparatuses, then to a great risk of arbitrariness and injustice during the transition period. This is the nub of Norberto Bobbio's critique of direct democracy and his spirited defence of 'the rule of law against the rule of men'.[75] It undoubtedly contains an element of truth.

As in the case of universal franchise, the long, traumatic experience with fascist, military, Stalinist and post-Stalinist dictatorships has taught all socialists that written law is a necessity if the dangers of arbitrary justice – that is, injustice – are to be at least restricted. This threatens workers and peasants in post-capitalist societies much more than it does intellectuals and bureaucrats.[76] Revolutionary Marxists did not wait for the current revolutions in post-capitalist societies before stressing this point.[77]

However, a purely formal definition of the problem – such as Bobbio proposes, following the tradition of Weber and earlier liberal philosophers – does not help to reduce the sources and extent of arbitrariness and injustice.[78] To counterpose 'the rule of law' to 'the rule of men' is an example of fetishistic thinking, not really valid even if the latter is interpreted as meaning the rule of despots.[79] It overlooks the fact – well documented in the history of the USA, for example – that the people who write and apply laws are not simply machines programmed by juridical procedure but flesh-and-blood human beings bound up with specific social conditions and material interests.[80]

The only 'rule of law' divorced from the 'rule of men' would be a justice applied by robots. It is an open question whether that would be radically better, but it will not in any case come about in a foreseeable future. In the meantime, innumerable examples could be cited of blatantly unjust verdicts in spite of 'the rule of law' in conditions of bourgeois democracy. The systematic way in which judges in the Weimar Republic let off murderers of workers or left-wing leaders is one of them. Another is the scandalous freeing of the extreme right-wingers responsible for the Bologna bombing in Italy.[81]

Human beings must have the material possibility of defending themselves with some effectiveness against what they feel to be unjust laws, enforced by unjust judges. The 'rule of law', with a minimum of equal justice for all, must therefore be backed up by equality of access to lawyers, trial by jury as a norm, and a system for the election (and deselection) of judges. In theory, this too could lead to cases of injustice or what conservatives call 'mob rule'. But in either case, we have a combination of 'rule of law' and 'rule of men', not a separation between them.

Self-administration linked at once to written law, direct democracy, pluralism and public control seems to us the ground for a qualitative decline in arbitrariness and injustice – not for their total disappearance, which would be utopian. But this implies that conflicts of material, social interest should be recognized as such, and that the administration of justice should not be subordinated to a need to avoid explosive conflicts – that is, to the preservation of the basic social order. It is extremely easy, in the name of tolerance and consensus, to become more and more intolerant to the victims of the existing order who rebel against it.[82]

In the Soviet Union neo-liberals adopted a similar intolerance that borders on the cynical. Efrim Cherniak, for example, writes as follows with regard to the French Jacobins' attitude to slavery: 'It is necessary to refer to the principles of historicism, which do not allow one to judge the qualities of a historical figure in isolation from the specific features of the epoch. An apology for slavery, though inadmissible by twentieth-century criteria, was not so for men in the seventeenth and eighteenth centuries.'[83] Which men? one would like to know. Were slaves not 'men' as much as the slave-owners and their apologists? Did they not rise up against slavery? Is not Toussaint L'Ouverture part of the history of the eighteenth century in the same way as Robespierre, the defender of slavery? Was he wrong to rebel? And what of Condorcet, who strongly condemned the institution of slavery? In the name of 'objective needs' and 'objective possibilities', borrowed in fact from the Stalinists, these nice neo-liberals intolerantly project outside history all those who break the consensus with the triumphant bourgeoisie.

10. Is the Search for the Best an Obstacle to Achieving the Good?

Since the collapse of the Stalinist and neo-Stalinist regimes in Eastern Europe, a large number of neo-conservatives, liberals and even social democrats have taken up the old refrain that Marxism has a dangerously chiliastic thrust. Of course, there is something grotesque in the notion that cynical realpoliticians like Stalin were driven by the desire to realize a 'utopia'. But, so the argument goes, the utopian passion to achieve a 'perfect world', 'heaven on earth', 'a total reconciliation of man and nature, individual and society' is likely to inspire a ruthlessness in the choice of means which will lead on to the horrors of state despotism. In this way, a direct link is drawn between, on the one hand, not only Lenin and the Bolsheviks but even Marx and all socialists, and on the other hand, the sad realities of the USSR, China, Eastern Europe and even Pol Pot's Kampuchea.

In its main substance, this line of argument simply misses the mark. It involves a crass misunderstanding, if not deliberate falsification, of Marx's thought and writings, and of the theories and practices of classical socialism.

There is no element of chiliasm or 'secularized religion' in Marxism. There is no childish dream of completely reconciling man and nature, individual and community. There is no prediction that social conflicts and contradictions will totally disappear. Nor is there any project for forcing such utopias down people's throats. Marxism is by no means blind to the means–end dialectic.[84] And it is a key theme of this book that the very essence of Marxist socialism is *self*-emancipation of the toilers, not 'making people happy against their own wishes'.

What Marxists do claim is that it is both possible and necessary *drastically* to reduce the conflicts between human practice and nature, between blind egoism and the general needs of the community. But today an increasing number of non-socialists also see this as an urgent imperative, for reasons of self-preservation of our species, of sheer physical survival.

Insofar as the equation 'Marxism = utopianism = road to Stalinism and serfdom' is not just a perverse ideological construct, it poses a series of real questions about socialist theory and action, and their consequences from the point of view of progressive politics. Is the building of a classless and stateless society not a utopian project? Would the energy devoted to it not be better spent on gradual reform of the existing 'open' society, at least as it exists in the West? Is there not a basic contradiction between the struggle for attainable reforms and pursuit of the 'final goal' of a different society? Do not systematic denunciations and 'hardline' challenges to the ruling classes and the state stoke up their resistance to immediately achievable reforms and provoke them into violent reprisals? Does this not objectively undermine the institutions of political democracy, which can function only on the basis of consensus around a given set of social values?

Now, the charge of utopianism that is made against Marxian socialism implies a restrictive definition of the term 'utopia' itself – which in turn takes us deep into the materialist interpretation of history.[85] If 'utopian' is defined as meaning impossible or unrealizable, then evidently it is a waste of time and effort to struggle *politically* for what is utopian – although it could still have a moral significance and even be a means of better understanding reality.

But the content of 'utopia' changes as soon as one breaks from this formalist, mechanistic and undialectical definition, which sets up an absolute opposition betweeen 'the possible' and 'the impossible', 'the real and the unreal'. Lenin of all people, and in *What Is To Be Done?* of all his writings, actually drew attention to the 'right to dream', nay the 'need to dream', provided that the dream is about what does not yet exist but could come about under a certain set of circumstances.[86] To make such dreams 'come true' implies both the existence of the material preconditions, and human endeavour, projects, the will to act, and the capacity for effective action.[87]

The platitude that 'Marxian socialism' does not exist anywhere in the world today is tirelessly repeated as, in effect, an argument against all human progress. But was it utopian to fight for the abolition of slavery, which existed on a large scale for more than a thousand years? Was it utopian to seek an end to serfdom? Religious oppression, including the burning of heretics at the stake, was a 'fact of life' for at least five centuries. Was it then utopian to try to establish freedom of conscience and freedom of thought? Parliaments existed for many hundreds of years on the basis of an extremely narrow franchise. Was it therefore utopian to fight for universal suffrage? Why should it be utopian today to try to do away with wage-labour and gigantic state bureaucracies, which after all have been central structures of society for no more than two hundred years.

It is both necessary and empirically justified to cut right across the gradualists' argument. Utopia, in the broad sense of the word, has been one of the great motors of the eventual achievement of historical progress. In the case of slavery, for example, its abolition would not have happened when and as it did if revolutionary or 'utopian' abolitionists had limited themselves to a struggle to better the conditions of slaves within the 'peculiar institution'.

In assessing a particular project from the point of view of historical progress, we have to ask two kinds of questions. Is it *desirable* because it seeks to eliminate inhuman conditions – which is sufficient reason to struggle for it? Is it *realizable*, in the sense that the conditions for its existence, though not yet grown to full maturity, have been developing within existing society? This was Marx's own approach, which we have followed in this book, to the problem of creating a classless and stateless society.

As we have already argued, there is no contradiction between the struggle for reforms and propaganda (preparation) for revolution. Indeed, whereas 'consensus politicians' turn away from reforms, or even try to erode previous gains, as soon as the higher goal of capitalist profit is threatened, revolutionary socialists are the most resolute fighters for immediately realizable reforms. The real contradiction is the one between unfettered mass action (including extra-parliamentary action) and consensus politics.

This commitment of revolutionary socialists to radical reforms has deeper roots than the need to defend the immediate material and democratic interests of the mass of the exploited and oppressed. It is closely bound up with the basic psychological– political prerequisites for rising self-activity and self-organization of the toilers.

Revolutions do not and cannot occur every day; they do not even occur every year. They are periodic results of explosive social contradictions on the one hand and explosive mass actions on the other. Great self-confidence of the broad masses is necessary if these two elements are successfully to fuse together, and that has to develop through the experience of self-activity and self-organization under non-revolutionary circumstances, in the struggle for radical reforms.[88]

In the last analysis, the branding of revolutionary socialists as dangerous utopians rests on a defence of consensus politics, with its 'mutual tolerance', as a necessary safeguard of political democracy understood in purely parliamentary terms. For some authors, moreover, such institutions as workers' or people's councils would not only be impracticable over any long period of time but even pose a potential threat to civil liberties.[89]

The fatal flaw in this argument is the one-sided character of any consensus in class society, which rules out any serious challenge to the status quo. In India, for example, it is considered normal that more than 50 per cent of the population (the *shudra* and the Muslims) get a mere 4 per cent of top government and public-sector jobs, while upper-caste brahmins, fewer than 20 per cent of the population, cream off 68 per cent. A consensus accepting that basic injustice is deemed indispensable to the 'stability of democratic institutions'. Any proposal to make the distribution more equitable, even if backed by a parliamentary majority, is considered dangerously 'subversive'. Similarly, the exploited are supposed to consent to capitalist exploitation, so long as this is subject to some regulation. The exploiters are not asked to consent to the abolition of exploitation, even when this is requested by the majority of the people.

Sometimes an attempt is made to counter these points by invoking the political philosophy of gradualism, with its allegedly superior wisdom. Consensus politics, it is said, will gradually reduce ruling-class opposition to reforms. If everybody accepts the 'rules of the game' (that is, the parliamentary–electoralist game), social legislation will eventually whittle away the basic evils of capitalism and the bureaucratic state: softly, softly catchee monkey. The equivalent Italian proverb is: *chi va piano va sano* – although popular wisdom has fittingly added: *ma non arriva mai.*[90]

What this overlooks is the *structural character* of the basic relations of production and of political and social class power, which are backed up by an increasingly independent and uncontrollable executive. These relations cannot be changed piecemeal, just as one cannot get a little bit pregnant. There is no way of reducing the power of big money wealth without suppressing big money wealth. Olaf Palme, the late and sadly regretted social-democrat leader, conducted his final election campaign under the slogan: Give us a parliamentary majority; otherwise the fifteen families which dominate Sweden's economy will dominate Parliament too. But if, after forty-five years of reforms and nearly uninterrupted social-democratic rule, Sweden's economy was still dominated by fifteen families, it is very hard to see why that would not still be the case after a hundred years. Is that not the clearest expression of the historical failure of gradualism?

It is not a question of pursuing some far-fetched goal for dogmatic or 'idealist' reasons. Of course, Swedish capitalism *anno* 1990 is different and less obnoxious than Swedish capitalism *anno* 1932, not to speak of *anno* 1890 or 1832. But it is still capitalism, and still obnoxious. Capitalist competition and the profit motive still imply that periodically factories are closed down, workers are thrown on the dole, wages are cut, social security benefits are reduced. Inside the factory, the pace of work is speeded up and its alienating character increased.[91] We are against capitalism because we are against these social evils. We note that even the best and most consistent gradualists have not succeeded in eradicating them. So the case for consensus politics is historically weak, implying as it does the survival of capitalism and the a priori rejection of revolution.

Furthermore, consensus politics carries a grave risk of sowing political frustration among an ever larger section of the population. Especially in the age of 'television politics' and 'opinion poll politics', it leads to further erosion of the difference between 'left' and 'right', which tend to become 'centre-left' and 'centre-right' with few nuances between them. The feeling that there is no longer any real political choice can breed a kind of political apathy that is obviously dangerous for the survival of democratic freedoms. Paradoxically, then, it is the very same people who accuse revolutionary socialists of undermining parliamentary democracy who produce exactly that result through their day-to-day policies.[92]

In the end, consensus politics raises the bourgeois welfare state to the level of the only possible, progressive and realizable alternative to a 'jungle type' of capitalism. The *tertium non datur* exclusion appears once again. 'Marxian socialism', not to say socialist revolution, is held to be neither a possible nor even a desirable option.

We say advisedly the *bourgeois* welfare state, for the underlying assumption of present-day social-democratic gradualism is precisely this: let the capitalists produce the goods, so that governments can redistribute them in a juster way. But what if capitalist production demands a more unequal, more unjust distribution of the 'fruits of growth'? What if there is no economic growth at all as a result of capitalist crisis? The gradualists can then only repeat mechanically: there is no alternative; there is no way out.

Now, a number of studies have been made of the limits of the welfare state. The German Civitas Society, for example, has raised general theoretical questions about the relations between state and market, about the 'limits' of public-sector growth and income redistribution in an essentially market (that is, profit-oriented) economy, and about the implications of social security for economic growth.[93] The final conclusion to be drawn is that it is the intrinsic logic of capitalism which hedges in the dimensions of welfare. Citizens should not lose the sense of 'realities'. They should not forget the 'rules of the struggle for life'. Indeed they should not. The 'struggle for life', the struggle of all against all, is the very heart of 'capitalist culture'.

The ultimate argument deployed against opponents of consensus politics is that they lose sight of the electoral facts of life. How can you push through social legislation if you don't win elections? And how can you win elections with anti-capitalist propaganda if it does not appeal to the great majority of voters? But such a line in rhetorical questions can cut both ways. How can you change voters' minds about capitalism unless you try to propagate alternative ideas? And what if they suddenly vote in favour of radical change, of an alternative 'model of society', as the French electorate clearly did in 1981–82? Why do you then suddenly accept the social status quo and refuse to accept their mandate? Is it because you want to maintain at any cost the consensus with the bourgeoisie?

In a way which borders on the tragic, André Gorz concentrates the

236

historical *impasse* of gradualism. His *Critique of Economic Reason*, which we have already had occasion to mention, is a brilliant exposure of the character of wage-labour and the trends towards a 'dual society' in capitalism, which spell a massive resurgence of poverty and physical and mental suffering for a new 'Lazarus layer' of the contemporary proletariat. This critique gives Marxists a series of new and powerful arguments in favour of socialism.[94] Similarly, his plea for a radical reduction in the working week as the key demand for the trade-union movement, and for a radical change in our understanding of the relationship between work and leisure, is identical with the position we have been arguing for many years.

Yet when Gorz advances his proposals for radical reform – all of which we endorse, as far as they go – he does not touch on the basic power relations within the factory and the firm, or within the economy as a whole. Nor does he question the fundamental structures of the bourgeois state. All he wants to do is 'democratize' them. No wonder that he has ended up as an adviser for the new programme of German Social Democracy. Once you say 'farewell to the working class', it is not long before you are saying hello to reformed welfare-state capitalism. If there is no longer a potentially revolutionary subject, then capitalists, like diamonds, are forever – so long as they don't blow up our little planet.

11. Bobbio and the Marxian Concept of the Withering Away of the State

Bobbio's defence of 'the rule of law' against 'the rule of men', which we discussed earlier in this chapter, is not his only major contribution to the debate about bureaucratic despotism. He also offers a systematic critique of the Marxist conception of the state and of its withering away.

Bobbio gives the following definition of the 'rules of democracy', as a minimum without which political democracy cannot be said to exist:

1. All citizens who have attained their majority are entitled without distinction of race, religion, economic conditions, sex, etc. to political rights, i.e. to the right to express, through the casting of votes, their own opinion, and/or to elect the person who expresses it for them.

2. The vote of all citizens must have an equal weight (i.e. must count as one voting unit).

3. All citizens who are entitled to political rights must be free to vote in the light of their own opinion – one which has been formed freely as far as possible, i.e. in a free competition between organized political groups who vie with each other for aggregate demands and transform them into collective decisions.

237

4. They must also be free in the sense that real alternatives must be made available to them so that they can choose between different solutions.

5. Both in collective decisions and in the election of representatives the rule of the numerical majority applies. . . .

6. No majority decision can restrict the rights of the minority, in particular the right to become a majority, subject to the same condition.[95]

We shall perhaps surprise Bobbio, but as an orthodox Marxist we would approve of all these rules and indeed argue for further measures to safeguard them. As the reader can judge, there is nothing in the present book which contradicts them – quite the contrary.

But we must immediately point out that *nowhere in the world are these six rules fully put into practice*. At best, they apply 50, 66 or 75 per cent, certainly no more. The restrictions prevailing under bourgeois parliamentary democracy thus make it a partial democracy which has still to be perfected. They confirm the Marxist critique of its validity.

We are not at all talking of some minor shortcomings. Foreign residents and migrant workers are denied the right to vote in all capitalist countries – the first Soviet constitution, let us remind Bobbio, gave them this right from the moment they had settled in the country. Real alternatives do not exist in most countries which have moved towards a tweedledum-tweedledee 'Americanization' of politics. Not insignificant minorities are excluded from parliamentary representation by means of electoral thresholds and systems that distort or even reject proportionality.

Most important of all, however, is the fact that competition among rival political parties is neither completely free nor particularly equal, since their access to money and other means of influencing the electorate is highly differentiated. We might very well ask Bobbio if he would contemplate adding one more to his list of 'rules of democracy' – one which, in line with our previous suggestions, would grant all citizens access to the media and hence the material possibility of exercising equal political rights.

Here Bobbio's 'paradoxes of democracy' explode on him, showing apologists of *purely* representative (that is, indirect) democracy to be inconsistent with their own profession of faith. We need not pay much attention to the trite argument according to which Marxists, and especially Leninists, tend to substitute 'party rule' for the rule of the masses. We have dealt with that ahistorical approach at various points in this book. For Marx, direct democracy was an instrument for self-emancipation of the toiling masses, not a pretext for party rule. And at least after 1905 – with the exception of the dark years – Lenin had a similar view of things.

We come to the heart of the matter in Bobbio's contention that 'to demand the extension of democracy means asking for decisions to become the responsibility of people who, given the objective conditions which accompany the development of modern society, are less and less competent to take them. This is especially [!] true of the manufacturing sector, i.e. precisely the sector which has up to now been effectively removed from any sort of popular control.'[96]

Bobbio's further criticisms of direct democracy focus on what, in his view, are four key weaknesses: (a) mass actions tend to promote demagogy; (b) referenda are impractical except occasionally on a few limited questions; (c) institutions of direct democracy could not work for any large community; (d) the recallability of elected delegates would mean that some mediator would step in to take the initiative. We have already largely answered these points. But they all basically revolve around the question of whether the masses are competent or not.

Bobbio takes for granted that our 'industrial society' is run by 'competent experts', whereas everything suggests rather that it is run by financial tycoons in the West and by the top nomenklatura in the East. Is the historical balance-sheet of the rulers' competence really so convincing that the extension of human rights should be made secondary to it? Are broad masses themselves really incapable of becoming more and more 'competent', as a result both of higher levels of education and of the practice of self-management?

Two examples will have to suffice. It was recently reported that one of the British navy's nuclear submarines, the *Warspite*, had to be scrapped shortly before the end of a refit costing a hundred million pounds, and ten months after a fault, thought to be a hairline crack, was discovered in the reactor's cooling system. We shall not dwell on the original costs of producing and maintaining the *Warspite* for twenty-three years, nor on the number of hospital beds that could have been provided instead for life-saving surgery. We shall just ask: where was the expertise? Who was competent, and who incompetent, among the supposedly irreplaceable masters of society?

After an official enquiry into the Piper Alpha oil rig disaster, in which 167 workers died, the Scottish judge Lord Cullen proposed that the responsibility for offshore safety should be transferred from the Department of Energy to the Department of Health – a move which, ten years before, had been refused by the government and Occidental Oil. A Department of Energy report, which was never published, had noted a breach of safety regulations in a previous explosion. Yet workers and trade unionists had been consistently campaigning for the tougher mainland regulations to be applied to offshore platforms, and a rank-and-file committee led by shop stewards had organized a number of unofficial strikes around that demand. Again we ask: where was the competence? Where was the sense of social responsibility?[97]

Bobbio does not address these questions, as he does not seriously address the core of the Marxist critique of purely representative bourgeois democracy: namely, its structural entanglement with unequal economic powers, and with an ever-stronger 'executive branch of government' freed from any democratic involvement by the mass of citizens.

Thus, when all is said and done, Bobbio remains trapped within a technocratic justification for the growth of bureaucracy. Far from advocating an extension of democracy as the only means of countering this, he rejects such an alternative as unrealistic and impractical. He even quotes in his support a passage from Kautsky which neatly complements the one quoted above, and which makes Kautsky – not Lenin – the real source of substitutionism, the theoretical fountainhead of Stalinism.

> Public affairs are today too complicated, too intricate and wide-ranging to be dealt with like a secondary activity by dilettantes who work in their hours of leisure. . . . The idea of a government of the people by the people who work for nothing in their spare time, is a utopia, and what is more, is a reactionary and anti-democratic utopia.[98]

Logically one ought to add with Stalin that 'cadres' (that is, expert bureaucrats) 'decide everything'. That would square the circle. But it is not Marx's circle. It is not the circle of radical defenders of human rights.

From Bobbio's soul-searching investigation, we fully share his dedication to formal democratic rules that provide guarantees to all. But precisely for that reason, we refuse to subordinate such rules to the alleged 'expertise' of bureaucrats or technocrats, as we refuse to subordinate them to 'economic efficiency' or to a hypothetical 'stability of the institutions'.

12. The New Impetus for Self-administration

However many the obstacles in its path, the goal of building a classless, socialist society is neither impossible nor located in an ever receding future. It emerges from tendencies already visible in the world around us, economic, social, cultural and psychological processes that are pushing in the direction of self-administration.

The third technological revolution, with its trend towards the computerization of economic activity in production, distribution, accounting or transport, contains a powerful dynamic for a reduction in the working week and a major extension of group cooperation as the basic social structure. Society is faced with a critical choice. Either it evolves into a 'dual society' in which a sector of skilled labour, more or less protected and even 'scarce' in periods of economic expansion,[99] coexists with another sector of degraded, unskilled and, to varying degrees, unprotected labour. Or else it imposes a new homogenization of labour, with an end to unemployment, a shortening of the working week to 30, 24 and 20 hours, and an enhancement of the role of education, skill formation and retraining during the producer's lifetime.

In point of fact, even the more 'enlightened' capitalist employers understand that a country's (we would add: humanity's) macro-economic productivity is much more a function of the workforce's skill and adaptability to new technological processes, than it is of increases in the current extraction of surplus-value. Marx's prophetic vision of a society in which leisure and full development of the personality were the main source of wealth is thus, in a certain sense, beginning to become reality as a result of the development of the productive forces under late capitalism.[100]

The GDR Marxist Ulrich Hedtke has correctly pointed out:

> On top of the retail shortages in the state economy, we should not forget the profusion of ideas, capacities, talents and productive necessities that had to be spoiled and driven out of people in this country. Manual workers, scientists, skilled workers, economists and pedagogues, engineers and doctors all had first to learn through practical experience that they were sought after only as bearers of *assumed* and therefore systemically defined capacities. They were not accepted as persons who could bring effectively into play within society the development of their capacity to create something new. . . . This aspect of the history of working people in the GDR remains completely to be written – the real everyday and social history of the *blocking of that productive force.*[101]

However, we should not interpret the relatively greater innovative success of late capitalism as implying that the same phenomenon does not exist there too. Indeed, both late capitalism and bureaucratized post-capitalism are unable to allow the productive or creative potential of the great majority of men and women to develop freely. Only in a socialist commonwealth of associated producers/consumers/citizens will the 'free development of each' become the real condition for the 'free development of all' – an interconnection that contemporary technology is literally crying out for.

An associated trend is the decline of the so-called work ethic, not only in the protestant lands of its historical origin but also in those parts of the world, Japan and Asia, with which it has more often been identified in recent times.[102] Leisure and 'the quality of life' are coming to the fore and progressively replacing the desire for greater consumption.[103] One of the main pillars of late capitalism is thereby undermined, while one of the principal sources for self-administration is opened up.

The growth of ecological, feminist, minority-ethnic, anti-militarist, anti-racist and anti-imperialist awareness in broad layers of the population, coupled with the emergence of the so-called new social movements in which millions have taken part in recent years, really implies a new way of conceiving political activity by large masses of people.

These movements have real limitations, due to the lack or weakness of a counter-model of society in their ranks, and they also display a tendency to neo-reformism and absorption into the establishment, at least in political terms. The latest sad example in this respect is the 'Realo' wing of the German Greens.

Nevertheless, at the level of mass activity, they are surprisingly fresh and full of emancipatory potential. They rebound again and again. And they represent a definite trend toward mass involvement in the political process, outside the channels of established and bureaucratic states, governments, parties, and Big Business lobbies. Such new conceptions point to the huge possibilities of institutionalized direct democracy after the downfall of capitalism. They indicate that self-administration, far from being a utopia, is actually the wave of the future.

In spite of all the propaganda presenting 'market economy' as a panacea, urgent problems of everyday life – beginning with the asphyxiation of big cities by irrational use of the motor-car and emission of industrial pollutants[104] – have again called into question the exercise of consumer choice purely through unevenly distributed 'effective demand', that is, through money income and money wealth. There is also a growing awareness of the threat to civic coexistence represented by stress, psychological imbalance, violence, drug addiction, the lack of hope and perspective for young people, and the general spread of demoralization. Even the more intelligent conservative circles are gradually, if reluctantly, coming to accept that more egoism, more social strife, more energy wasted on the pursuit of wealth offer no solution whatever to these problems, and indeed actually lie at their source. It follows that a whole range of social needs, going well beyond the safety-net level, must take precedence over manipulated individual choices.

Contrary to a fairly common misconception, Marxists and socialists do not maintain that human choices and struggles are exclusively, or even predominantly, driven by rational motives. In fact, such a belief is far more typical of the liberal myth of *homo oeconomicus* – however great the contradictions that subsequently emerge from it. Socialists are well aware that irrational drives, passions and preferences play an important role in individual behaviour, and therefore in the life of society.[105] Their cautious historical optimism bases itself on the capacity of human beings gradually to understand and control these irrational aspects of their behaviour. This capacity is proved by the development of civilization, though certainly not in a linear, non-contradictory fashion: epochal advances are always accompanied by, and in most cases combined with, partial regressions.

The fundamental argument in favour of socialism today is precisely that humankind can no longer endure the costs of aggregate irrationality. It has become a life-and-death question to master the most serious irrational tendencies of social evolution. Awareness of this necessity is today more and more widespread, at least with regard to the danger of nuclear and other weapons of mass destruction, and the threat of environmental disaster. If irrationality continues to prevail in these areas, humankind is doomed to extinction.

There is a structural link between these threats to the species, the capitalist mode of production and all the 'values', mentalities and motivations which spring from it. Capitalism means in the last instance the quest for short-term private profit and private wealth, capital accumulation spurred on by competition. That quest implies a basic tendency to disregard long-term macro-social effects of human action, in favour of short-term gains. We are not just referring to the 'writing off' of externalities – a problem that neo-liberal conservatives and their neo-reformist disciples claim to be able to solve 'in principle' through the pricing of these externalities. The point is that decisions about current inputs altogether disregard the long-term effects of their implicit social priorities. There is no way in which you can 'price' or 'discount' the future revenue of unborn babies. And anyway cost–benefit analysis that 'discounts' human lives as a function of 'lost revenue' is pretty inhuman in itself.

The key question for human survival, then, is to achieve a qualitative increase in conscious control over social developments, instead of leaving these to spontaneous, uncontrolled and ever more destructive processes. The same applies even more to human relations with nature. Nothing clearer has been said on these matters than what Friedrich Engels wrote in 1876, anticipating the whole ecological movement.

> In short, the animal merely *uses* his environment, and brings about changes in it simply by his presence; man by his changes makes it serve his ends, *masters* it. This is the final, essential distinction between man and other animals, and once again it is labour that brings about this distinction.
>
> Let us not, however, flatter ourselves overmuch on account of our human victories over nature. For each such victory nature takes its revenge on us. Each victory, it is true, in the first place brings about the results we expected,

243

but in the second and third places it has quite different, unforeseen effects which only too often cancel the first. The people who, in Mesopotamia, Greece, Asia Minor and elsewhere, destroyed the forests to obtain cultivable land, never dreamed that by removing along with the forests the collecting centres and reservoirs of moisture they were laying the basis for the present forlorn state of those countries. . . .

Those who spread the potato in Europe were not aware that with these farinaceous tubers they were at the same time spreading scrofula. Thus at every step we are reminded that we by no means rule over nature like a conqueror over a foreign people, like someone standing outside nature – but that we, with flesh, blood and brain, belong to nature, and exist in its midst, and that all our mastery of it consists in the fact that we have the advantage over all other creatures of being able to learn its laws and apply them correctly.

And, in fact, with every day that passes we are acquiring a better understanding of these laws and getting to perceive both the more immediate and the more remote consequences of our interference with the traditional course of nature. In particular, after the mighty advances made by the natural sciences in the present century, we are more than ever in a position to realize, and hence to control, even the more remote natural consequences of at least our day-to-day production activities. But the more this progresses the more will men not only feel but also know their oneness with nature, and the more impossible will become the senseless and unnatural idea of a contrast between mind and matter, man and nature, soul and body, such as arose after the decline of classical antiquity in Europe and obtained its highest elaboration in Christianity.

It required the labour of thousands of years for us to learn a little of how to calculate the more remote *natural* effects of our actions in the field of production, but it has been still more difficult in regard to the more remote *social* effects of these actions. We mentioned the potato and the resulting spread of scrofula. But what is scrofula compared to the effect which the reduction of the workers to a potato diet had on the living conditions of the masses of the people in whole countries, or compared to the famine the potato blight brought to Ireland in 1847, which consigned to the grave a million Irishmen, nourished solely or almost exclusively on potatoes, and forced the emigration overseas of two million more? When the Arabs learned to distil spirits, it never entered their heads that by so doing they were creating one of the chief weapons for the annihilation of the then still undiscovered American continent. And when afterwards Columbus discovered this America, he did not know that by doing so he was laying the basis for the Negro slave trade and giving a new lease of life to slavery, which in Europe had long ago been done away with. The men who in the seventeenth and eighteenth centuries laboured to create the steam-engine had no idea that they were preparing the instrument which more than any other was to revolutionize social relations throughout the world. Especially in Europe, by concentrating wealth in the hands of a minority and dispossessing the huge majority, this instrument was destined at first to give social and political domination to the bourgeoisie, but later, to give rise to a class struggle between bourgeoisie and proletariat which can end only in the overthrow of the bourgeoisie and the abolition of all class antagonisms. But in this sphere, too, by long and often cruel experience and by collecting and analysing historical material, we are gradually learning to get a clear view of the indirect, more remote social effects of our production activity, and so are afforded an opportunity to control and regulate these effects at will.

This regulation, however, requires something more than mere knowledge. It requires a complete revolution in our hitherto existing mode of production, and simultaneously a revolution in our whole contemporary social order.

All hitherto existing modes of production have aimed merely at achieving the most immediately and directly useful effect of labour. The further consequences, which appear only later and become effective through gradual repetition and accumulation, were totally neglected. The original common ownership of land corresponded, on the one hand, to a level of development of human beings in which their horizon was restricted in general to what lay immediately available, and presupposed, on the other hand, a certain super-fluity of land that would allow some latitude for correcting the possible bad results of this primeval type of economy. When this surplus land was exhausted, common ownership also declined. All higher forms of production, however, led to the division of the population into different classes and thereby to the antagonism of ruling and oppressed classes. Thus the interests of the ruling class became the driving factor of production, since production was no longer restricted to providing the barest means of subsistence for the oppressed people. This has been put into effect most completely in the capitalist mode of production prevailing today in Western Europe. The individual capitalists, who dominate production and exchange, are able to concern themselves only with the most immediate useful effect of their actions. Indeed, even this useful effect – inasmuch as it is a question of the usefulness of the article that is produced or exchanged – retreats far into the background, and the sole incentive becomes the profit to be made on selling.
. . .

In relation to nature, as to society, the present mode of production is predominantly concerned only about the immediate, the most tangible result; and then surprise is expressed that the more remote effects of actions directed to this end turn out to be quite different, are mostly quite the opposite in character; that the harmony of supply and demand is transformed into the very reverse opposite, as shown by the course of each ten years' industrial cycle.[106]

In order to extend conscious, democratic control over the relations between humankind and nature on the one hand, over the mutual relations of human beings on the other hand, it is necessary to break the stranglehold exercised over society by capital, capital accumulation, generalized commodity production or market economy, and the structures of competition–monopoly–monopolist competition. It is necessary to make substantial, qualitative progress towards the withering away of institutionalized scarcity and the state – that is, towards abundance and self-administration. Our survival depends on a successful outcome.

Some may see this as a debate between realism and utopia. In our view, it is a contest between pessimists-cum-misanthropes and moderate optimists. To believe that the trend towards self-destruction of humankind can be stopped without overcoming competition and long-term global irrationality, 'the war of all against all', the universal rule of greed, is in no sense realistic. It is utterly utopian. It points straight to Doomsday.

Socialists believe that Doomsday can still be averted if we increase the degree of rationality of our collective behaviour, if we strive to take the future into our own hands. That is the freedom and self-determination we are fighting for. To believe that humankind is incapable of it is not 'being realistic'. It is to assume that men and women are congenitally unfitted for self-preservation. But that is utter superstition, a new version of the myth of Original Sin.

The final word remains with Karl Marx: 'The bureaucracy can be superseded only if the universal interest becomes a particular interest *in reality* and not merely in thought, in *abstraction*, as it does in Hegel.'[107] In other words, it can be superseded only if the great majority of producers/consumers/citizens gradually take into their own hands the management of the 'general affairs of society'. This is possible only under the rule of the freely associated producers, in a socialist commonwealth.

NOTES

1. I. Deutscher, *The Prophet Outcast*, Oxford 1963, pp. 311–13.
2. See M. Gorbachev, *Perestroika*, London 1987.
3. T. Zaslavskaia, *Die Gorbatschow-Strategie*, Vienna 1989, pp. 28, 30, 224, etc.
4. As we saw in Chapter 1, this outcome is implied by theories that the bureaucracy is a new ruling class, or a fortiori that the USSR is a totalitarian society. The most seminal of many works on this question is probably Hannah Arendt, *The Origins of Totalitarianism*, new edn, New York 1966. It is crucially important to distinguish between the concept of a 'totalitarian society' (which has never existed and never will) and a 'totalitarian regime' (which is, of course, a bitter reality of the twentieth century).
5. See Gorbachev, *Perestroika*; Mandel, *Beyond Perestroika*, London 1989; Abel Aganbegyan, *Moving the Mountain: Inside the Perestroika Revolution*, London 1989.
6. L. Trotsky, *The Revolution Betrayed*, London 1967, pp. 241–42.
7. A distinction should be made between money–commodity relations and the accumulation of capital. The first evolves into the second only under specific social circumstances that can be avoided or at least held in check.
8. See the positions of Alec Nove in *The Economics of Feasible Socialism*, London 1979, as an example in the West; and those of Tsypko, Afanasiev and E. Yakovlev, the editor of *Moscow News*, in the USSR.

9. Rödel, Frankenberg and Dubiel (*Die demokratische Frage*, Frankfurt/Main 1989) point cautiously in the same direction when they plead for a broader sphere of active exercise of power by citizens' bodies. See also André Gorz, *Critique of Economic Reason*, London 1989.

10. Leszek Kolakowski attributes to Trotsky the idea that 'since only the genuine vanguard of the proletariat is to exercise power, that vanguard must also have the right to decide which parties are "Soviet" and which are counter-revolutionary. In Trotsky's eyes, the upshot seems to be that socialist freedom means freedom for Trotskyists and no one else.' (*Main Currents of Marxism*, vol. 3, London 1981, p. 197.) This is a blatant distortion of the position taken by Trotsky at least after 1935, if not earlier. He came out clearly in favour of a multi-party system, of the exercise of power by freely elected soviets and not by any 'genuine vanguard': 'The workers and peasants themselves by their own free vote will indicate what parties they recognize as soviet parties.' *The Transitional Programme for Socialist Revolution* (1938), New York 1973, p. 105.

11. The USA during the Cold War, or Israel today provide striking examples in the capitalist countries, with Mrs Thatcher's Britain showing many of the same signs. The trend was recently codified, as it were, in a judgement of the West German Constitutional Court: 'Inhuman treatment like torture is not as such admissible according to the letter and spirit of the constitution. Things would stand rather differently, however, if the torture was inflicted on someone because of their assault on a political object of legal protection and thus because of its danger to state unity and the foundations of the state.' (*Süddeutsche Zeitung*, 23 February 1990.) Hitler and Stalin could hardly have come up with anything better.

12. *Le Monde Diplomatique*, October 1989.

13. In the heyday of Yugoslav self-management, between 1957 and 1971, the commune system made significant progress in that direction.

14. See the interesting book on this subject by Rödel, Frankenberg and Dubiel, *Die demokratische Frage*. The reservations held by socialists mainly concern the plebiscitary potential of referenda, and the possibility that results could be manipulated through misleading ways of posing the issue. But one answer would be to move away from simple 'yes or no' questions, perhaps with the presentation of three or four alternatives from which to choose. On the historical balance-sheet of the use of the referendum in Switzerland, see Jean-François Aubert, *Institutions politiques de la Suisse*, Lausanne 1983.

15. A referendum initiated by the Swiss Left in 1989 recorded a third of all votes (more than half among the younger generation of military age) for the immediate abolition of the army.

16. A recent example was Fujimori's presidential campaign in Peru in 1990, which secured him victory by portraying him as a 'defender of the poor' against the neo-liberal/conservative Mario Vargas Llosa. Hardly elected, Fujimori imposed an austerity pro-gramme which made five million more people poor. See *Le Monde*, 10 September 1990.

17. Quite a number of functions exercised today by state apparatuses are unnecessary and should not be performed by anyone. Examples include: the executioner, the torturer, the nuclear-war 'planner', the protector of 'state secrets', and the listener to private telephone conversations.

18. There is a growing literature on this subject which correctly stresses the dual aspect of computerization under capitalism: its destruction of skills, and its creation of new potentials. See among others Klaus Haefner, *Mensch und Computer im Jahre 2000*, Zurich 1986; Barbara Garson, *All the Livelong Day: The Meaning and Demeaning of Routine Work*, Harmondsworth 1977; and the work of Ashley Montagu.

19. The fact that the amount of information, mostly stored on computer, is growing exponentially is no argument against self-management, unless it is considered an argument against rational management in general. It does not stand to reason that a small group of professional managers are better able than a large number of producers to digest a huge mass of information, especially if the producers can sift the useful from the less useful in the course of their everyday activity.

20. On this and other objections to a self-managed economy, see among others Jan Osers's critique of my positions in his *Sozialistische Wirtschaftsmodell*, Frankfurt 1990.

21. It should not be forgotten, moreover, that the ending of permanent large-scale unemployment would be a major economic effect of a democratically planned economy.

22. Michael Harrington, *Socialism Past and Present*, New York 1989.

23. Etzioni, *Complex Organizations*, New York 1975, p. 472.

24. A number of interesting studies on the conflict-defusing potential of debates show the inherent dynamics of genuine direct democracy. See among others the textbook *Decision by Debate*, eds, D. Ehminger and Wayne Bockriede, New York 1978; and chapter nine, 'Participation and Self-Management', in Carol C. Gould's excellent *Rethinking Democracy*, Cambridge 1988.

25. Unfortunately Agnes Heller, who should know better, repeats this absurd idea in her book *The Theory of Need in Marx*, London 1974.

26. The rather conservative though critically minded American sociologist Vance Packard recently interviewed a number of multi-millionaires and billionaires about their life-style. He found that while there are some exceptions, the majority lead a rather simple life, much like that of average upper-middle-class people. It is an instinctive reaction: why trouble yourself with spending ever vaster sums of money, if it only complicates your existence? Even for billionaires, a figure of $150,000 was often quoted as the maximum level of annual personal expenditure. *The Ultra-Rich*, New York 1989.

27. Among innumerable sources we shall mention only: The World Commission on Environment and Development, *Our Common Future*, Oxford 1987; B. Wiesberg, *Beyond Repair: The Ecology of Capitalism*, Boston 1971; Christian Leipert, *Die heimlichen Kosten des Fortschritts*, Bonn 1989; World Watch Institute, *State of the World 1990*, London 1990; and Peter Hennicke and Michael Müller, *Die Klima-Katastrophe*, Berlin 1989.

28. Such arrogance is indeed present in the neo-Stalinist proposals of Harich and others, who allege that a technocratic dictatorship is necessary to save the environment by forcing people to lower their consumption. For their part, neo-liberal conservatives want to impose upon people, against their will, passive acceptance of supposedly unavoidable 'laws of market economy', such as structural unemployment, mass poverty and rising inequality.

29. See chapter 15 of our *Marxist Economic Theory*, London 1968.

30. As we have pointed out many times, this does not require a fall in living standards for the working masses in the advanced industrialized countries, provided that the resources uselessly and dangerously consumed in arms production are converted into free gifts to the Third World, and that the huge waste involved in the underemployment of resources is eliminated.

31. A good answer to the neo-Malthusian population scare is offered by M. Bookchin, *Toward an Ecological Society*, Montreal 1980. See also S. Weissman, 'Why the Population Bomb Is a Rockefeller Baby', *Ramparts*, May 1970.

32. Heller, *The Theory of Need in Marx*; Etzioni, pp. 470–73.

33. *Institutional Investor*, April 1989. Examples of this practice are offered by the Trump and Kashoggi cases.

34. A Gallup poll commissioned by the New York Business Group on Health found that, in certain companies, a full 25 per cent of the workforce may suffer from anxiety disorders or stress-related illnesses. *The Wall Street Journal*, 20 October 1989.

35. Carol Gould has presented a convincing argument – which will be very difficult to counter – that social justice, even as defined by neo-utilitarians or neo-libertarians like Rawls and Dahl, cannot be served by the system of private property in the means of production, with freedom to hire and fire wage-labour. However, Gould still maintains that enterprises run by workers' self-management should connect with one another essentially through the market. See also Amartya Sen, *Choice, Welfare and Measurement*, Oxford 1982.

36. See his article in Robert Ware and Karl Nielsen, eds, *Analysing Marx*, Calgary 1989.

37. It should be mentioned that van Parijs establishes, as we do, a basic causal link between needs satisfaction and the decline of work compulsion. The withering away of bureaucracy thereby becomes possible under growing abundance.

38. In *Marxist Economic Theory* (chapter 15), we made the point that economic growth is not in and of itself a goal of human endeavour, and that one day it would have to

stop. But we did not then take into consideration that ecological factors would eventually make this necessary.

39. There is a large and constantly increasing literature on the inter-related questions of controlled/uncontrolled economic growth, needs satisfaction in the so-called Northern hemisphere and the Third World, the threats to the environment and to human survival, the necessary adaptation of socio-economic structures to these needs, and the task of rethinking economic science (including Marxist economic theory) in the light of our present-day ecological understanding. Here we shall only mention one outstanding recent contribution to the debate: Keekok Lee, *Social Philosophy and Ecological Scarcity*, London 1989. We shall deal more extensively with all these subjects in our forthcoming book *Restating Marx's Case at the End of the Twentieth Century*.

40. See, among recent authors, Gérard Roland, *Economie politique du système soviétique*, Paris 1989. The argument is more than a hundred years old.

41. See, for example, the excellent study by Andy Pollack, 'Socialist Planning and the National Question', a still unpublished manuscript.

42. This point is ignored in Makhaisky's classic anarchist case against socialist planning, but only at the price of rehabilitating market economy in the Proudhon tradition. Apart from the alienating consequences for the producers, this would be unjust towards the least protected sectors of society, for the elderly and permanently disabled, as well as schoolchildren and full-time students, would be denied the right to intervene in allocation decisions. J.W. Makhaisky, *Le socialisme des intellectuels*, Paris 1979. See also Claude Lefort, *The Political Forms of Modern Society: Bureaucracy, Democracy, Totalitarianism*, Cambridge 1986.

43. A major debate is taking place on this question in the USSR, as reported in *Moscow News* and elsewhere. It also plays a key role in current debates within the Soviet working class – for example, the striking miners in 1989 and 1990 – about the concrete ways and means of transforming state (despotic) property into really social, workers' property.

44. See the works by Makhaisky and Lefort quoted in footnote 42.

45. L. von Mises, *Bureaucracy*, 1st edn, 1944, Yale University Press, and 2nd edn, Arlington House, 1969, chapter one. (The pagination is identical in the two editions.) Cf. F.A. von Hayek's famous book *The Road to Serfdom*, London 1944.

46. See the Nove/Mandel debate in *New Left Review*, Nos. 159, 161 and 169.

47. Von Mises, pp. 10, 20.

48. Ibid., pp. 38–39.

49. *Sunday Times*, 4 November 1990. According to an enquiry by the *Harvard Business Review* (quoted in Gorz, p. 172), 85 per cent of top managers recognized that advertising campaigns often led to the sale of products for which the buyers had no use and (in the case of 51 per cent of respondents) which the customers did not really want to buy.

50. *Bureaucracy*, p. 21.

51. Milton Friedman, *Market or Plan*, Centre for Research into Communist Economics, 1984, p. 9.

52. Neither von Mises nor Hayek nor even Friedman mentions the disastrous impact on wage-earners' income of employment fluctuations completely outside their control. In the days when capitalism was 'unhampered' by the welfare state, these could literally condemn workers to starvation.

53. *Times Saturday Review*, 3 November 1990.

54. See the table in *Die Zeit*, 27 October 1989.

55. In opposition to the Malthus–Ricardo–Lassalle demographic theory of wages (the so-called 'iron law'), Marx showed that the wage has two components: a physiological minimum below which it cannot fall; and a moral–historical element whose fluctuations, though overdetermined by the level of employment, depend in the last analysis on the class struggle between capital and labour.

56. If the average wage or salary earner could really save enough out of current income to start a business, the share of independent businessmen in the total active population would be on the rise. In reality, it has been constantly declining for more than a century, while the proportion of wage-and salary-earners has steadily increased to its present level of 90 per cent and more in countries like the USA, Britain and Sweden.

57. Von Mises held that since all investment is risky, and since new businesses are continually destroying the old, uninterrupted capital accumulation (and hence the rise of money dynasties lasting several generations) was extremely unlikely if not impossible. (*Socialism*, London 1951, pp. 379–80.) Empirical evidence proves the contrary. The continuity of 'super-rich' families in the USA, and in most cases in Western Europe and Japan, now stretches over a century. Once wealth passes a certain threshold, it accumulates without any risk other than that of a total collapse of the banking system and public finance.

58. A powerful left-wing critique of liberal (and neo-liberal) dogmas in this regard may be found in Gunnar Myrdal, *The Political Element in the Development of Economic Theory*, London 1953.

59. Following writers such as Gossen, Pareto, Barone and Pierson, Ludwig von Mises gave the classical formulation of this positiion in *Archiv für Sozialwissenschaft*, vol. 47 (April 1920) and vol. 51 (1921), pp. 490–95.

60. F.A. Hayek, *The Fatal Conceit: The Errors of Socialism*, London 1988, p. 134.

61. Of course, monopolists and 'central planning authorities' (that is, nomenklatura bureaucrats) are also ever seeking to tighten their control over such innovations.

62. 'In ordinary language we describe by the word "planning" the complex of interrelated decisions about the allocation of our available resources. All economic activity is in this sense planning [. . . another] question arises here, that of who is to do the planning.' (F.A. Hayek, 'The Use of Knowledge in Society', *American Economic Review*, September 1945.) The Swiss professor Norbert Thom, who heads the management training programme at the University of Fribourg, states just as categorically: 'Like planning and control, organization is a fundamental instrument for managing firms.' *Neue Zürcher Zeitung*, 9 October 1990.

63. This long tradition began in the thirties with Lange and Taylor (*On the Economic Theory of Socialism*, Minneapolis 1938) and Abba Lerner ('Economic Theory and Socialist Economy', *Review of Economic Studies*, October 1934, and *The Economics of Control*, New York 1944). More recent contributions have been made by German social democrat Heimann, H.D. Dickinson, Maurice Dobb and James E. Meade.

64. A. Nove, *The Economics of Feasible Socialism* pp. 33–34.

65. Wide differences in production costs can lead to the subcontracting of certain parts of the finished product. But for technical and organizational reasons, this cannot become a general practice. No combine will allow cars to be produced by subcontractors.

66. *Forces of Production*, New York 1984, p. 217.

67. Ernst Fehr (*Oekonomische Theorie der Selbstverwaltung*, Frankfurt/Main 1988) has tried to prove with neo-classical analytical tools that enterprises under workers' self-management would be more efficient than capitalist ones. A similar thesis has been defended by Yaroslav Vanek.

68. The German liberal weekly *Die Zeit* calculated that two million unemployed in Germany cost the state nearly DM60 bn ($40 bn) a year: DM27.3 bn in dole payments and DM31.4 bn in lost revenue, or DM3,000 per jobless person. Moreover, if these two million were to be employed outside the market economy in reforestation, municipal house-building, pollution control, etc., they could increase the national product by as much as DM120 bn a year, without any 'negative competitive effects'. Quite apart from the human toll in anxiety and lower standards of living, then, unemployment is sheer macro-economic inefficiency.

69. Without talking of macro-social rationality or optimization, André Gorz argues along exactly the same lines in his *Critique of Economic Reason*.

70. Von Mises, *Bureaucracy*, pp. 46, 50 and *passim*.

71. F.A. von Hayek, *Law, Legislation and Liberty*, Chicago 1979, vol. 3, pp. 112–13. Bruno Coppieters ('La Critique de l'utopie dans la théorie politique de Friedrich August von Hayek' in *Tijdschrift voor de Studie van de Verlidrting*, Free University, Brussels) correctly stresses the authoritarian character of Hayek's assaults against universal franchise and majority rule, in spite of Hayek's own denials. For Hayek's defence of traditional values see *The Fatal Conceit*, pp. 136–37, 157.

72. See the report by J.-M. Chaviez, 'La perestroika "new look" en quête d'un pouvoir fort', *Le Monde Diplomatique*, November 1990.

73. Cf. Kamenka, *Bureaucracy*, Oxford 1989, pp. 74–75.

74. The real point here is that such conflicts, if handled in a helpful, therapeutic way, will gradually lose their explosive character, and in no case lead to social catastrophes like wars, civil wars, mass imprisonment, torture or wide-scale repression. People engaged in conflict-solving would have no vested interest in repression – on the contrary, their interest would be in seeing a gradual withering away of conflict.

75. N. Bobbio, 'The Future of Democracy', *Telos*, Fall 1984. See also *Liberalism and Democracy*, London 1990.

76. One of the most tragic examples is that of the *ukazniks* under Stalin – hundreds of thousands of male and female workers condemned to years of hard labour by simple decree, with no possibility of ever defending themselves. The alleged offences generally related to absenteeism, including uncertificated sick-leave on days when a doctor was called to the worker's home but failed to appear.

77. See the document *Dictatorship of the Proletariat and Socialist Democracy*, adopted by the Twelfth World Congress of the Fourth International.

78. For an interesting critical examination of the concept of a 'law-based state' (*Rechtsstaat*), see the article by the Swiss social-democratic professor of constitutional law Andreas Auer, 'L'Etat de droit: sens et non-sens d'un concept prétentieux', *Plaidoyer*, April 1990.

79. It should not be forgotten that the Nazi persecution of the Jews began with the so-called Nuremberg Laws, and that democratically elected parliaments have proved quite capable of enacting unjust, repressive and racist legislation. As for the judicial system, in April 1941 a gathering of all the main German judges and all public prosecutors decided to legalize the Nazis' mass killing of the mentally ill ('Aktion T-4') and to block any attempt by family members to prosecute the perpetrators of these crimes which eventually wiped out seventy thousand people. See *Die Zeit*, 26 October 1990.

80. In the United States reactionary legislation severely restricts the capacity of workers to defend themselves by means of normal trade-union activity. See Christopher L. Tomlins, 'The State and the Unions', Cambridge 1985. The *Economist* (10 November 1990) notes: 'Many Italians find the revelations disquieting. Giovanni di Lorenzo, the head of the Italian secret service who appears to have founded Gladio in 1956, was later suspected of planning a coup.'

81. There is a growing literature on 'state-induced massacres' covered up by the Italian judiciary. See *inter alia* Edgardo Pellegrini, *Gli Ermellini da Guardia: Magistratura e repressione in Italia 1968–1973*, Rome 1973. As we were finishing this book, the Glavio scandal erupted. It appears that since the creation of Nato, a secret network of right-wing terrorists has been working hand in glove with the secret services and Nato officers in illegal anti-working-class activities. (See *Panorama*, 4 November 1990.) It extended all over Western Europe, and was possibly instrumental in triggering the putsch by the Greek colonels.

82. In recent debates concerning German reunification, bourgeois politicians in both East and West insisted that 'the right to property' should be included in an eventual treaty, while 'the right to work' (or, we would rather say, the right to a guaranteed income without the pressure of unemployment) should be excluded.

83. E. Cherniak, 'La Grande Révolution française: l'année 1794', *Sciences Sociales* (Moscow), No. 2, 1990, p. 83.

84. Cf. Karl Marx, 'But an end which requires unjustified means is no justifiable end.' 'Debates on Freedom of the Press', in Marx and Engels, *Collected Works*, vol. 1, London 1975, p. 164.

85. See, for instance, Hand, Jung and Braun, eds, *Utopien: Die Möglichkeit des Unmöglichen*, Zurich 1989.

86. Lenin, *What Is To Be Done?*, in *Selected Works*, vol. 1, London 1947, pp. 261–62.

87. Ernst Bloch's monumental work *Das Prinzip Hoffnung* offers many insights into this problem. English translation: *The Principle of Hope*, London 1986.

88. Cf. Karl Marx: 'is this saying that the working class ought to renounce their resistance against the encroachments of capital and abandon their attempts at making the best of the occasional chances for their temporary improvement? If they did, they would be

degraded to one level mass of broken wretches past salvation. . . . By cowardly giving way in their everyday conflict with capital, they would certainly disqualify themselves for the initiating of any larger movement.' 'Wages, Price and Profit', in *Marx–Engels Selected Works*, p. 225.

89. For a recent statement of this position, largely following the work of Nicos Poulantzas, see Antonio Santesmases, *Marxismo y Estado*, Madrid 1986, pp. 253f.

90. The new official anthem of the SPD actually says: 'drop by drop we'll change things'!

91. See among other sources: Sven Ljungren, *Det plundrarde boet*, Stockholm 1987; Eva Nickell, 'Visst tusan är det kris', *Internationalen* 8/90; Maria Sandvall, 'The End of the Social-Democratic Miracle' and 'The Crisis of the Swedish Model', *International Viewpoint*, 26 February and 2 July 1990.

92. This is clearly revealed in the declining participation in US Congressional elections. See *La Repubblica*, 8 November 1990.

93. Koslowski, Kreuzer and Löw, eds, *Chancen und Grenzen des Sozialstaats*, Tübingen 1983.

94. Gorz does Marx an injustice, however, when he attributes to him an ambivalent attitude to technology and the 'work ethic' and even suggests that he dreamt of a 'paradise of work'. We have already referred to all the prophetic statements in the *Grundrisse* which predict that leisure and not work will become the real measure of human wealth.

95. N. Bobbio, *Which Socialism?*, Cambridge 1988, p. 66.

96. Ibid., p. 72.

97. On the *Warspite* scandal see the *Sunday Times*, 11 November 1990; and on Piper Alpha, the *Times*, 13 November 1990.

98. K. Kautsky, *Die Agrarfrage*, Stuttgart 1899, quoted by Bobbio from the Italian edition, Milan 1959, p. 473.

99. The Hungarian Marxist economist Franz Janossy has analysed the inherent tendency of capitalism to underdevelop highly skilled labour, which generally leads to its scarcity in longer periods of expansion. See *Das Ende der Wirtschaftswunder*, Frankfurt 1969.

100. *Grundrisse*, p. 706.

101. U. Hedtke, *Stalin oder Kondratieff?*, Berlin/GDR 1990, pp. 24–25.

102. Contrary to Max Weber, Marx stresses that before people internalized this work ethic, it was imposed upon them – against resistance and periodic revolt – by means of political violence, economic compulsion and deprivation.

103. On Japan see *Tagesspiegel*, 15 April 1990, and on the USA, *International Herald Tribune*, 28 September 1989, referring to the recent book by Donald Kanter and Philip Mirvis, *The Cynical Americans: Living and Working in an Age of Discontent and Disillusion*. On West Germany see two recent studies reported in *Frankfurter Allgemeine Zeitung*, 13 September 1989.

104. See the excellent book by Winfried Wolf, *Eisenbahn und Autowahn*, Hamburg 1986.

105. See, for example, Engels, 'Ludwig Feuerbach and the End of Classical German Philosophy' and 'The Origin of the Family, Private Property and the State', both in Marx and Engels, *Selected Works*.

106. Engels, 'The Part Played by Labour in the Transition from Ape to Man', pp. 182–86.

107. 'Critique of Hegel's Doctrine of the State', p. 109.

Printed in the United States
by Baker & Taylor Publisher Services